IMAGES
of America

CLAIBORNE PARISH

On the Cover: Residents of Claiborne Parish found numerous ways to enjoy the lazy days of summer. There were baseball games and swim meets for the young and picnics and family reunions for those of all ages. These men are taking advantage of the shade on the courthouse lawn to play a friendly game of dominos. (Courtesy of the Ford Museum.)

IMAGES
of America

CLAIBORNE PARISH

The Herbert S. Ford Memorial Museum, Inc.

ARCADIA
PUBLISHING

ISBN 978-0-7385-5412-9

Published by Arcadia Publishing
Charleston, South Carolina

Printed in the United States of America

Library of Congress Catalog Card Number: 2008921696

For all general information contact Arcadia Publishing at:
Telephone 843-853-2070
Fax 843-853-0044
E-mail sales@arcadiapublishing.com
For customer service and orders:
Toll-Free 1-888-313-2665

Visit us on the Internet at www.arcadiapublishing.com

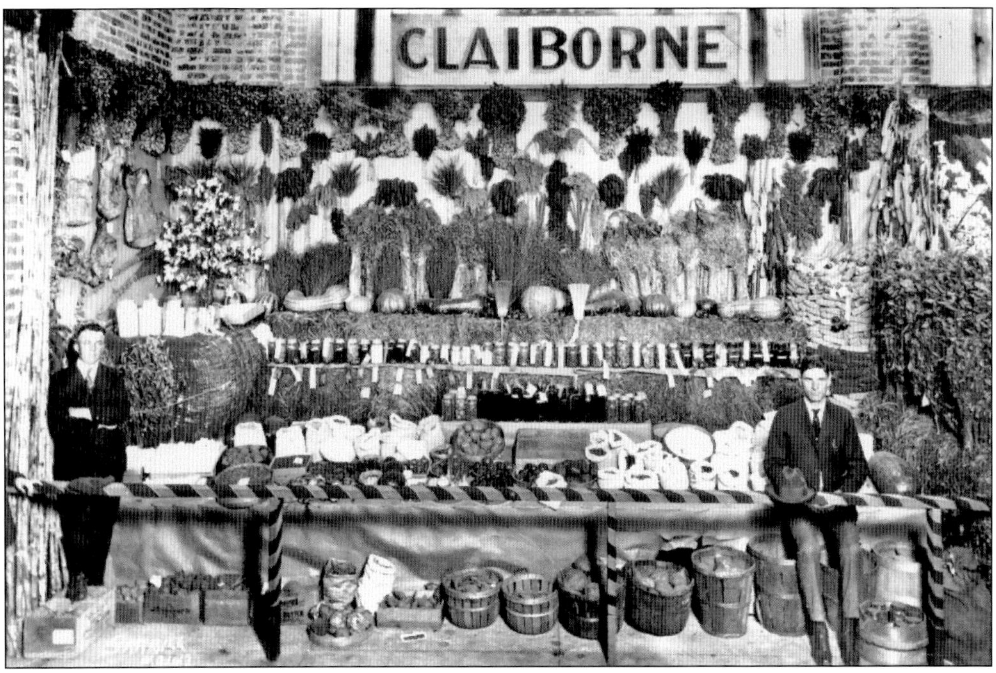

Claiborne Parish's agricultural bounty was the theme for this display at the Louisiana State Fair in the 1920s. The baskets of farm produce, the smoked meats hanging from the walls of the partition, and the canned and preserved items in the foreground all promote the image of Claiborne Parish as a place of plenty. (Courtesy of LSU Shreveport Archives–Noel Memorial Library.)

Contents

ACKNOWLEDGMENTS

The efforts, past and present, of many people have made publication of this book possible. In particular, we wish to express our appreciation to those individuals and groups who allowed their photographs to be included in this work. Their generous spirit reflects the love we have in common for Claiborne Parish, Louisiana. The Ford Museum has evolved from a small private collection of artifacts to a mature institution whose mission is to promote and preserve the history of Claiborne Parish and the North Louisiana Hill Country. We wish to acknowledge the contributions of all those past caretakers of the museum whose work has provided the foundation for its growth and expansion. We would be remiss if we failed to acknowledge the Town of Homer for their continuing support and interest in helping us maintain our level of excellence as a museum. Last, but certainly not least, we wish to acknowledge the enthusiasm and dedication of our project director, Linda Volentine; the book committee; and Bill and Kathy Hightower of the *Guardian-Journal*, whose Herculean efforts have made this book a reality. We feel privileged to have been a part of this worthy undertaking. To you, the public, we extend an ever-open invitation to join us in carrying the enduring legacy of our past into the bright light of our future. Additional information concerning some of the photographs and their captions has been posted on the Ford Museum Web site: ford.claiborneone.org. Contact us at fordmuseum@bellsouth.net for comments or questions.

INTRODUCTION

Claiborne Parish was originally part of Natchitoches Parish, which was created in 1806. By 1828, the population in the northern part of old Natchitoches Parish had increased sufficiently to warrant the creation of a new parish. In that year, the northeastern portion of old Natchitoches was detached, and a new parish was formed. It was named for the first American governor of Louisiana, William C. C. Claiborne.

The settlement of Claiborne Parish took place as part of the great westward movement of Americans into lands made available as a result of the Louisiana Purchase. The earliest settlers left their homes in North Carolina, South Carolina, and middle Tennessee and reached north central Louisiana by way of the Cumberland, Mississippi, and Red Rivers. In some instances, these early settlers reached their destinations by leaving the Mississippi River and traveling overland through the Arkansas Territory.

On August 6, 1818, John Murrell and his wife, Margaret, their six children, a packhorse, two dogs, and a rifle settled on a tract of land approximately 6 miles west of present-day Homer. The Murrell family is considered to be the parish's first permanent settlers, and their home served as the unofficial seat of government prior to the organization of Claiborne Parish in 1828.

As population in the region increased, portions of old Claiborne Parish were detached and new parishes formed. Claiborne Parish is known as the "Banner Parish of North Louisiana" because so many parishes were wholly or partially created out of her original territory: Bossier Parish in 1843, Bienville Parish in 1848, Webster Parish in 1871, and portions of Jackson, Red River, and Lincoln Parish in 1845, 1848, and 1873, respectively.

The new residents of Claiborne Parish opened roads, bridged bayous and creeks, and established churches and schools. Names of some of the early communities of the parish were Antioch, Arizona, Blackburn, Camp, Colquitt, Dykesville, Gordon, Hurricane, Mahon, Sharon, and Weldon. Communities that have persisted to the present day are Homer (1850), Lisbon (1850), Summerfield (1868), new Athens (1888), Junction City (1894), and new Haynesville (1898).

In 1828, the police jury of the new parish selected the home of Samuel Russell in the Allen settlement community to be the seat of parish government. The community would later be known as Russellville, located approximately one-half mile northeast of present-day Athens. In 1836, the parish seat was moved to Overton, then a thriving port town on Bayou Dorcheat. The Overton location proved to be unhealthful and prone to flooding, so in 1846, the parish seat was moved to old Athens. It remained there until the night of November 6, 1849, when a fire consumed the court building, destroying all public records. Following the fire, the police jury acted to move the parish seat to Homer, where it is still maintained.

The Claiborne Parish Courthouse was completed in 1861 at a cost of $12,304.36. It is one of the oldest public buildings still in use in the state today. Of the four antebellum courthouses remaining in Louisiana, the Claiborne Parish Courthouse is the only one still serving its original purpose.

The citizens of Claiborne Parish were self-sustaining. Every family had its wool and cotton cards, spinning wheel, and loom. Every family grew its own vegetables. The first cotton gin in the area that would become Claiborne Parish was erected in 1824. From that time until well into the 20th century, cotton served the farmers as their chief money crop. Schools were established in almost every settlement, and Claiborne soon became well known as an educational center.

When the War Between the States commenced in 1861, many Claiborne Parish men answered the call to arms. No battles took place on its soil, but Claiborne Parish mustered 10 and a half companies of infantrymen, and many more individuals enlisted in several cavalry, artillery, medical, ordnance, or other units to fight for the Confederate cause. On the home front, the citizens of Claiborne Parish cared for sick and wounded soldiers and opened their homes to refugees fleeing Union-occupied territories.

The Civil War created a hiatus in the economic development of Claiborne Parish, but prosperity returned at the end of the 19th century, due in large part to the coming of the railroad. The Louisiana and North West Railroad (L&NW) impacted the parish in numerous ways. In 1888, as the line was being built two miles to the west of old Athens, the townspeople began moving their homes and businesses to positions alongside the new railroad tracks, ultimately creating a ghost town at the old location. Ten years later, as the building of the line continued northward, the people of old Haynesville were also drawn away from their old location to a new town site beside the railroad tracks.

The first segment of the L&NW Railroad, which was completed in 1888, was a 19-mile line from Gibsland to Homer, thus connecting Homer with the east-west line of the Vicksburg, Shreveport, and Pacific Railroad. The northward extension of the line from Homer to Magnolia, Arkansas, was completed in 1898. At the present time, the L&NW hauls freight five days a week along its 62.5-mile route from Gibsland, Louisiana, to McNeil, Arkansas.

In the early years of the 20th century, the discovery of oil in Claiborne Parish brought further social and economic change. The Consolidated Progressive Oil Company drilled the first commercially successful well of the Homer Field in January 1919. By 1920, the Homer Oil Field was producing the largest portion of total oil production in North Louisiana. The Haynesville Field was brought in on March 30, 1921, causing Haynesville to mushroom from a town of 1,000 inhabitants to a boom town of over 10,000 people. The discovery well of the Lisbon Field was brought in on December 18, 1936. By 1946, there were 785 producing oil wells and 46 gas wells pumping in Claiborne Parish.

Although no volume this size can tell the entire story, the images in this book portray many of the people, places, and events that have shaped the development of Claiborne Parish. Many more images are needed. Photographs representing early Claiborne Parish businesses have proved difficult to find. As well, photographs representing the history of our black citizens are underrepresented in this volume. It is our hope that, by publishing this collection of retrospective images, the families and friends of Claiborne Parish will be motivated to further search their scrapbooks and attics for additional photographs to be included in future histories of Claiborne Parish.

One

A Beautiful Legacy

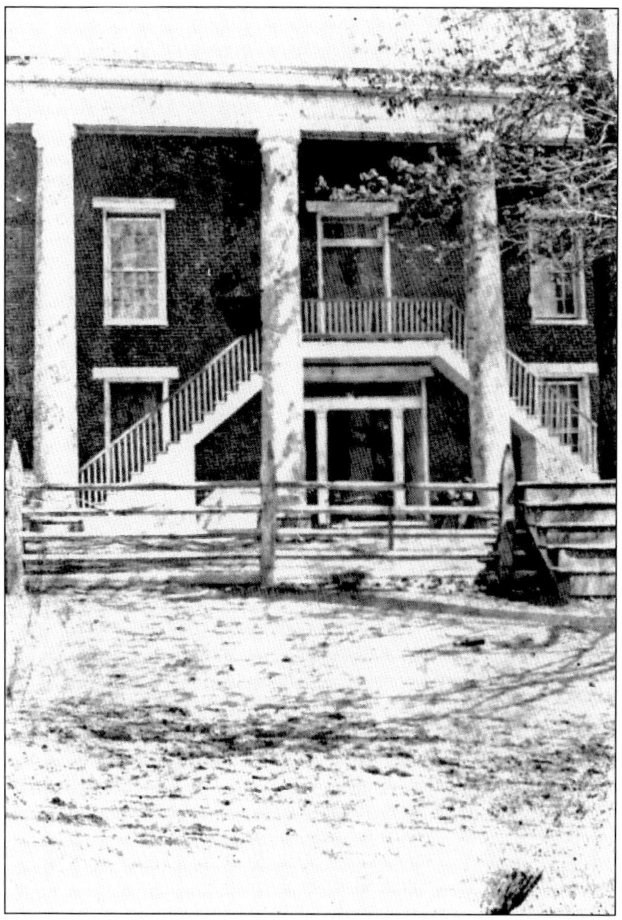

After the courthouse at old Athens burned on November 6, 1849, the police jury selected a centrally located site for the new parish seat. Using land patented to Tillinghast Vaughan and the Claiborne Parish Police Jury, lots for the town of Homer were laid out. The courthouse, costing $12,304.36, was constructed of red brick fired in a local kiln and lumber from Middlefork Bottom. Final settlement was made with contractor W. C. Crutcher on September 3, 1861. (Courtesy of the Ford Museum.)

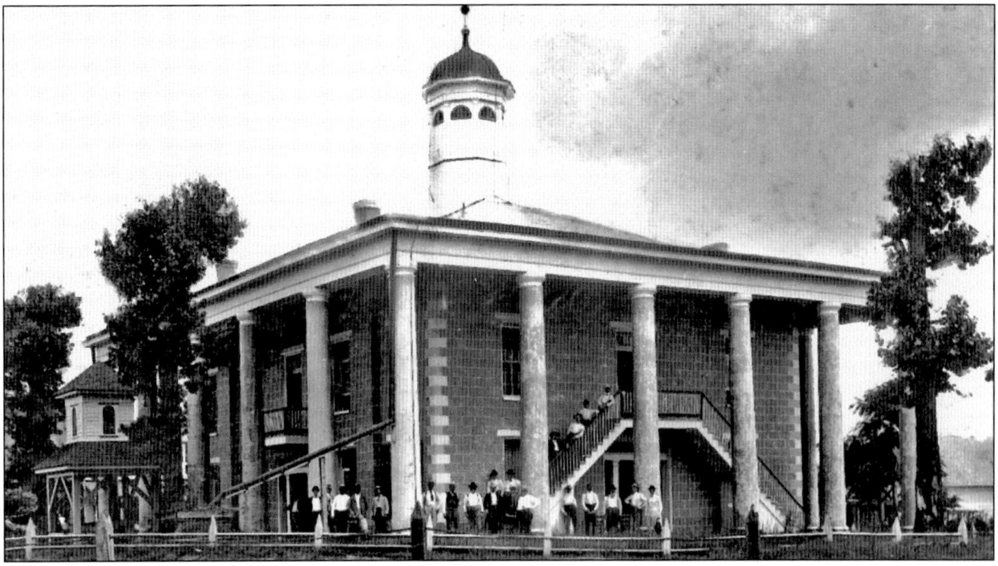

The building is a classic example of Greek Revival architecture. The 30-inch bell housed in the octagonal-shaped roof dome summoned citizens to court sessions, to community events, and to town fires. Later, when supporting beams weakened, the bell was removed. The iron hitching posts and rails that bordered the courthouse grounds provided a secure place to tie teams of horses and mules while their owners conducted business around the town square. (Courtesy of the Ford Museum.)

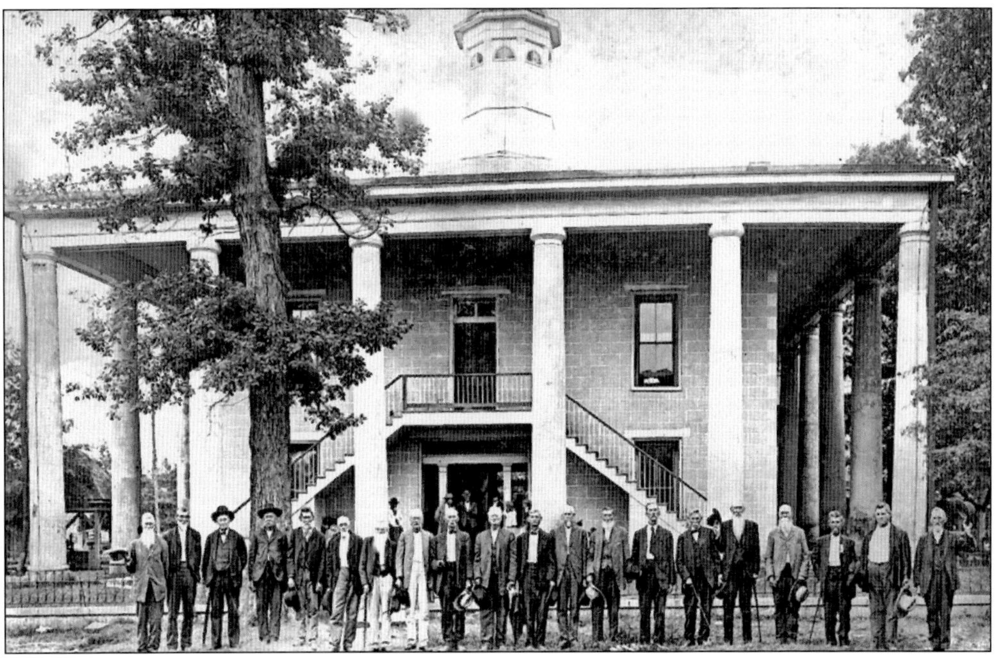

The courthouse was a departure point for Civil War troops. The 20 Confederate veterans gathered for this 1905 photograph are, from left to right, J. F. Peterson, W. W. Houston, G. G. Gill, B. B. McCasland, J. M. Taylor, W. R. Fortson, Seab Heard, H. W. Menefee, Joe Simmons, John M. W. Camp, W. L. Hamil, W. G. Beauchamp, J. L. Brown, S. J. Meadows, A. N. Brown, L. R. Lay, W. M. Jarrell, J. H. Broadnax, Tom Harris, and W. S. Geren. (Courtesy of the Ford Museum.)

In May 1940, a statue honoring the 1,564 Claiborne Parish men who served in the Civil War was placed on the courthouse lawn. The 8,000-pound figure was cast by a Georgia monument company at a cost of $1,500. The project was financed from donations collected by the Woman's Department Club and the United Daughters of the Confederacy. At the dedication ceremony, a local CSA veteran, 92-year-old J. M. Brooke, raised the Confederate flag as the Homer High School band played "Dixie." (Courtesy of the Ford Museum.)

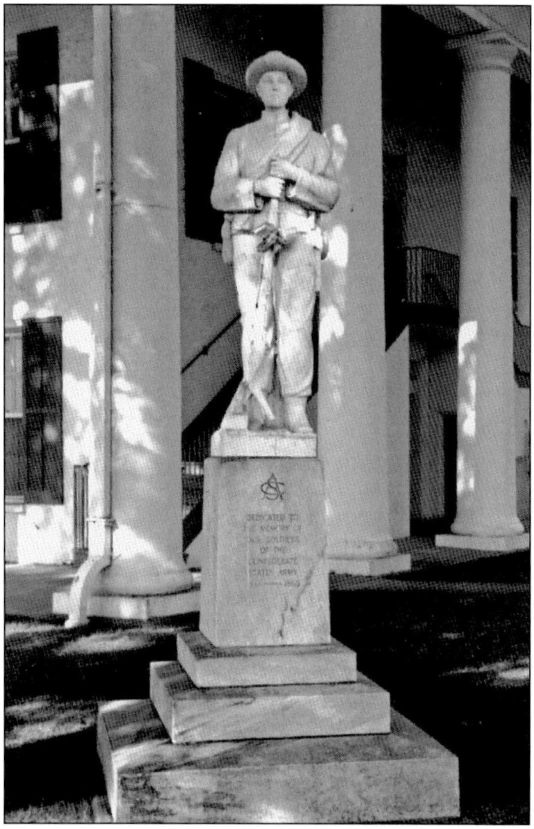

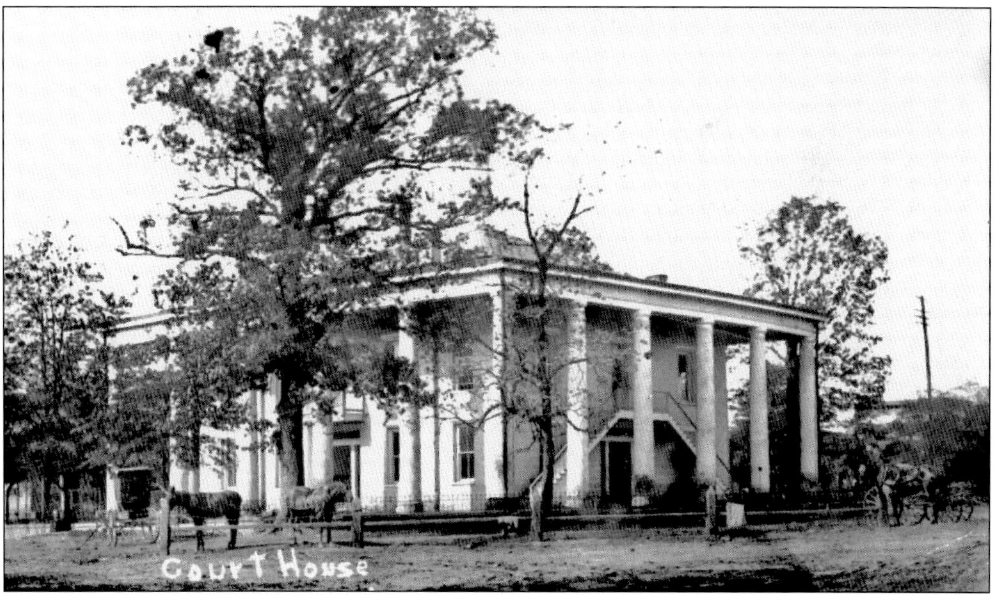

Although the courthouse appears to be square, it is actually a rectangle. The north and south sides of the building measure 63 feet in length, and the east and west sides are 53 feet in length. The 20 massive columns that surround the courthouse were placed closer together on the north and south sides, creating the illusion of a square. (Courtesy of the Ford Museum.)

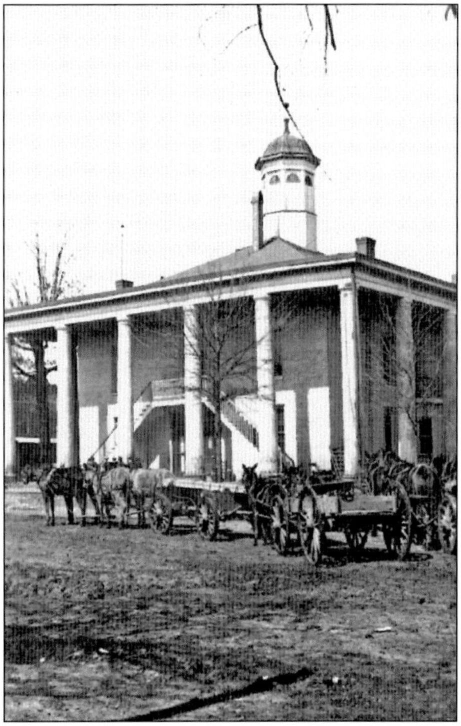

As seen in this photograph, the courthouse lawn originally extended approximately 40 feet farther in all directions. The lawn's size was reduced to allow the streets surrounding the courthouse to be widened. In 1918, the hitching posts were removed from the square and new hitching posts were erected on South Main and East Main Streets. (Courtesy of the Ford Museum.)

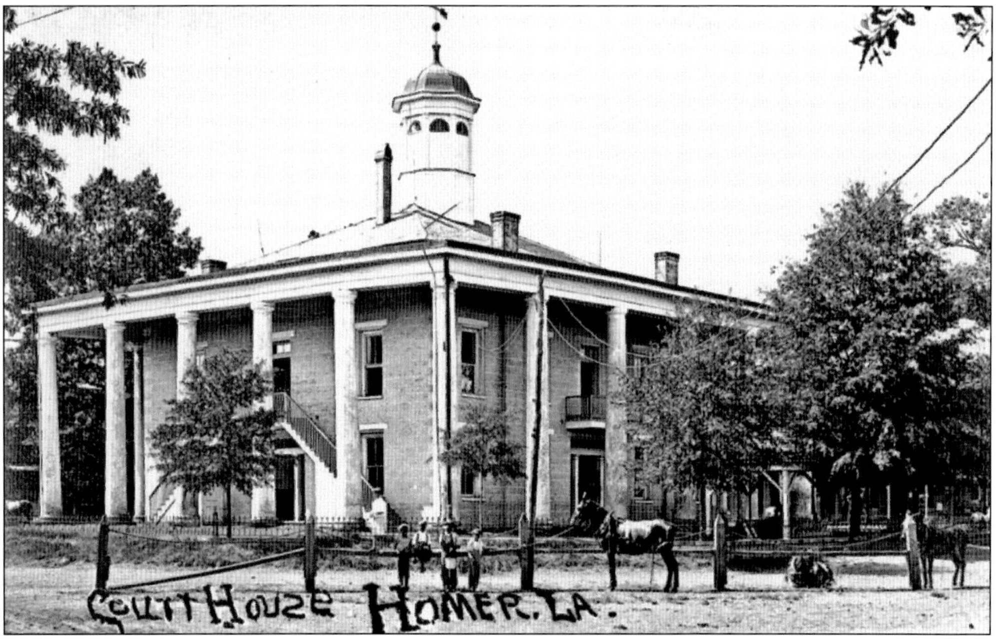

Two hallways, one running north and south and the other running east and west, once traversed the ground floor of the courthouse. The high ceilings and a substantial roof overhang allowed offices on the ground floor to receive maximum cooling during long, hot summer months. The east and west entrances were sealed in 1919 to provide additional office space. The second floor contained a large courtroom, jury room, and office for the district judge. (Courtesy of the Ford Museum.)

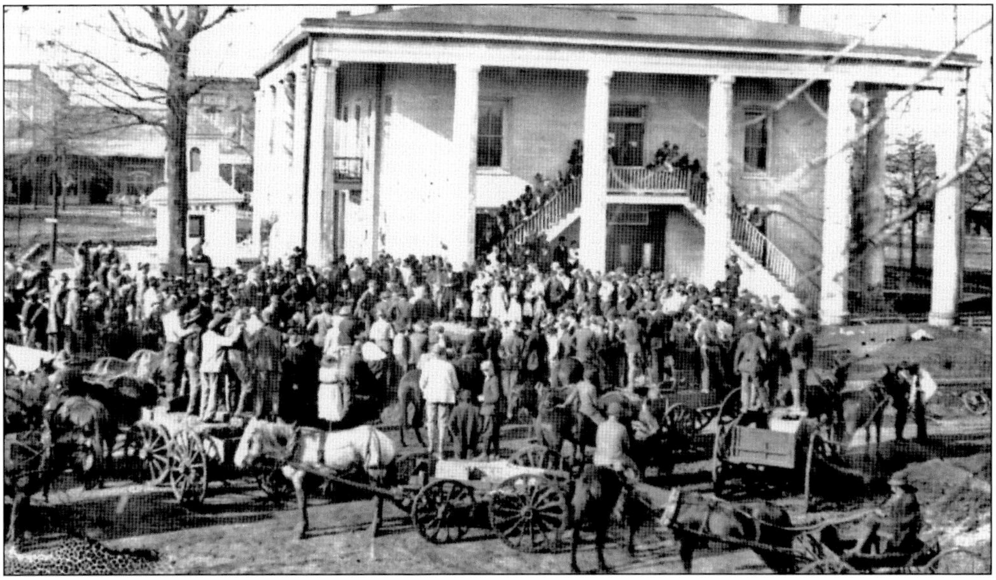

Saturday was the day when farmers brought their families to town. It was a time to sell crops and items produced on the farm and to buy supplies from town merchants. Farmers made an exception to their weekly Saturday visits whenever a much-anticipated trial was under way at the courthouse. Those unable to crowd into the courtroom gathered on the courthouse lawn to await the news of the trial. (Courtesy of the Ford Museum.)

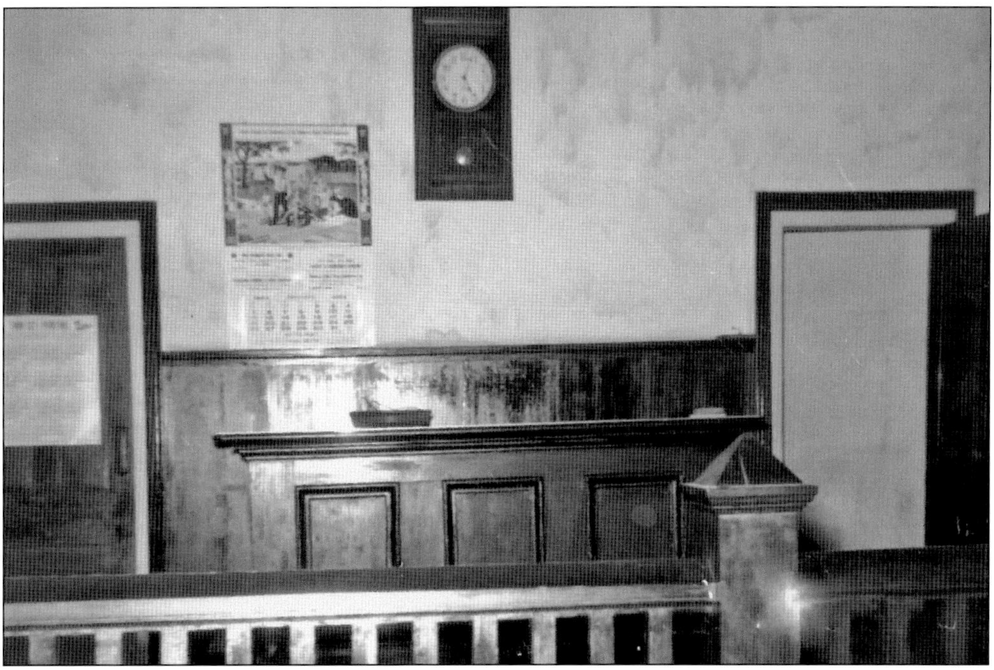

Justice was dispensed from behind this judge's bench in the second-floor courtroom. Both civil and criminal cases were tried, just as they are today. A newspaper account of an 1897 trial reports that the jurors were sequestered for three days and forced to sleep on a sawdust-covered floor with only a single blanket given to each juror. (Courtesy of the Claiborne Parish Sheriff's Department.)

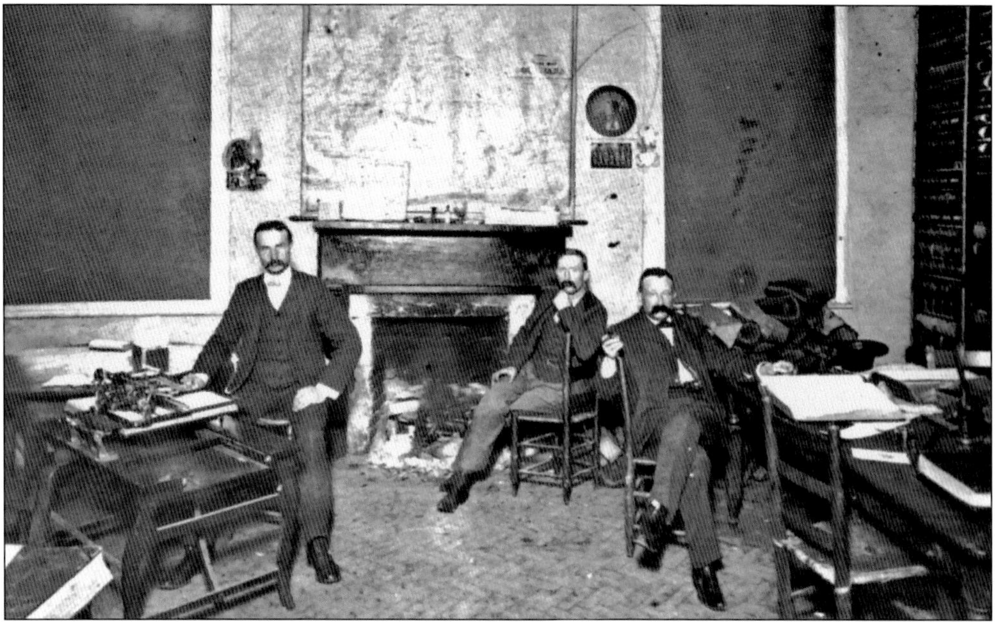

One of the parish offices housed inside the courthouse was that of the Claiborne Parish clerk of court. In this 1903 photograph are, from left to right, Edgar H. Fortson, deputy clerk; B. H. Moore, Claiborne Parish sheriff; and Drew Ferguson, clerk of court. Prominently seen are the wood-burning fireplace and some of the office's many record books stacked on shelves at the right. A calendar hangs on the rear wall denoting the 1903 date. (Courtesy of the J. J. Smith family.)

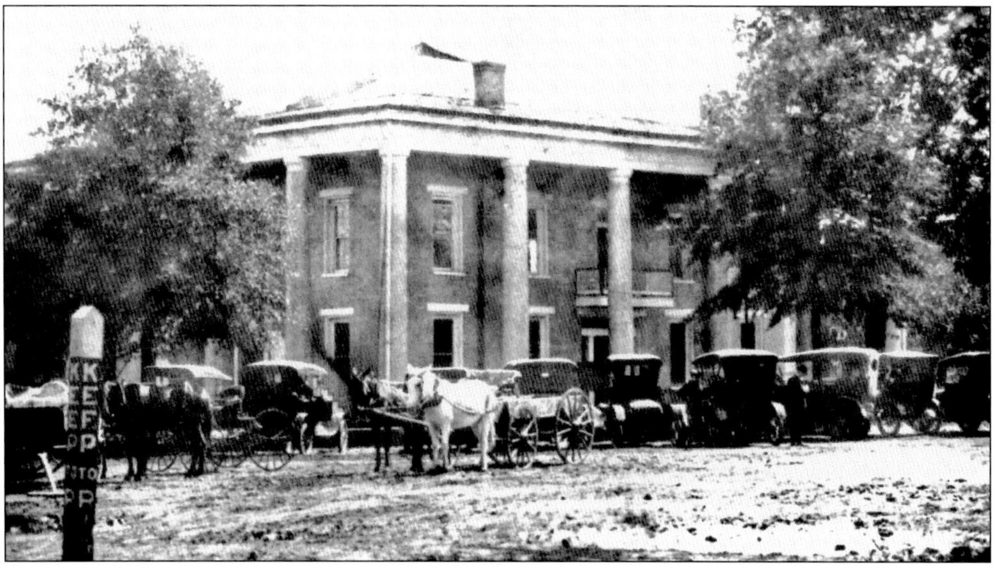

Methods of transportation were changing as the horse and wagon were being replaced by the automobile in the 1910 and 1920 eras. Here the Ford Model T and other automobiles have left few parking spaces for the wagons. The first automobile in Homer belonged to Dr. Philip Gibson, who received it by rail shipment from a New York factory in September 1908. By 1913, Homer Town Ordinance No. 135 set the first speed limit on the square at 12 miles per hour. (Courtesy of Frank and Jane Speer.)

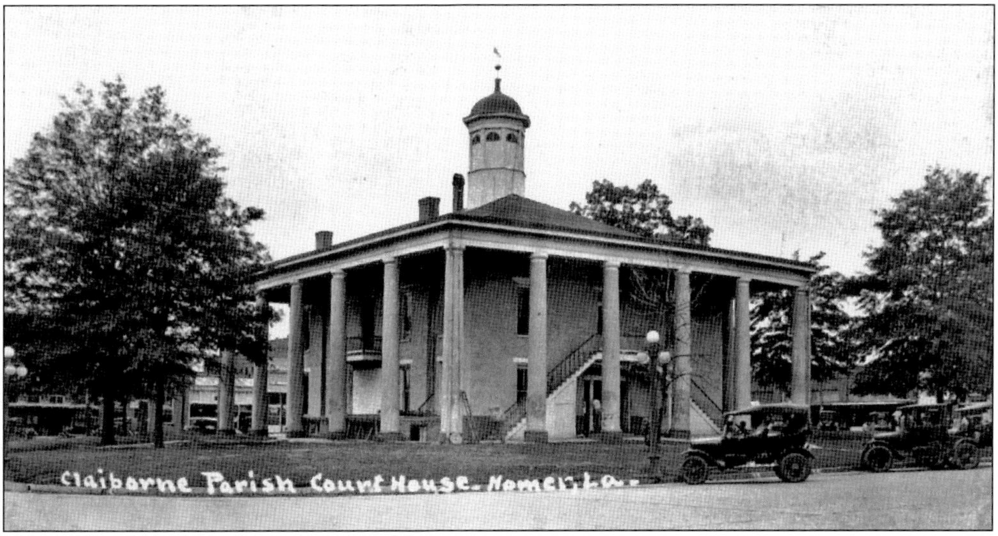

With increased revenues from the oil boom, the parish was able to fund renovation and improvement projects for the courthouse square. In April 1922, eight light posts, each with five electric light globes, were installed on the courthouse grounds. Sidewalks were laid around the courthouse, and the surrounding streets were paved. Underground restrooms were constructed on the east side of the building in 1924. One restroom entrance is seen between two column bases. (Courtesy of Bill W. Hightower.)

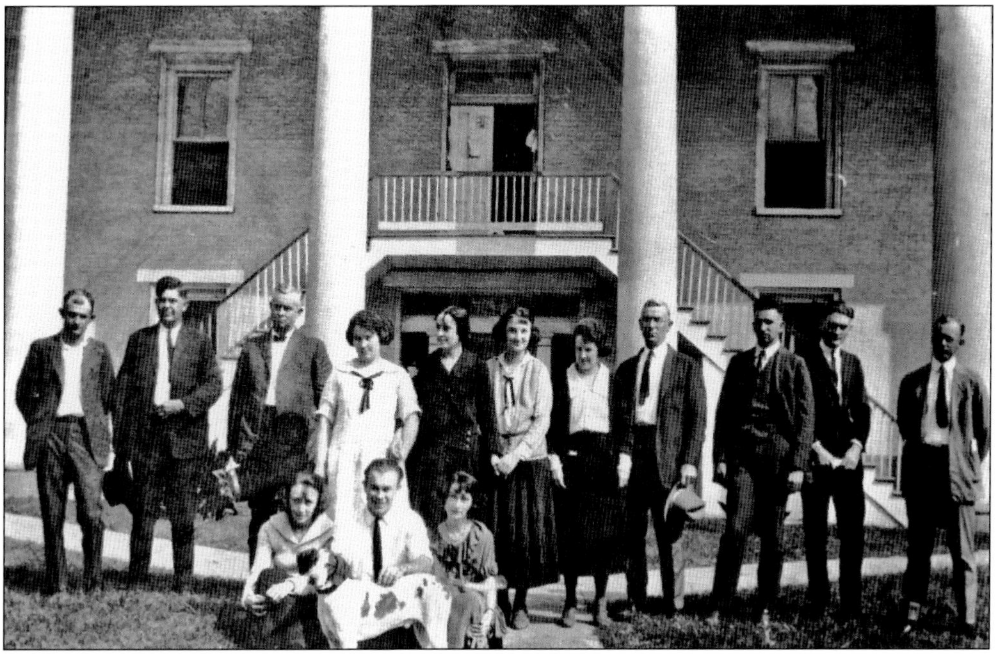

Many parish officials and personnel had offices on the first floor of the courthouse. Some of the officials and personnel shown in this 1923 photograph are, from left to right, (kneeling) Bonnie Martin, Fomby Coleman, Mertie Reece Webb, and Mack, Deputy Larry Sale's dog; (standing) E. S. Elkins, Deputy Baker Lay, Sheriff John W. Coleman, Bessie Gruner, Inez Barrow, Gertrude Gandy, Julia Moore, Dr. William L. Stone, Lester Kilpatrick, Neville Ward, and Fred Meadows. (Courtesy of the Claiborne Parish Sheriff's Department.)

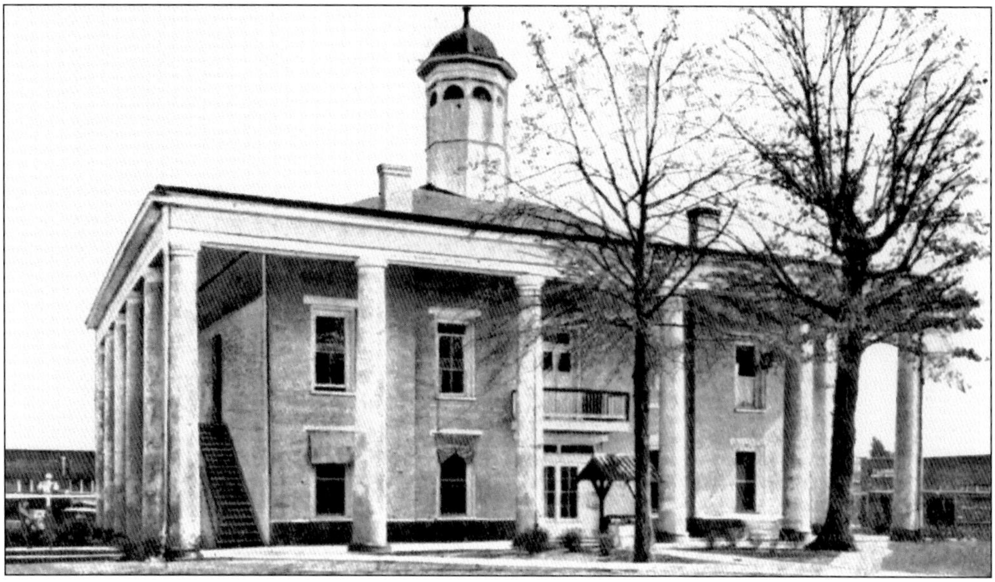

The decorative well shed, seen in this 1920s photograph, was constructed on the courthouse lawn in 1913 after a water tower for the town was erected and a water system installed around the square. Note the second-story window that is painted with signage indicating the location of the first Homer Chamber of Commerce office. (Courtesy of Bill W. Hightower.)

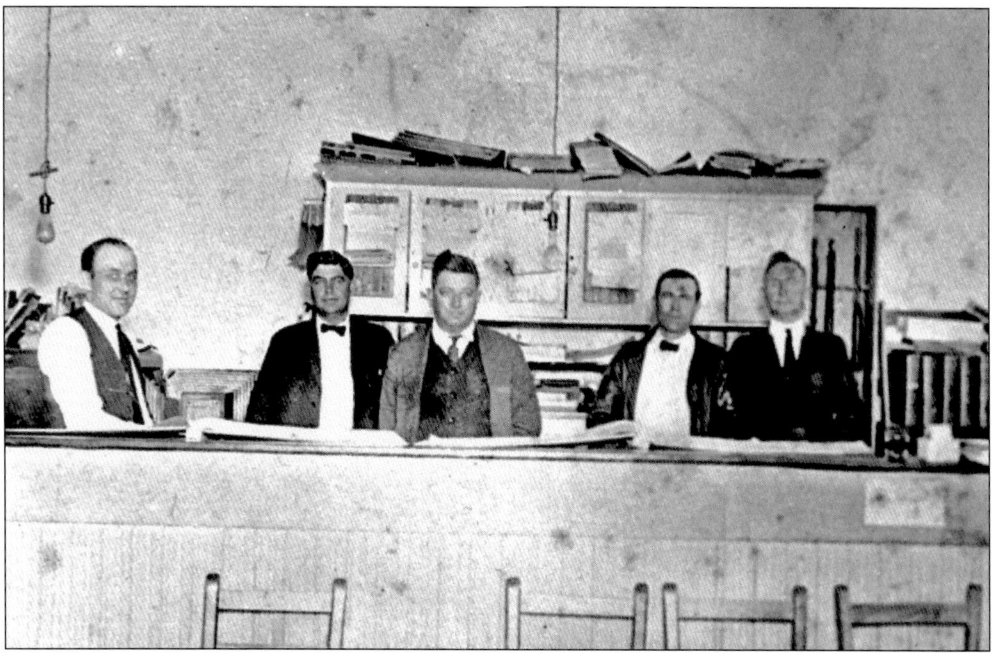

Sheriff's office personnel in this late-1910s photograph are, from left to right, Tom Robinson, Deputy Baker Lay, Deputy Larry Sale, Sheriff B. H. Moore, and an unidentified man. Emergency responses were often delayed because of poor roads, limited and often unreliable automobile transportation, and lack of parish-wide telephone service. (Courtesy of the Claiborne Parish Sheriff's Department.)

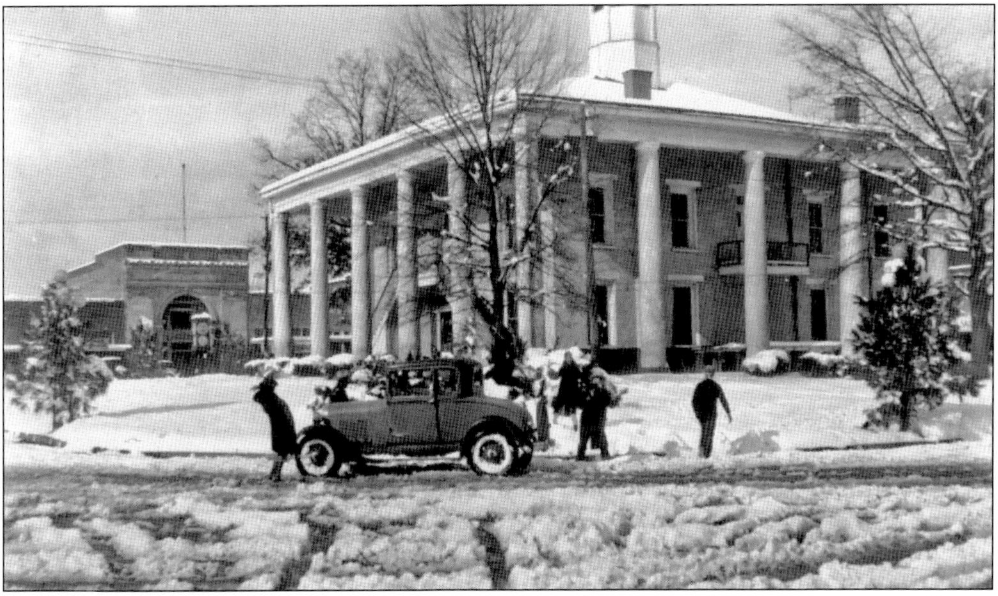

The snowballs are flying in this late-1920s photograph. The coldest temperature in Homer occurred on February 13, 1899. The *Guardian-Journal* and the *Clipper* both reported minus 17 degrees. The temperature had reached minus 10 degrees the previous morning and reached 10 degrees the following morning. The bitter cold, with several snowfalls, lasted two weeks. Merchants had goods freeze on the shelves, and canned items burst. Poultry and livestock suffered greatly, and much timber and shrubbery were damaged. (Courtesy of the W. M. Knighten Estate.)

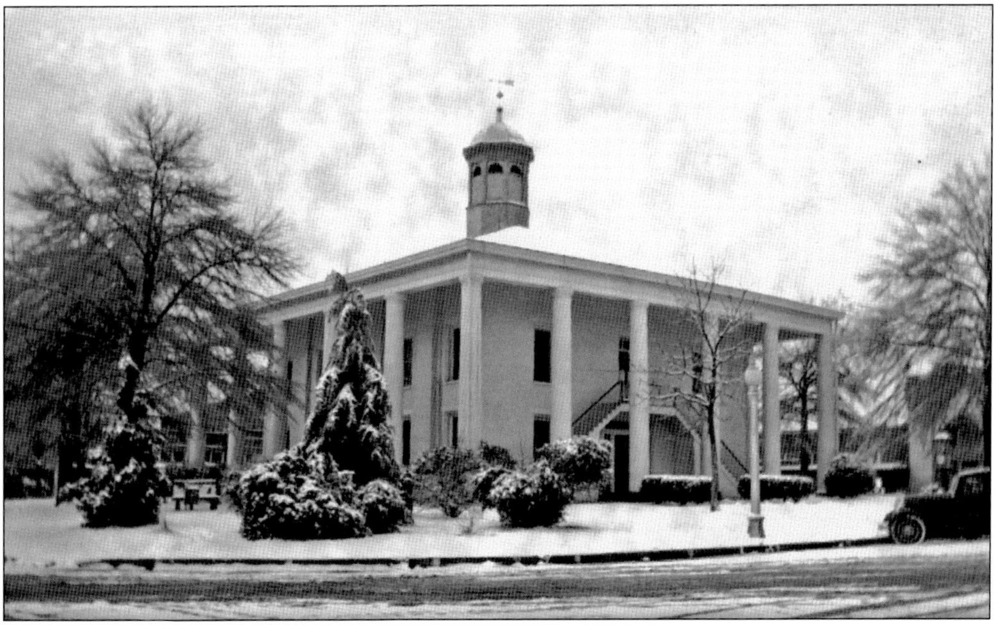

Another snowy scene shows the courthouse as it begins to take on a more modern appearance. The chimney tops have been removed from above the roofline, the five-globe light posts have been replaced with single-globe posts, and the streets around the square have been widened. Still unchanged are the wooden staircases and the roof dome. (Courtesy of Gil Dowies.)

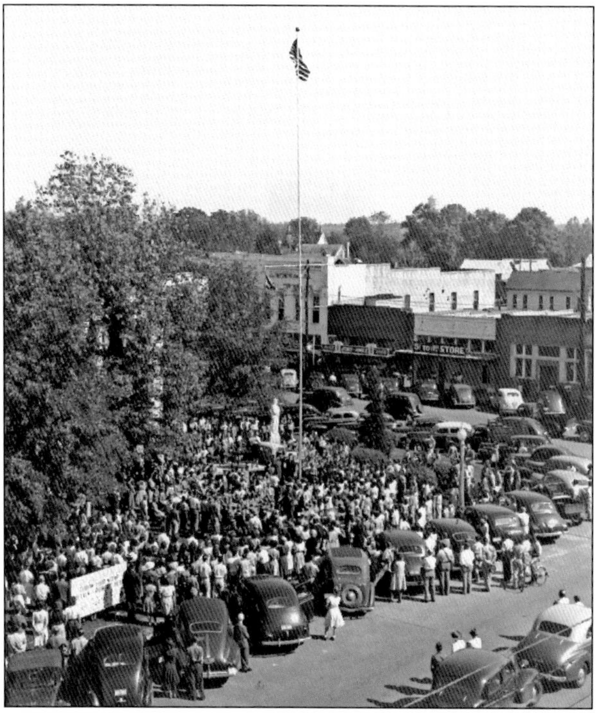

Citizens gathered on the courthouse lawn for a World War II war bond rally. Claiborne Parish citizens purchased enough war bonds to fund the building of a warship. Built in Nashville, Tennessee, the submarine chaser *PC-1247* was launched August 7, 1943, into the Cumberland River and commissioned as the USS *PC-1247* by the U.S. Navy on December 20, 1943. (Courtesy of the J. J. Smith family.)

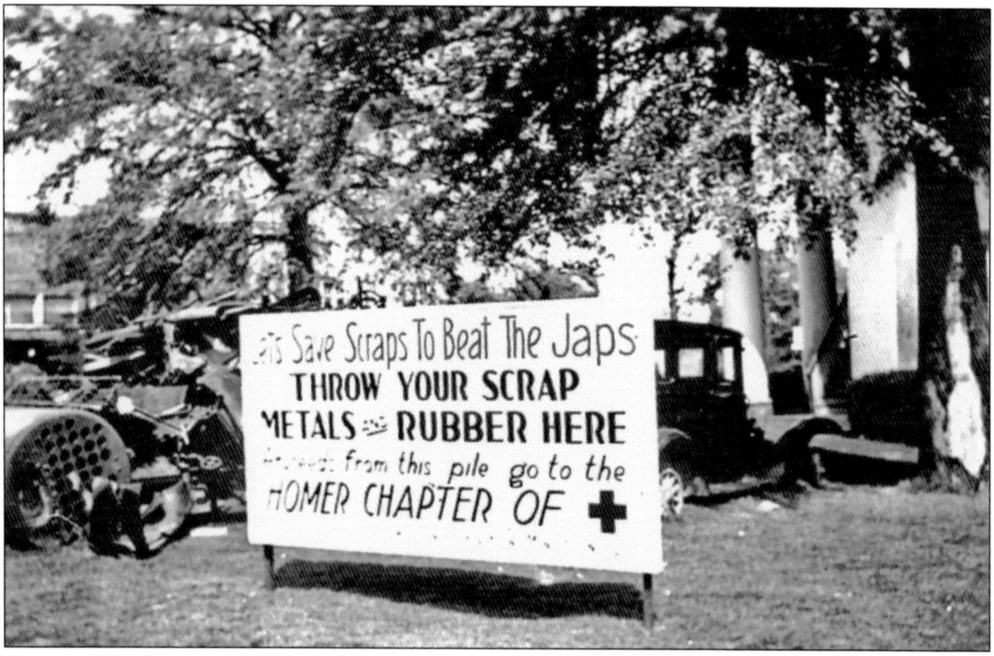

During World War II, patriotic drives were undertaken to stockpile scrap metal and other materials. The police jury temporarily abandoned all road work and turned its entire crew and equipment over to gathering scrap iron. The Homer city dump was dredged, quickly uncovering 550 tons of salvage. The L&NW salvaged two old locomotives. By April 1942, Claiborne Parish had collected approximately 1,000 tons of scrap iron and metal, which were sold for $9 a ton through a Shreveport junk dealer. (Courtesy of the J. J. Smith family.)

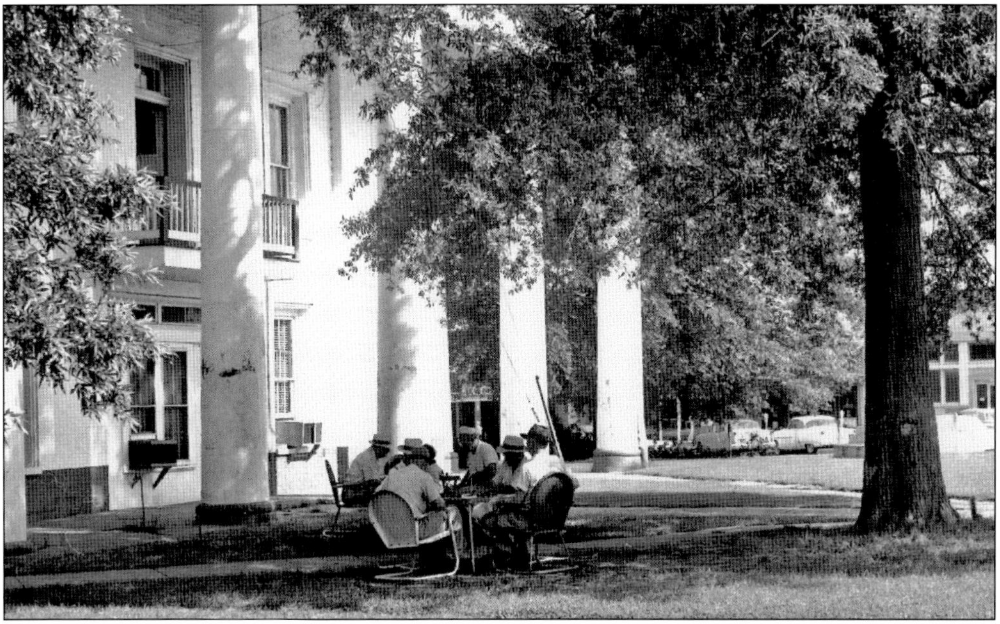

During the lazy days of summer, the courthouse lawn became a gathering place for a friendly game of dominos and afforded players a chance to swap tales. The huge oak trees provided the players shade from the blazing sun. Inside the courthouse, offices once cooled by the breezes blowing through the open hallways were now cooled by window air-conditioning units. (Courtesy of the Ford Museum.)

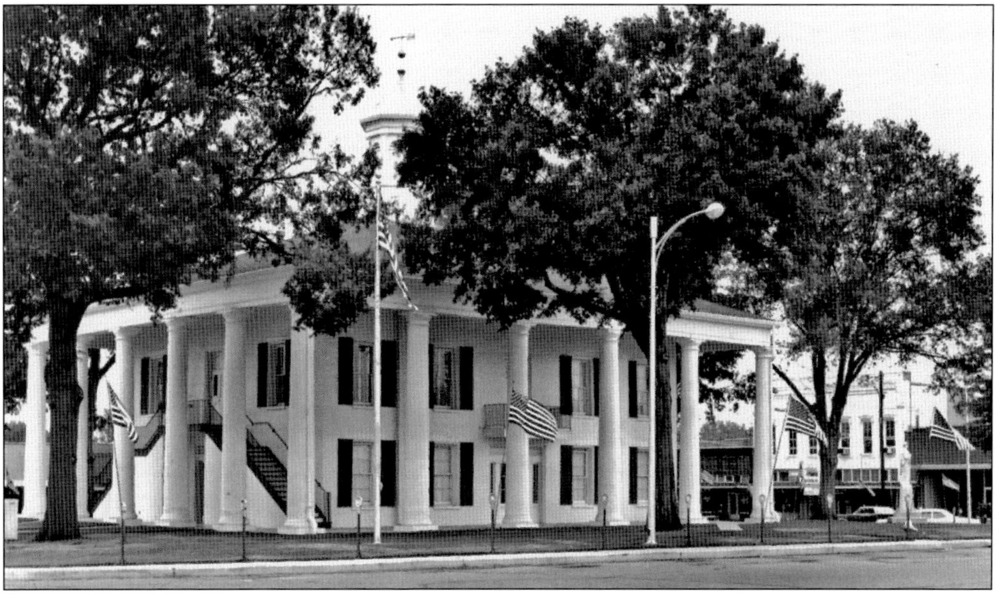

The 1960s brought the threat of losing the courthouse to make room for a modern structure to house parish offices, a courtroom, and a new jail. Ironically, the Courthouse Centennial Celebration was held July 20, 1961, just as plans were being made to demolish it. The demolition plans soon lost momentum as concerned citizens banded together to preserve this historic landmark, and instead of replacing the courthouse, efforts were turned toward renovating the building. (Courtesy of the *Guardian-Journal*.)

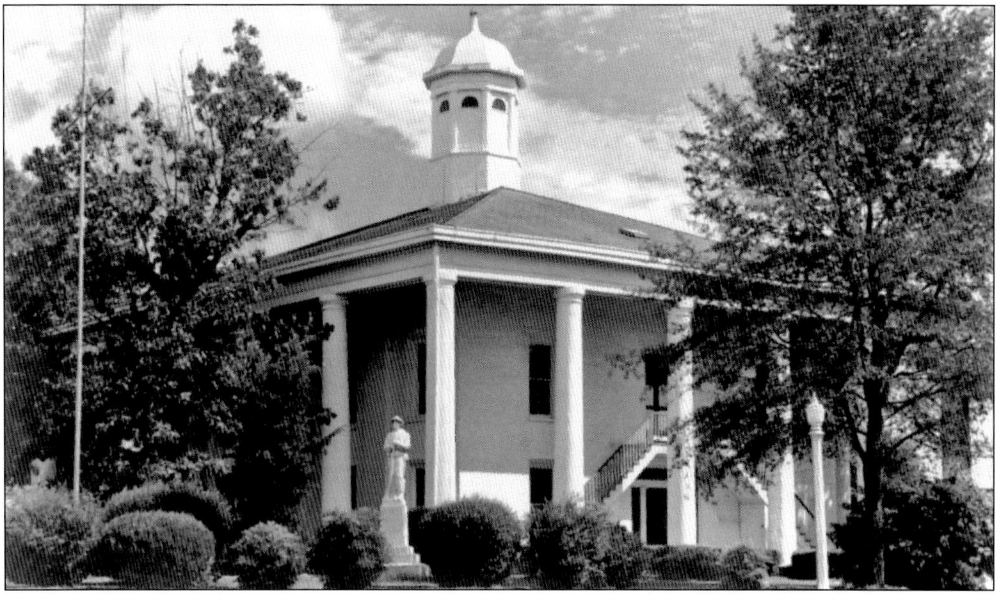

Through the years, picturesque oak trees have surrounded the courthouse, enhancing its beauty. A tradition of squirrels living in the courthouse oaks began in 1922 when Deputy Larry Sale donated a fox squirrel to start a colony; however, it soon disappeared. Later Caddo Parish officials presented three pairs of gray squirrels, and the courthouse squirrel population flourished for many years. In the 1990s, courthouse renovations, inclement weather, and disease resulted in the removal of some of the stately oaks, forcing the faithful squirrels to leave the square for better nesting areas. (Courtesy of Colynn Butler.)

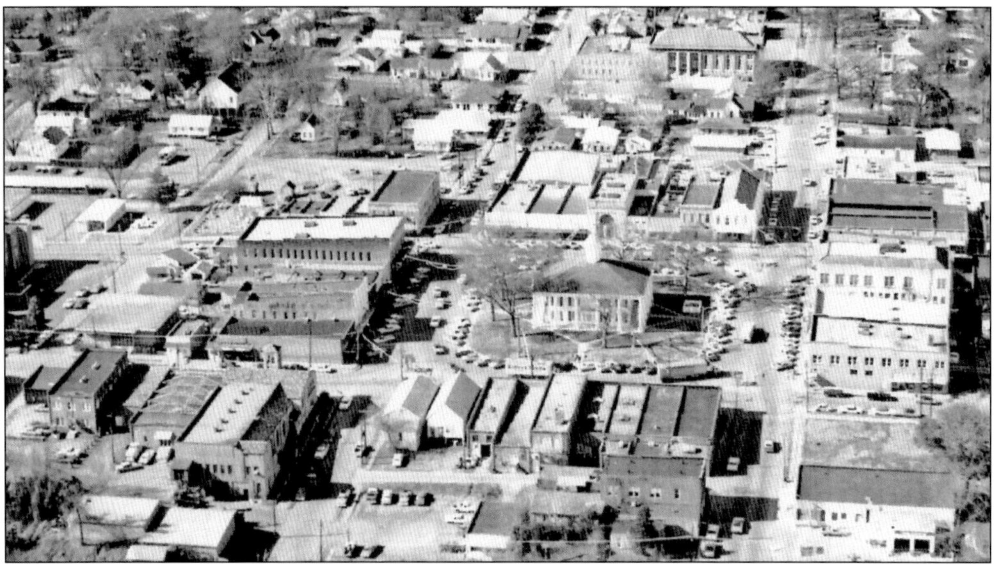

The Claiborne Parish Courthouse is one of the oldest public buildings still in use in the state today; of the four antebellum courthouses in Louisiana, it is the only one still serving in its original capacity. Tourists are amazed by its antebellum beauty and are quick to photograph the parish's best-known landmark. This lovely structure is a source of pride for all Claiborne Parish citizens, and it stands today as a symbol of its rich and varied historical past. (Courtesy of David Watson.)

Two

THE IRON HORSE

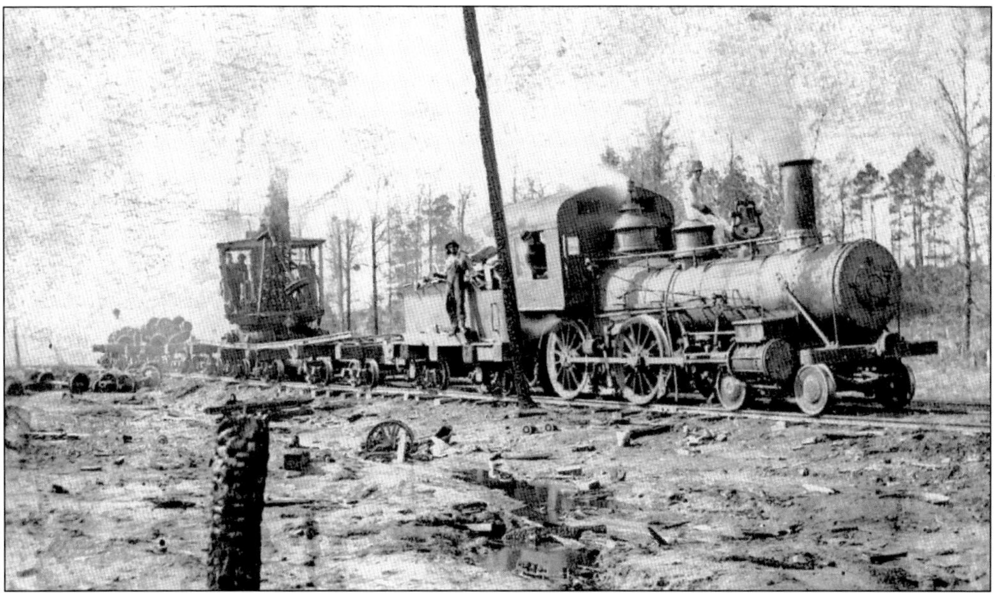

Development was slow in coming to North Louisiana's gently rolling hill country, prompting a group of 29 men from Claiborne and Bienville Parishes to organize a railroad that would connect their area with the rest of the world and ensure its future growth and development. The Louisiana North and South Railway Company was chartered on November 28, 1885. Due to a technical flaw in the charter, however, the company was reorganized as the Louisiana and North West Railroad Company on December 3, 1889. (Courtesy of C. C. Austin.)

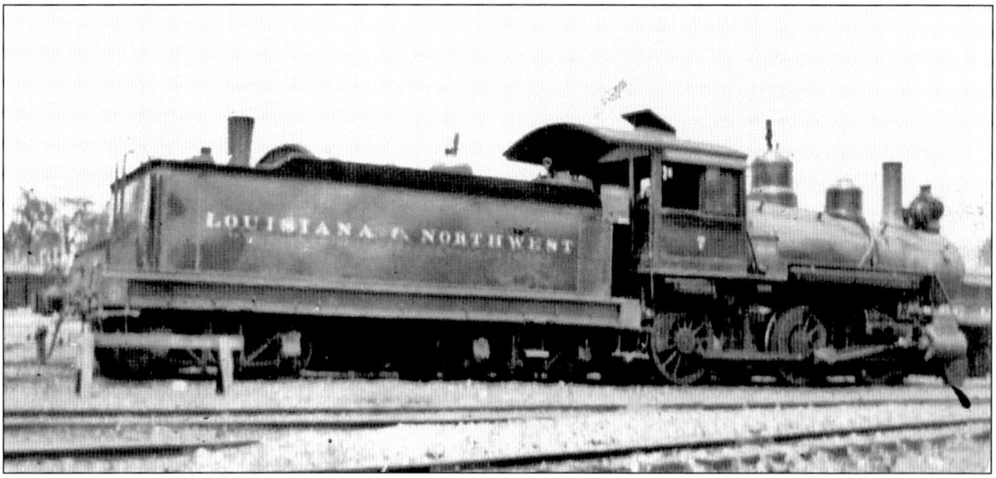

On April 30, 1887, the company signed a contract with J. D. Beardsley to construct 19 miles of track from Gibsland to Homer. This section was completed in 1888 and linked Homer with the east-west line of the Vicksburg, Shreveport, and Pacific Railroad. (Courtesy of the Ford Museum.)

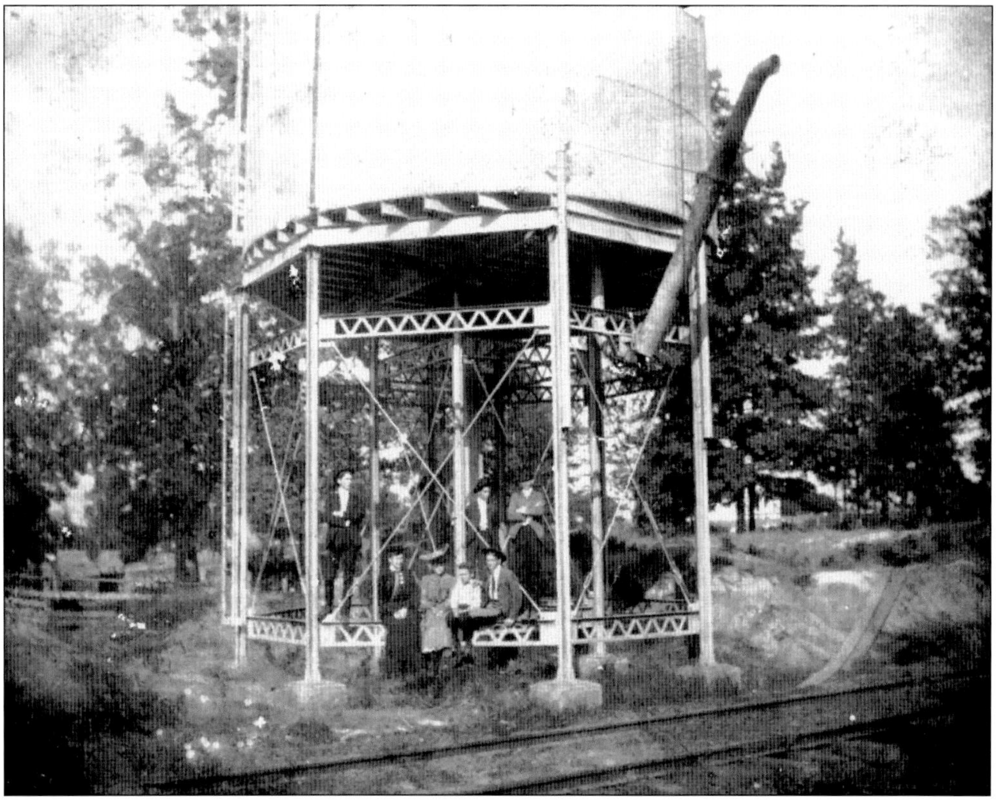

Watering stations were situated every 10 miles along the line to provide water for the boilers of the L&NW's steam engines. Watering stations were located at Gibsland, Athens, Homer, Standpipe, Haynesville, and Magnolia. The L&NW also purchased the lake on the Spring Lake Plantation south of Homer to serve as a watering stop. The railroad still owns this property. (Courtesy of the W. M. Knighten Estate.)

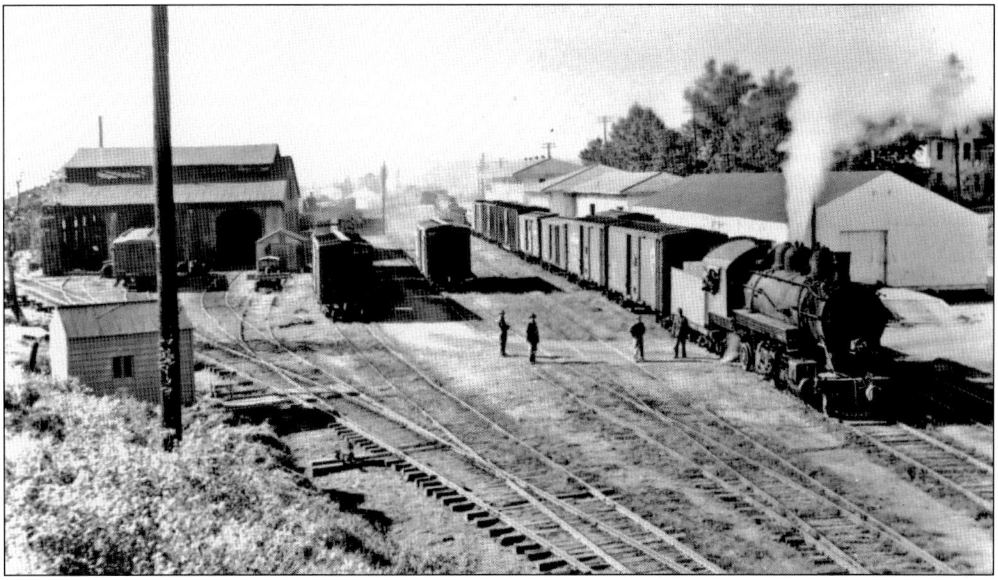

The newly founded L&NW was plagued by financial problems. Track expansion had created a $700,000 debt. On August 23, 1913, the company was placed in the hands of a receiver. Under the receivership, the property continued to decline to the extent that, when it was advertised for sale in July 1919, there were no bidders. On October 1, 1920, E. R. Bernstein of Shreveport was appointed as the new receiver. Under Bernstein's leadership, conditions began to improve. (Courtesy of the Ford Museum.)

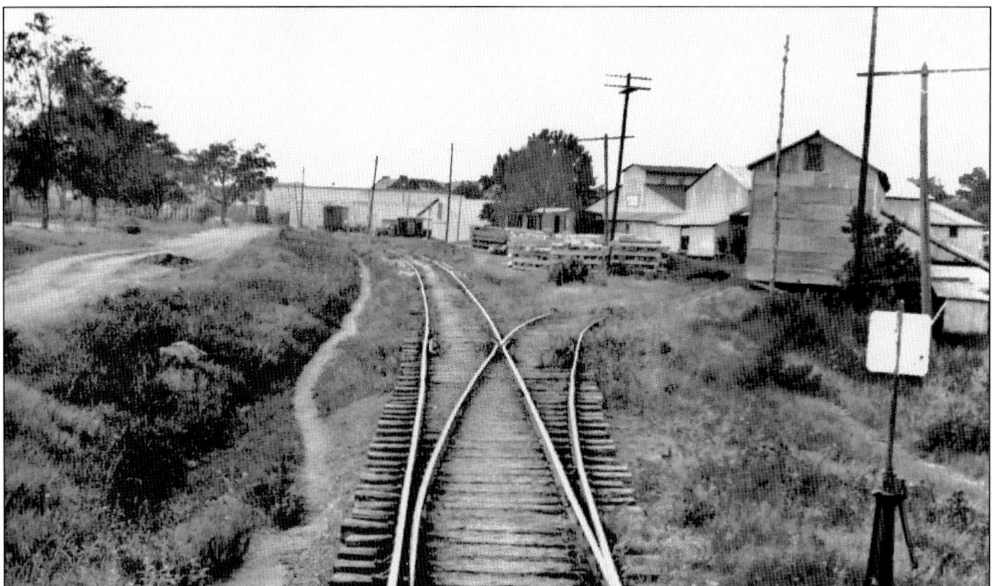

When the L&NW tracks were laid two miles east of old Haynesville in 1898, residents and businesses began moving to be closer to the new tracks, ultimately creating a ghost town at the old location. Old Town Cemetery serves as a reminder of the abandoned town site. The Haynesville Cotton Warehouse was built alongside the new railroad tracks. (Courtesy of the Ford Museum.)

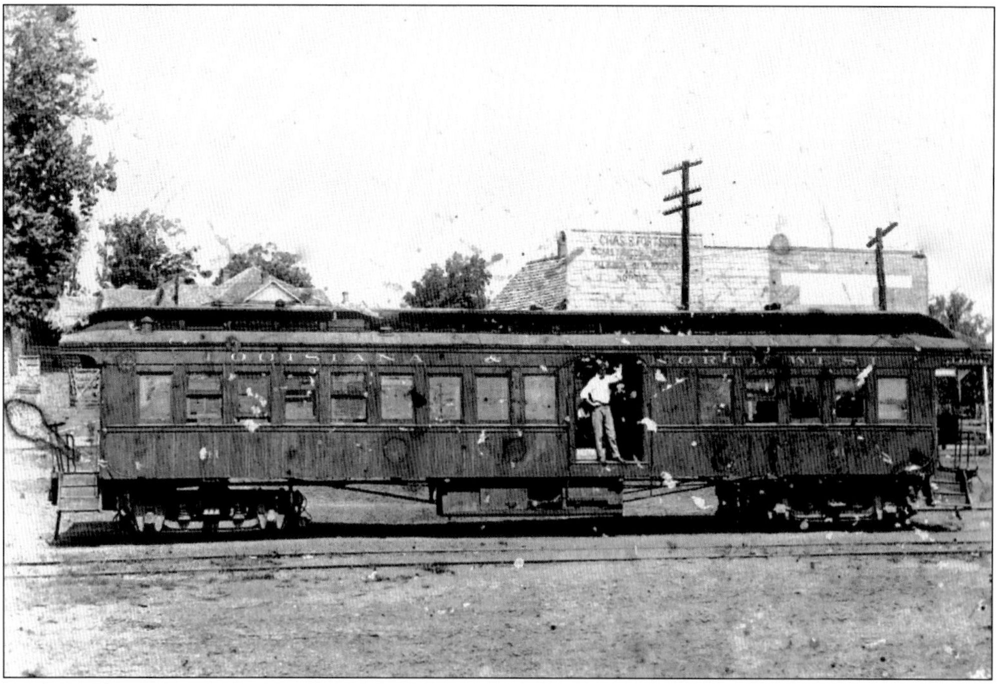

In the early 1900s, the L&NW, with its general offices in Homer, provided freight and passenger service Monday through Saturday, thus linking Claiborne Parish with major centers of trade. Charles Fortson's general merchandise store can be seen in the background of this photograph. (Courtesy of the Ford Museum.)

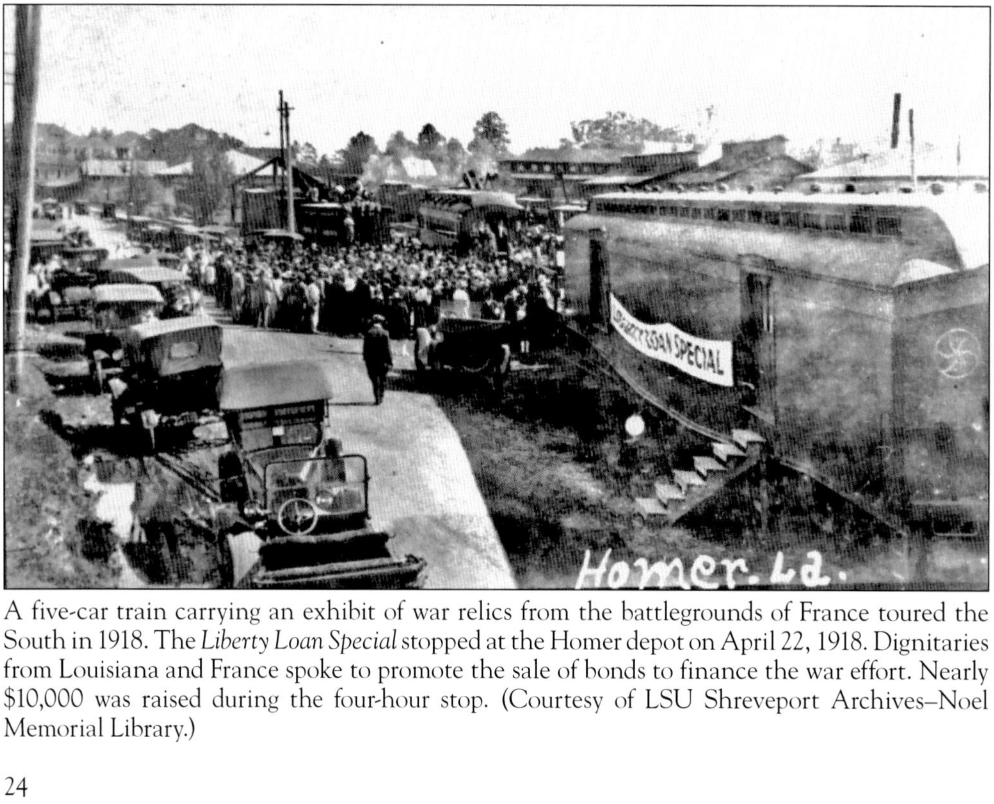

A five-car train carrying an exhibit of war relics from the battlegrounds of France toured the South in 1918. The *Liberty Loan Special* stopped at the Homer depot on April 22, 1918. Dignitaries from Louisiana and France spoke to promote the sale of bonds to finance the war effort. Nearly $10,000 was raised during the four-hour stop. (Courtesy of LSU Shreveport Archives–Noel Memorial Library.)

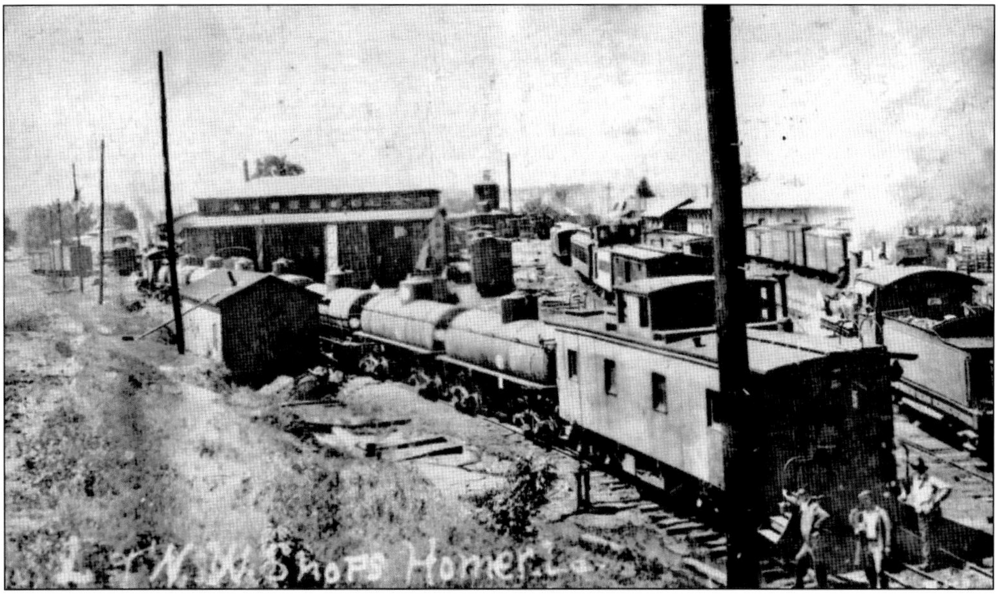

Much of the daily hustle and bustle of the railroad business took place in the Homer shop and yard. Locomotives, passenger cars, tanker cars, freight cars, and cabooses are all visible. (Courtesy of the Ford Museum.)

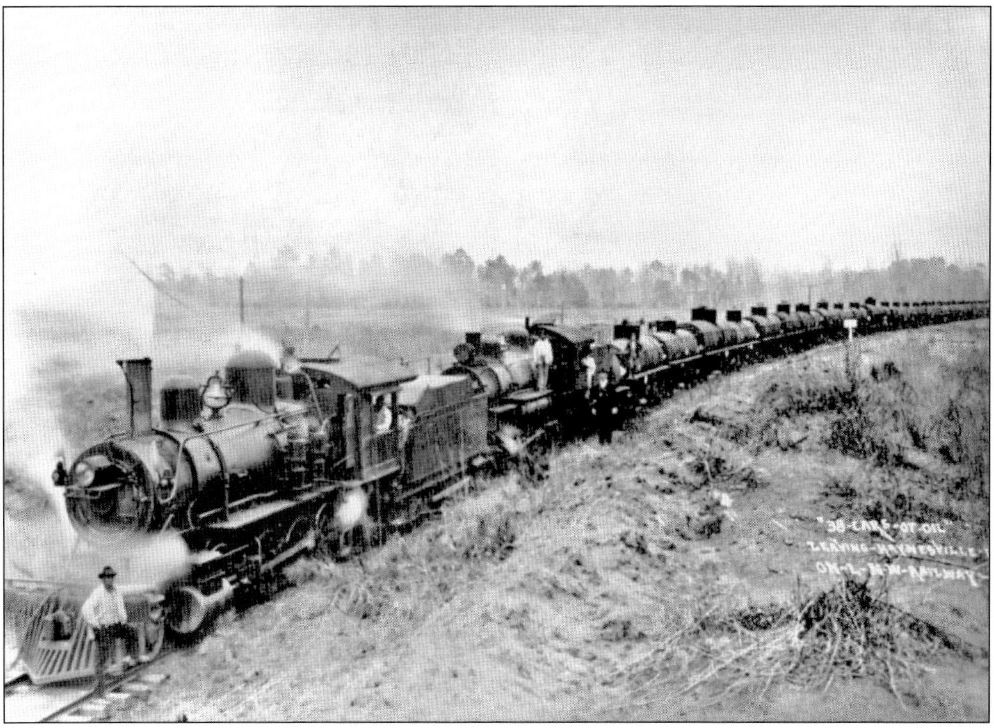

When oil was discovered near Homer in 1919 and near Haynesville in 1921, the L&NW began hauling tank cars filled with crude oil. A 38-car train pulled by locomotives No. 27 and No. 28 is transporting crude oil from Haynesville in the early 1920s. On the return trip, the railroad delivered necessary supplies and equipment to the oil fields. (Courtesy of the Ford Museum.)

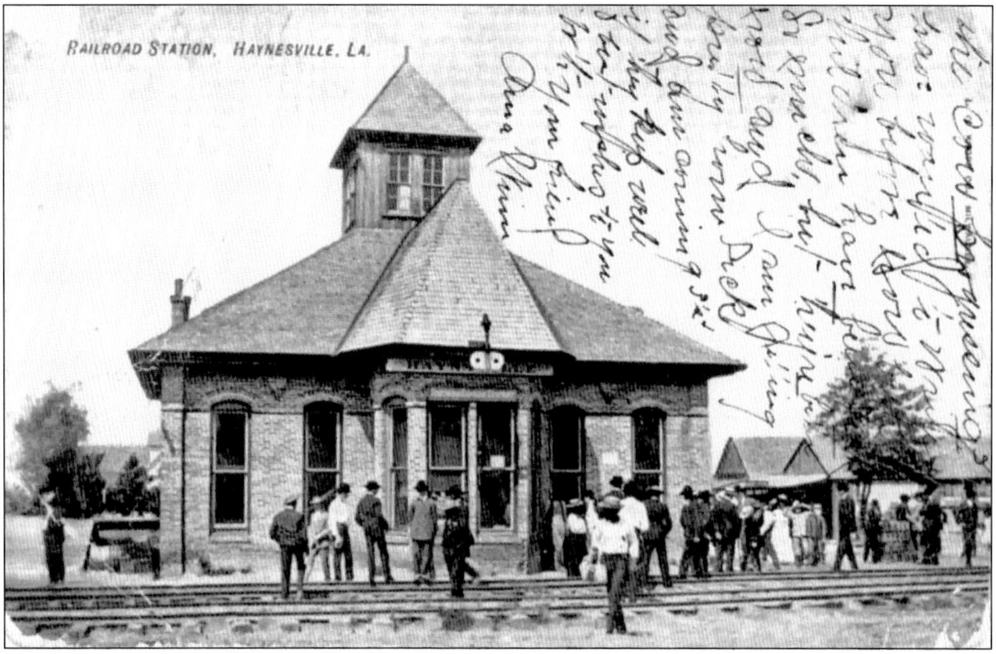

When the L&NW tracks reached Haynesville, the railroad used a boxcar as its first depot. Pictured here in 1908 is Haynesville's new brick depot building with its distinctive tall, narrow windows. A sign for the Southern Express Company hangs over the two center windows. (Courtesy of Bill W. Hightower.)

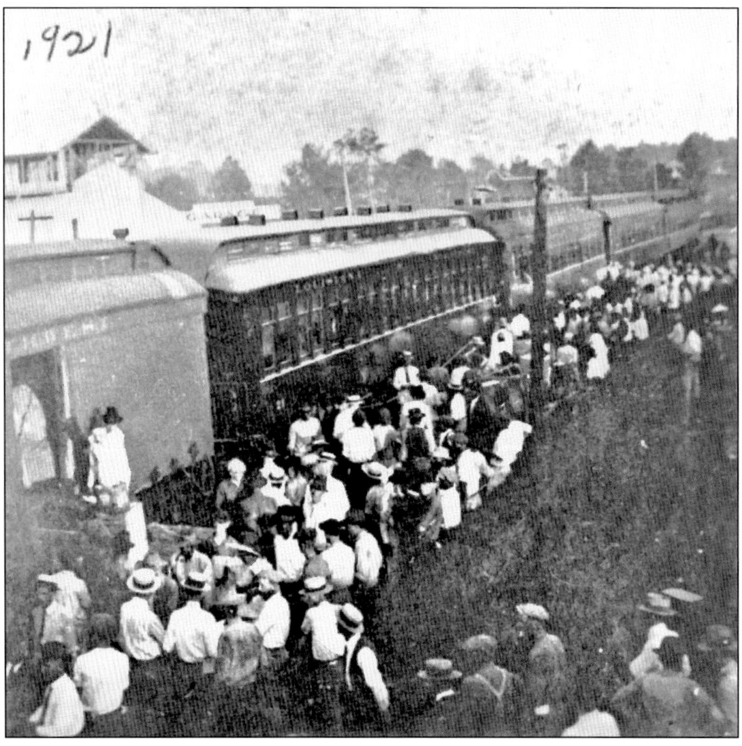

In addition to transporting crude oil from the fields, the L&NW also brought in hundreds of workers. Drillers, tool pushers, roustabouts, and roughnecks all came to work in the oil fields. Producers, promoters, engineers, oil well service crews, lease men, and lawyers also came to benefit from this newfound source of wealth. In this 1921 photograph, the Haynesville depot is shown congested with passenger traffic. (Courtesy of Tom Crocker.)

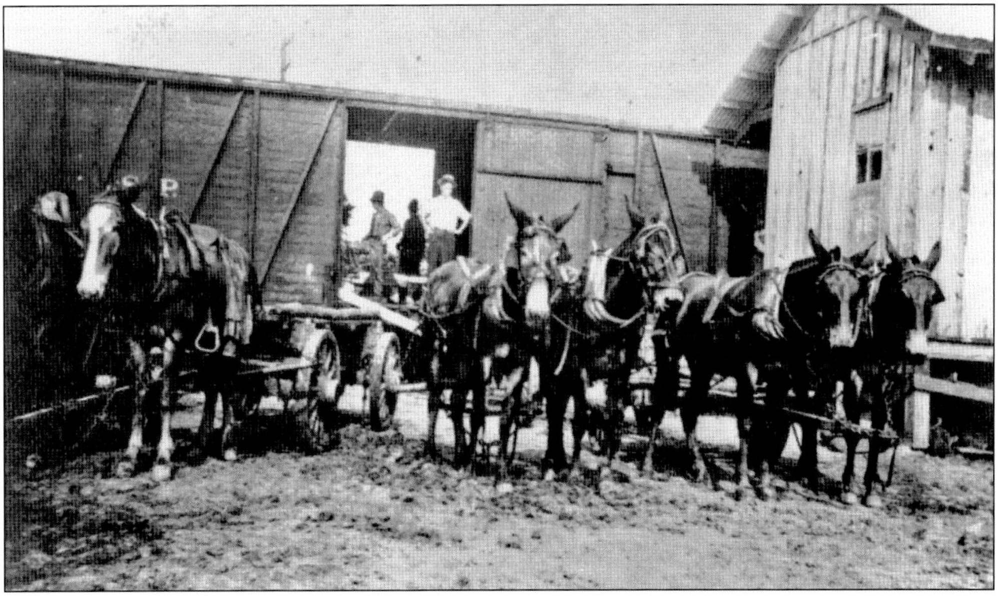

While work in the oil fields was booming, the L&NW profited from an increased freight volume, as well as increased passenger traffic. At one time, the daily volume of outbound freight for Haynesville was 185 tons, inbound 85 tons. Daily outbound freight for Homer was 150 tons, inbound 66 tons. Most incoming supplies were transported to the oil fields in wagons pulled by teams of mules. (Courtesy of the Ford Museum.)

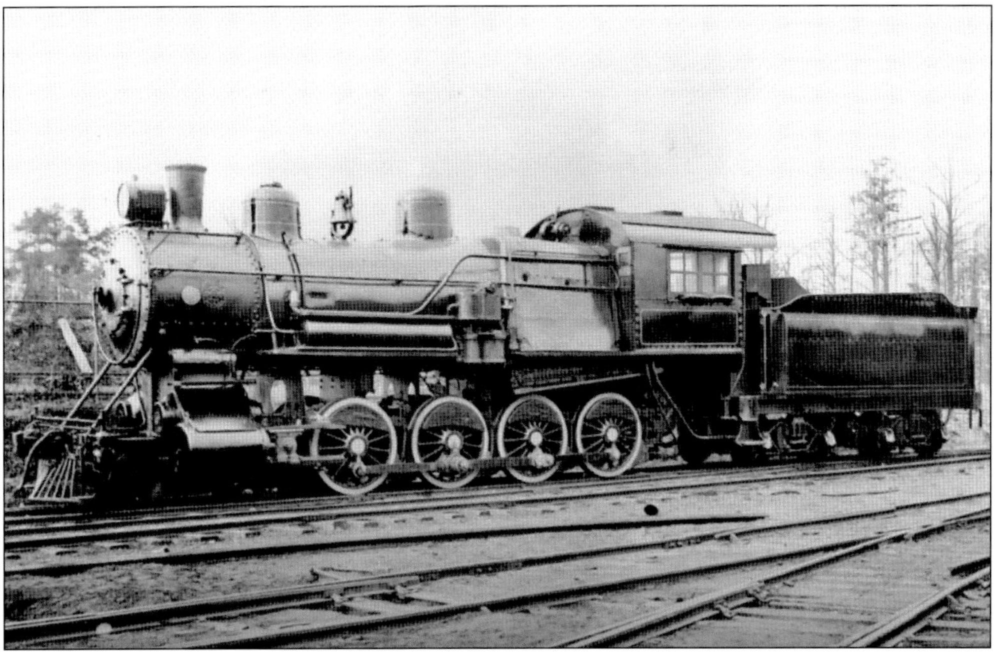

During the 1920s, the L&NW began burning the oil it hauled. Six locomotives were converted from coal to oil in 1922. Above is Engine No. 33, which had a rare 4-8-0 wheel arrangement. Built in 1900, No. 33 had been previously owned by four railroads before being purchased by the L&NW in 1926. Profits from the oil boom enabled the L&NW to make improvements to its tracks and bridges. (Courtesy of Bill W. Hightower.)

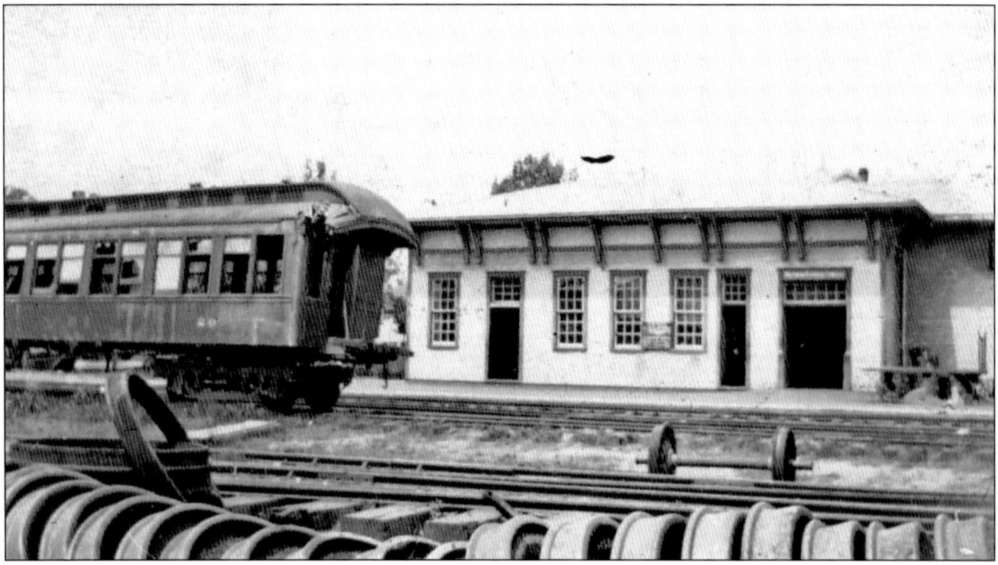

Passenger service was discontinued on January 31, 1948; however, the railroad continued to transport oil- and timber-related products. In 1949, the L&NW became the first railroad in the United States to be completely operated by radio. Note the idle passenger car in the background and the metal wheels stockpiled in the foreground. (Courtesy of the Ford Museum.)

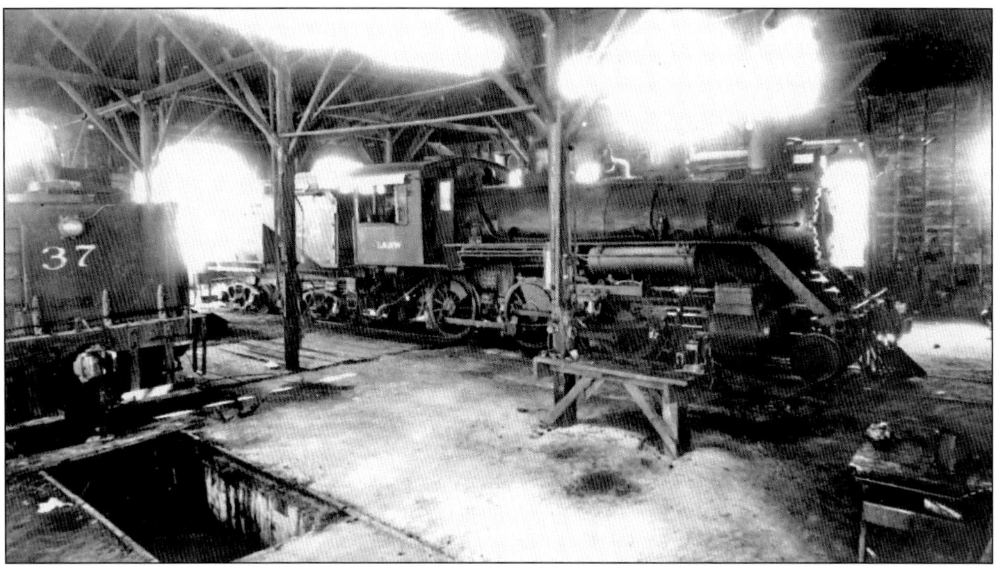

The L&NW maintained depots at Gibsland, Athens, Homer, and Haynesville, Louisiana, and at Emerson, Magnolia, and McNeil, Arkansas. The steam locomotive shop, shown above in November 1944, was located on the Homer yard. In 1950, when the railroad replaced its remaining steam-driven locomotives with diesel-powered ones, a diesel repair shop was established at Gibsland. (Courtesy of the Ford Museum.)

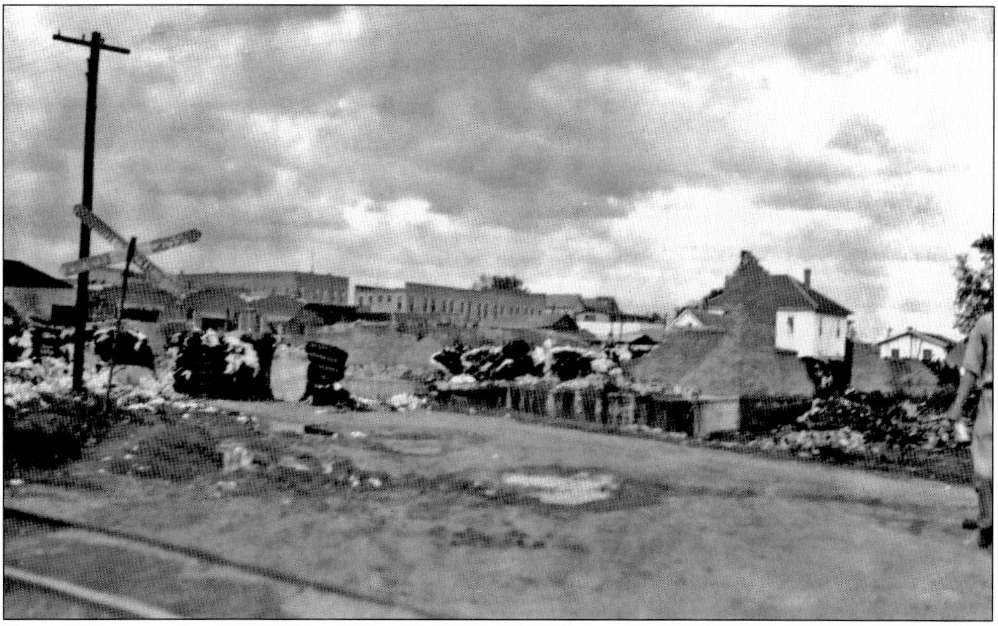

Over the years, the L&NW laid spurs to serve the various businesses along the railroad line. A spur connected the Haynesville Cotton Warehouse to the main line of the L&NW to facilitate the shipment of cotton to market. The Haynesville Cotton Warehouse burned in 1930, destroying the cotton held in storage. (Courtesy of the L&NW Railroad.)

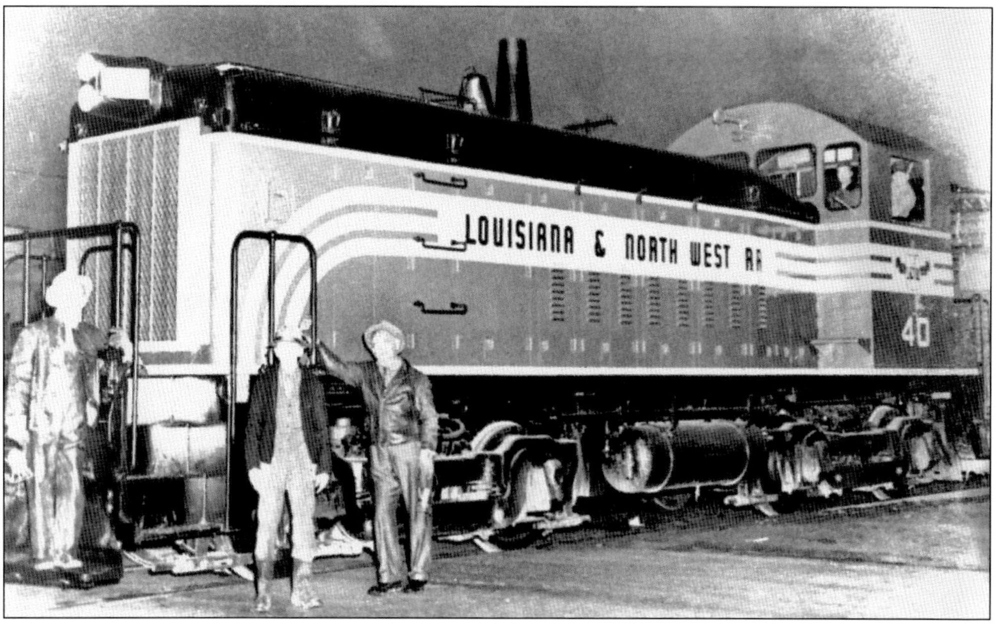

In December 1950, the L&NW purchased its first diesel-powered locomotives, Nos. 40 and 41, from General Motors Electro-Motive Division. These locomotives were the first to bear the L&NW's familiar red-and-yellow logo. The logo was designed by Charles Endom, whose father was the master mechanic and shop foreman in the Homer shops. The L&NW's last four steam-powered locomotives, Nos. 36 through 39, were sold for scrap in July 1951. (Courtesy of Tom Crocker.)

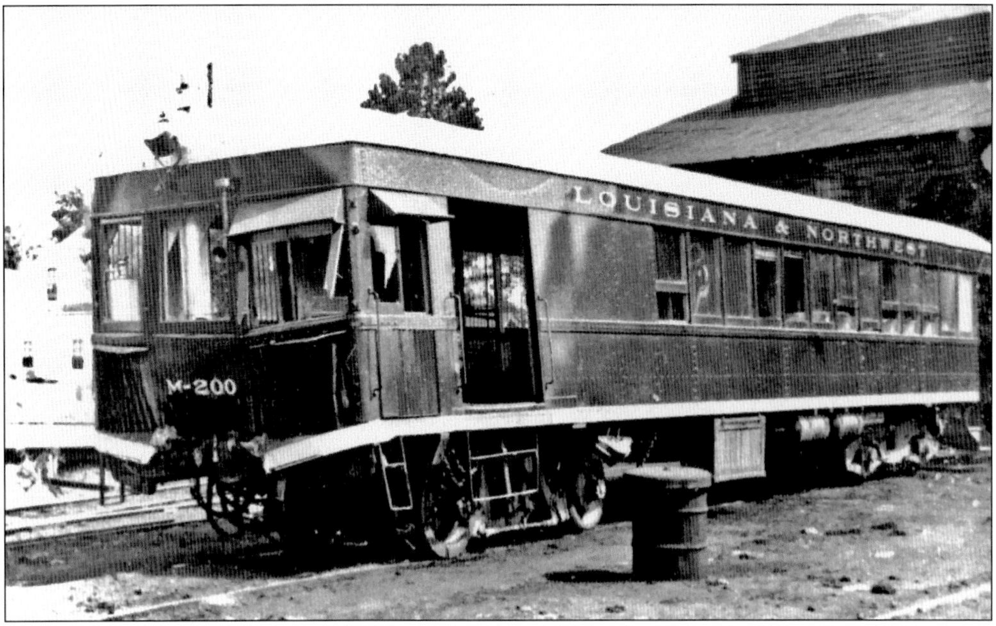

By 1925, wooden passenger cars had been largely put out of service. At that time, the L&NW purchased a new M-200 Brill motor car for $26,619 to provide passenger service. It was retired in July 1944, following a head-on collision with a freight train in Haynesville. (Courtesy of Tom Crocker.)

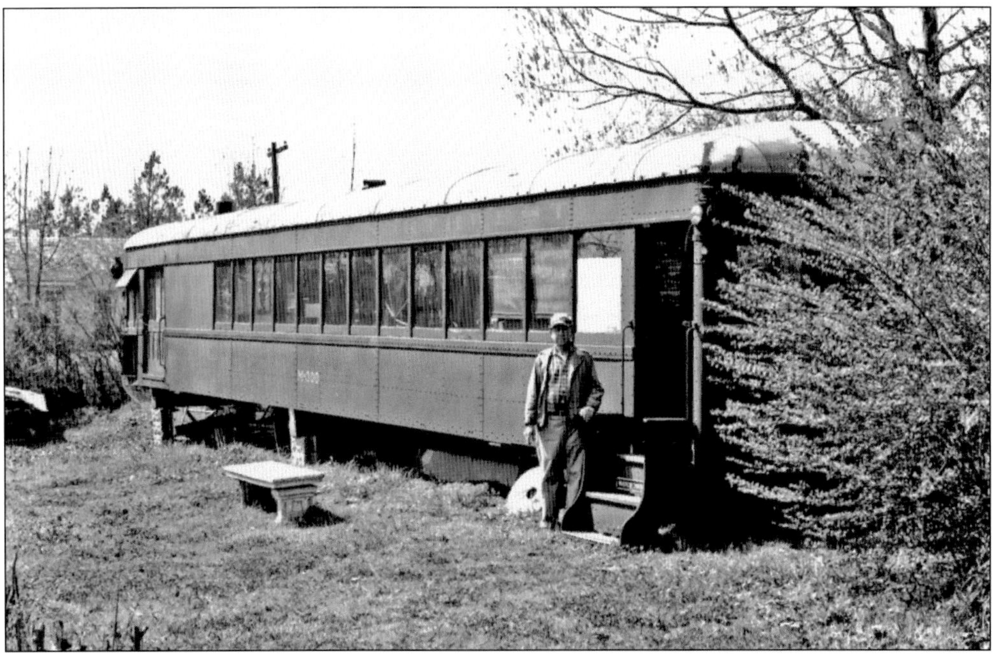

The L&NW purchased an M-300 Brill motor car in 1931. Herbert S. Ford later acquired a "Doodle," the nickname given to these cars, to house his growing collection of artifacts. Parked alongside Ford's home on North Main Street, the Doodle provided a unique setting for his museum. Through the years, many guests visited the museum in the Doodle for a glance back into Claiborne Parish history. (Courtesy of the J. J. Smith family.)

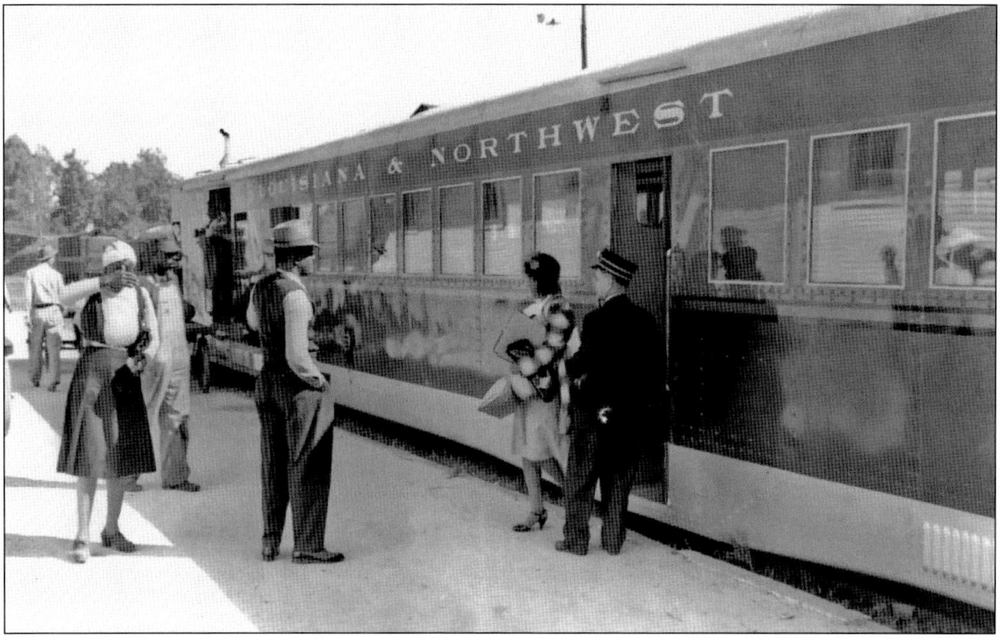

Conductor Chris Weaver is shown assisting passengers off the newly acquired M-400 Brill motor car in November 1944. The self-propelled Brill cars provided safe and inexpensive transportation to points along the railroad line. Competition from an increasing number of private automobiles following World War II ultimately caused the L&NW to discontinue its passenger service. (Courtesy of the Ford Museum.)

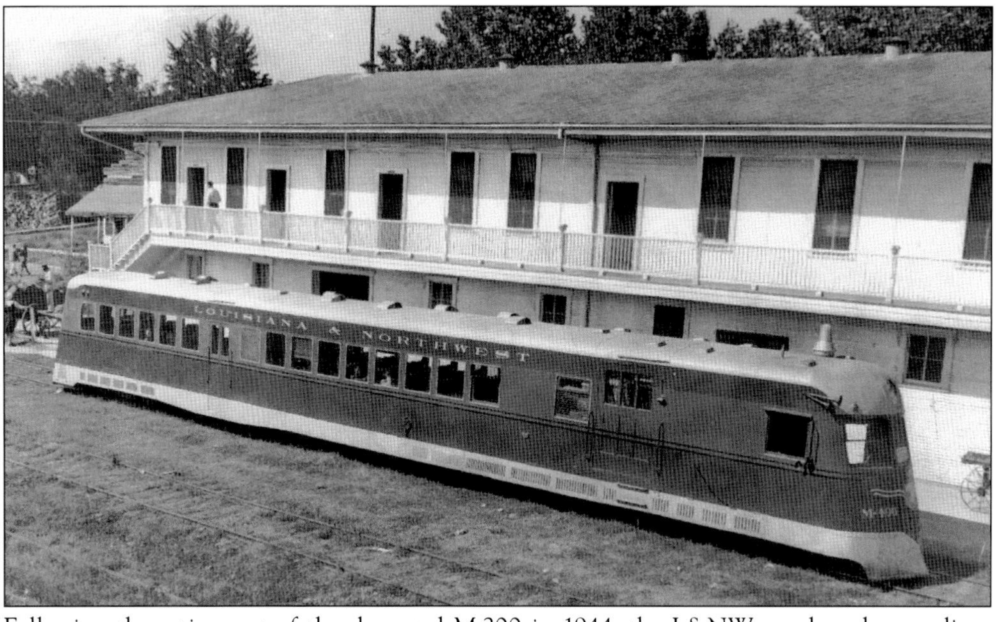

Following the retirement of the damaged M-200 in 1944, the L&NW purchased a gasoline-powered M-400 Brill motor car, designed to carry mail and express freight as well as passengers and baggage. Previously owned, it was acquired from the Chicago and Eastern Illinois Railroad for $15,000, plus $808.56 freight. The car was sold through a broker to Cuba in 1948. (Courtesy of the Ford Museum.)

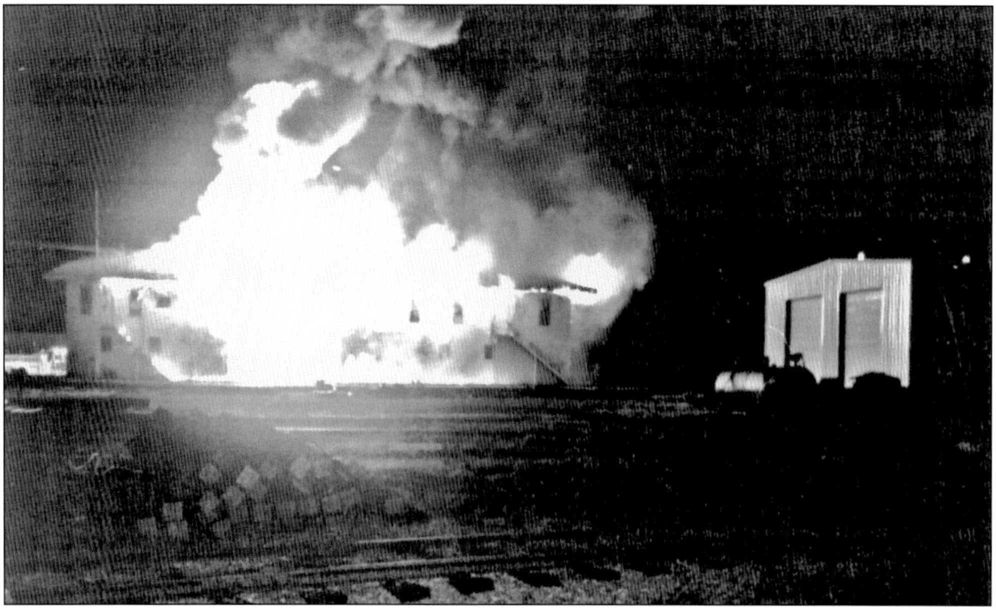

On July 6, 1998, an early morning fire destroyed the L&NW's general office building in Homer. Nine firefighting units responded to the alarm, and 60 volunteer firefighters battled the blaze for several hours. At the height of the fire, workers pumped 3,000 gallons of water per minute onto the burning building. (Courtesy of Gladney Dillon.)

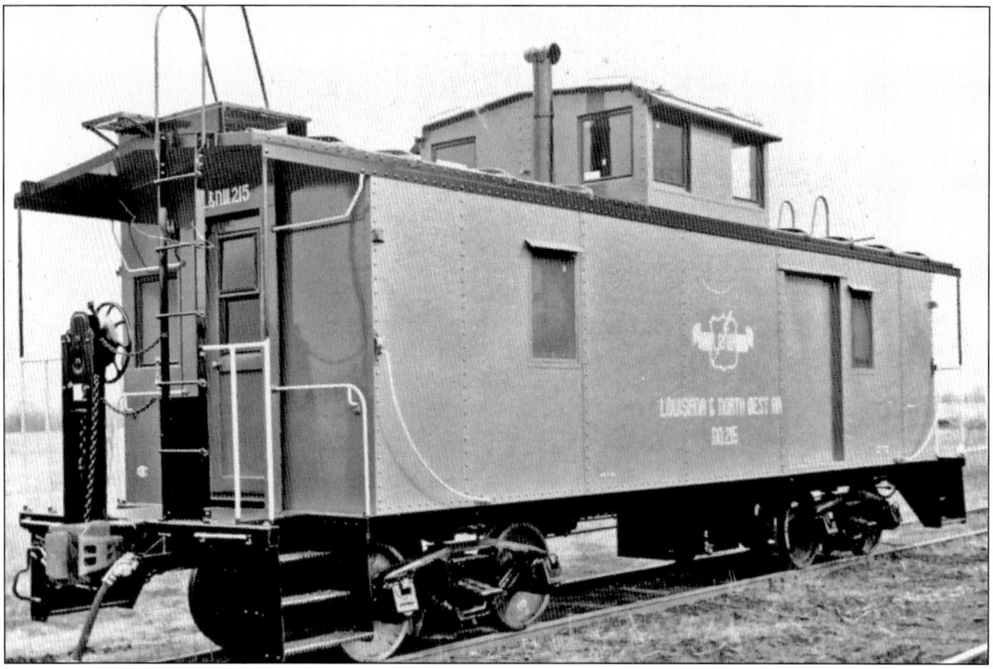

The traditional red caboose has been replaced by a "flashing rear-end device," or a FRED. The FRED is operated by air and battery power. It transmits a signal from the end of the train to the locomotive when the proper air pressure has been applied to all the cars. Today's children no longer know what it means to look for that distinctive red car that, for the older generation, signaled the end of a passing train. (Courtesy of Tom Crocker.)

Three

Reading, 'Riting, and 'Rithmetic

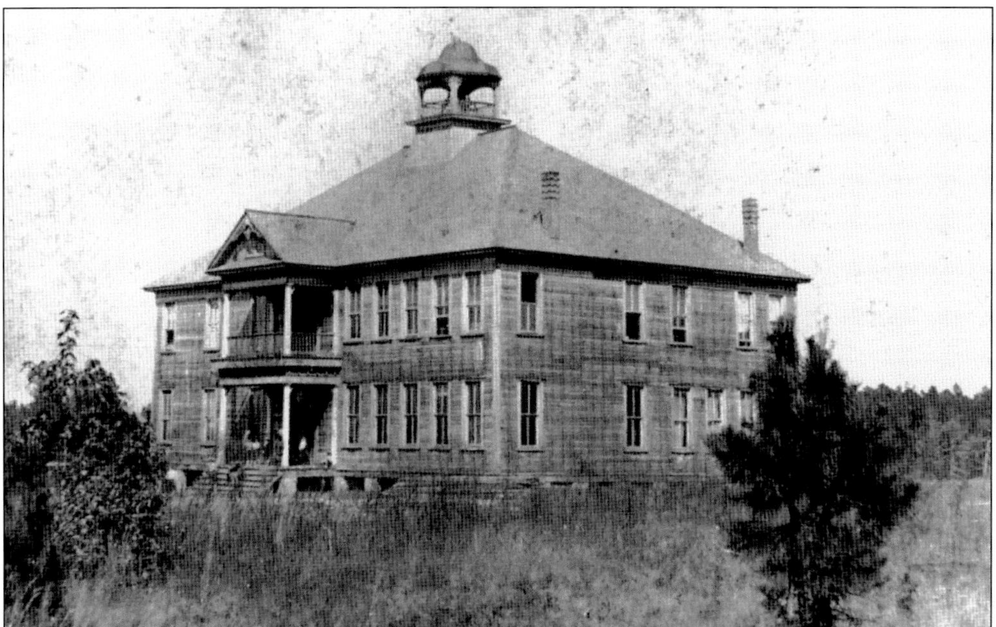

The cornerstone of the educational movement in Claiborne Parish was laid in 1822, when James A. Conley was hired by John Murrell, the first white settler in the area, to teach in his home. As population increased, one-room schoolhouses were built or abandoned structures were refurbished for use as school buildings. This photograph shows Haynesville School around 1915. The building burned in 1923. (Courtesy of Tom Crocker.)

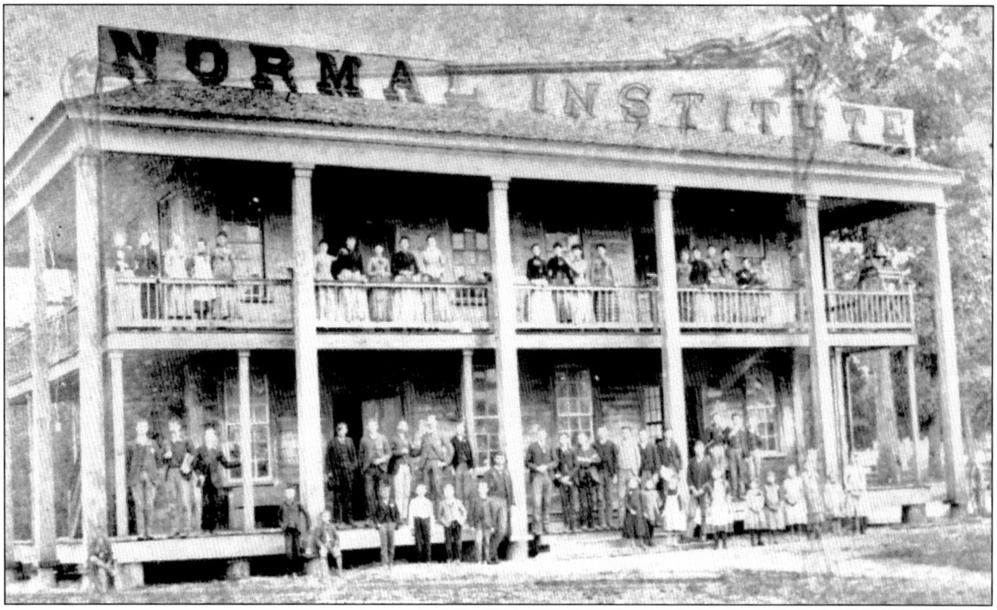

Haynesville Normal Institute served as a training school for teachers as well as a coeducational school for elementary and secondary students. Built in 1871 on the site of present-day Old Town Cemetery, it became a noted North Louisiana school with 200 students. According to the institute's history, Latin mottoes and classroom rules were written on darkened walls used as blackboards. One rule forbade boys and girls from speaking to each other during school hours. Punishments, such as wearing dunce caps, were carried out with each infraction. (Courtesy of the Ford Museum.)

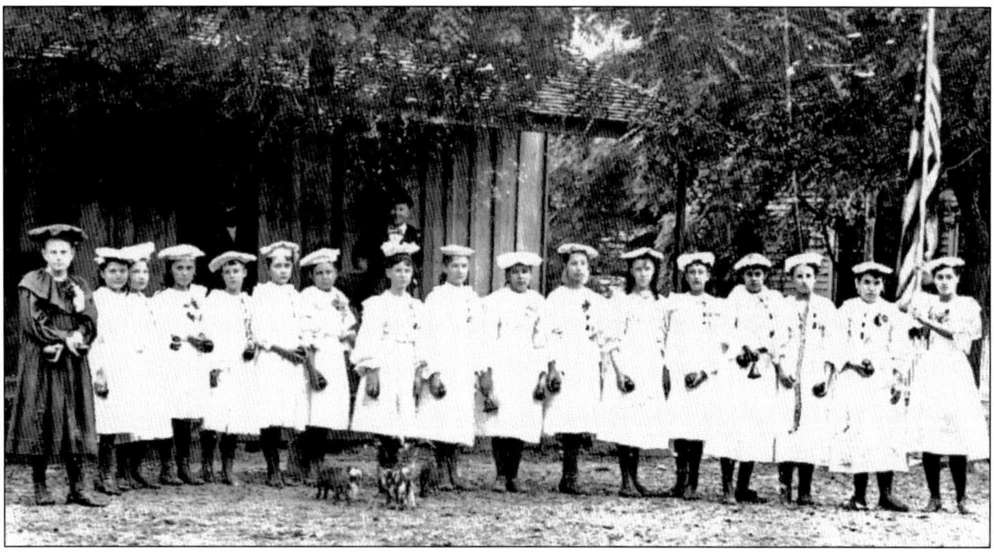

These young women attended the Homer Masonic Female Institute. Formerly known as the Homer Female College, the school was purchased in 1859 by Homer Masonic Lodge No. 152, F&AM, and renamed the Homer Masonic Female Institute. Under the able administration of Prof. L. F. Wilcox and Prof. T. S. and Mrs. Sligh, the institute flourished for many years. Some of the best-educated women of North Louisiana were graduates of this well-known school. (Courtesy of the Ford Museum.)

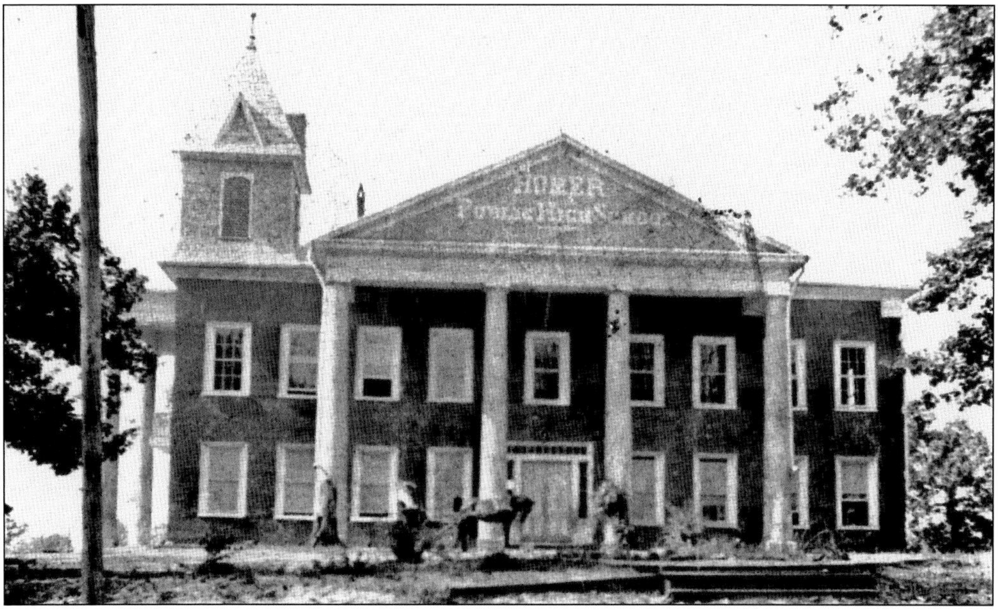

Under the supervision of a board of trustees appointed by the Louisiana Methodist Conference, the Homer Male College was chartered by the state legislature in 1855. The college opened its doors in 1859. Classes were suspended during the Civil War but resumed in 1867. Many notable men were educated here, including Col. James W. Nicholson, president of Louisiana State University and a distinguished professor of mathematics. Following the closure of the Homer Male College, the building was used to house Homer's first nine-month public high school. (Courtesy of the Ford Museum.)

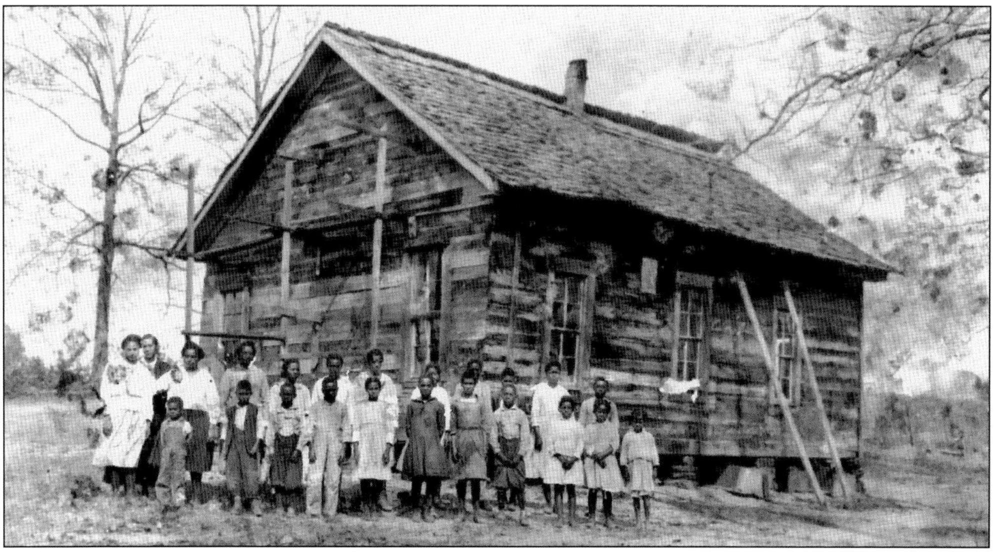

Most rural black schools employed a single teacher to teach grades one through eight. The curriculum included reading, writing, arithmetic, grammar, and geography. Physical education consisted of ring plays, rag ball, and basketball played in the schoolyard. Friday evening programs at the school gave people in the community an opportunity to get together to hear the students recite their lessons. Richland School, located northeast of Athens, was typical of one-room schools located in rural communities. (Courtesy of A. D. Williams.)

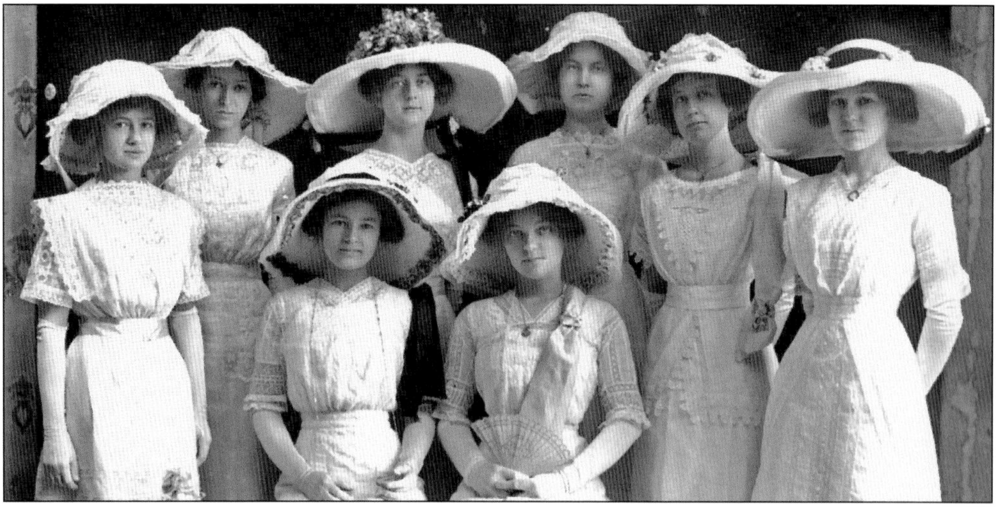

The Homer High graduating class of 1913 was made up of eight girls. Graduates were, from left to right, (seated) Bessie Bonner and Sarah Meadors; (standing) Ida Langston, Mary Tooke, Ruth Meadows, Ida Knighten, Sunshine Johnson, and Ruby Flynt. The friendships formed by the girls during their school years lasted a lifetime. (Courtesy of the Ford Museum.)

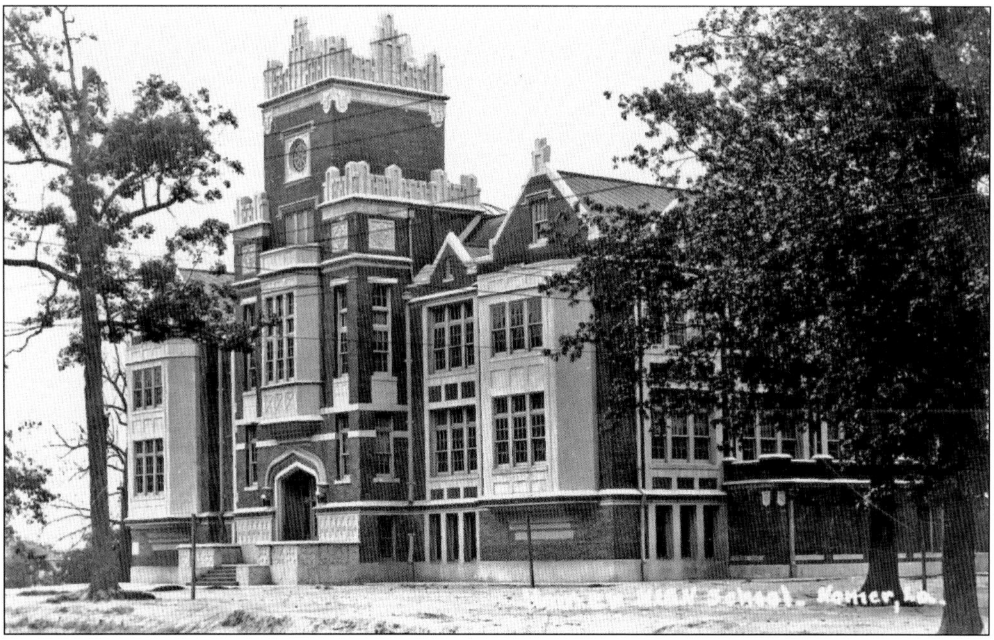

Homer's new high school building, dedicated on January 11, 1915, was erected on the site of the old Homer Male College. The school and furnishings were financed through the sale of a 40-year bond issue. This impressive structure served Homer's high school students until 1927, when the present high school building was completed. The Homer Grammar School occupied the building from 1927 to 1948. (Courtesy of the Ford Museum.)

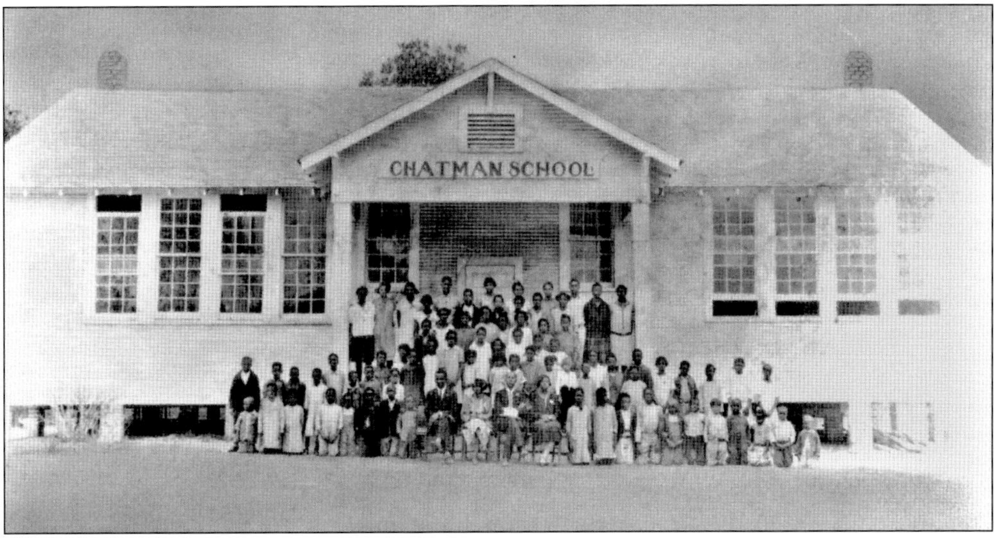

When oil was discovered on Bill Chatman's property in 1919, he and Rev. Andrew Rhodes, a Methodist minister and carpenter, donated land for a teachers' home and school to serve the children in their community. Construction of the buildings was financed, in part, by the Julius Rosenwald Fund. Rosenwald, a philanthropist who was president of Sears, Roebuck, and Company, donated money to build black schools throughout the South. Chatman School was one of 35 rural schools in Claiborne Parish financed through the Rosenwald Fund. (Courtesy of the William Chatman Estate.)

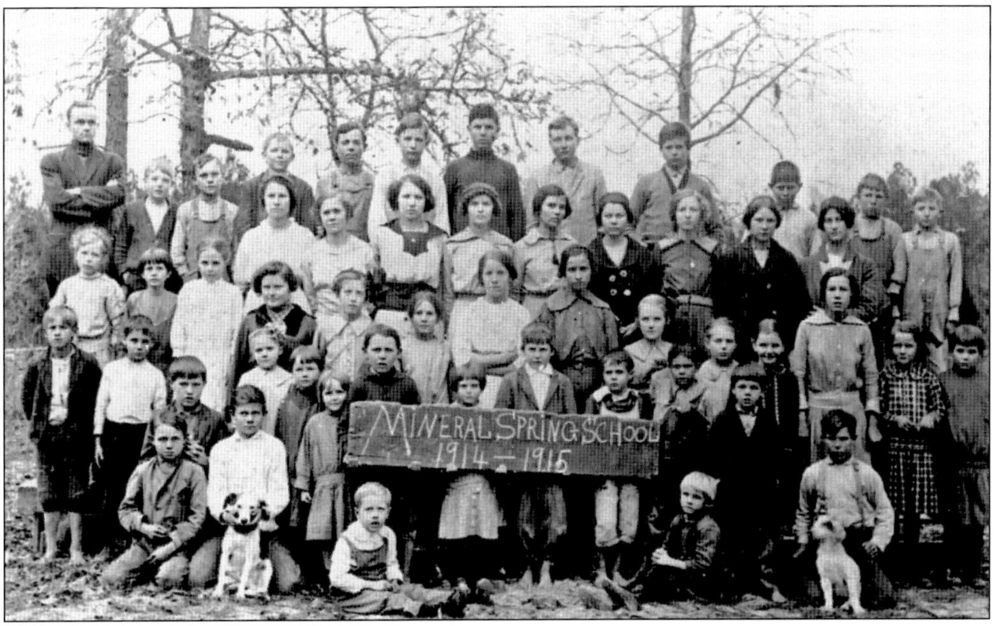

Mineral Spring School was one of many small schools established during the administration of E. H. McClendon, who served from 1900 to 1906 as Claiborne Parish's first superintendent of education. Teacher pay was low during this period, and classroom supplies were often meager. Despite difficulties, many Claiborne Parish students received good basic educations from teachers who were dedicated to the goals of public education. (Courtesy of LSU Shreveport Archives–Noel Memorial Library.)

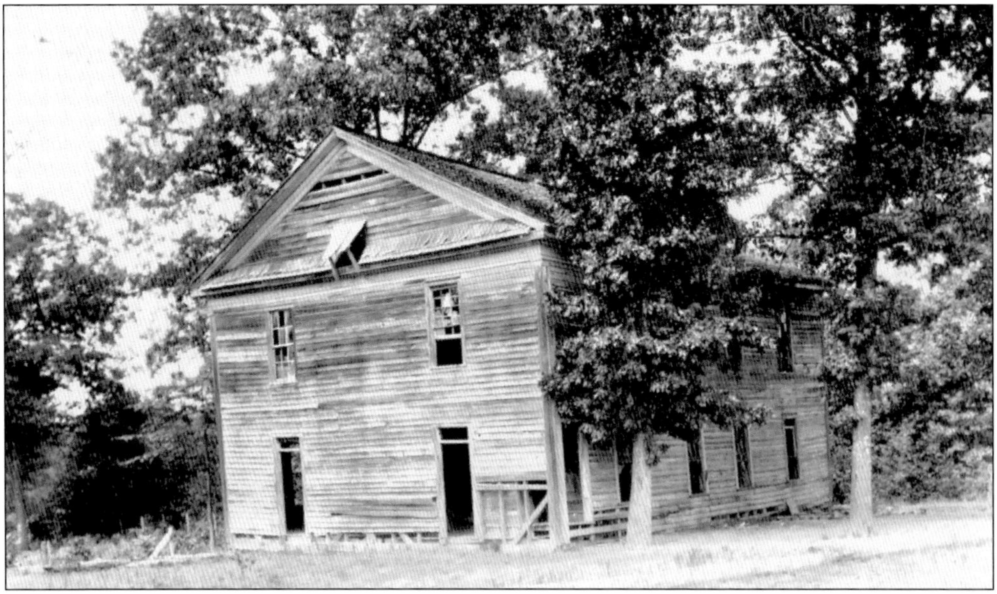

The first school building in the Summerfield community was a log structure erected in 1867. The two-story frame building above was constructed in 1872 on the site of the present-day Summerfield campus. E. M. Corry was the first teacher at the new building. The basic curriculum included lessons from the *Blue Back Speller*, *Davies' Arithmetic*, and *McGuffey's Reader*. Grade levels were not used at the school; instead, students advanced to the next level based on ability. (Courtesy of the Claiborne Parish School Board.)

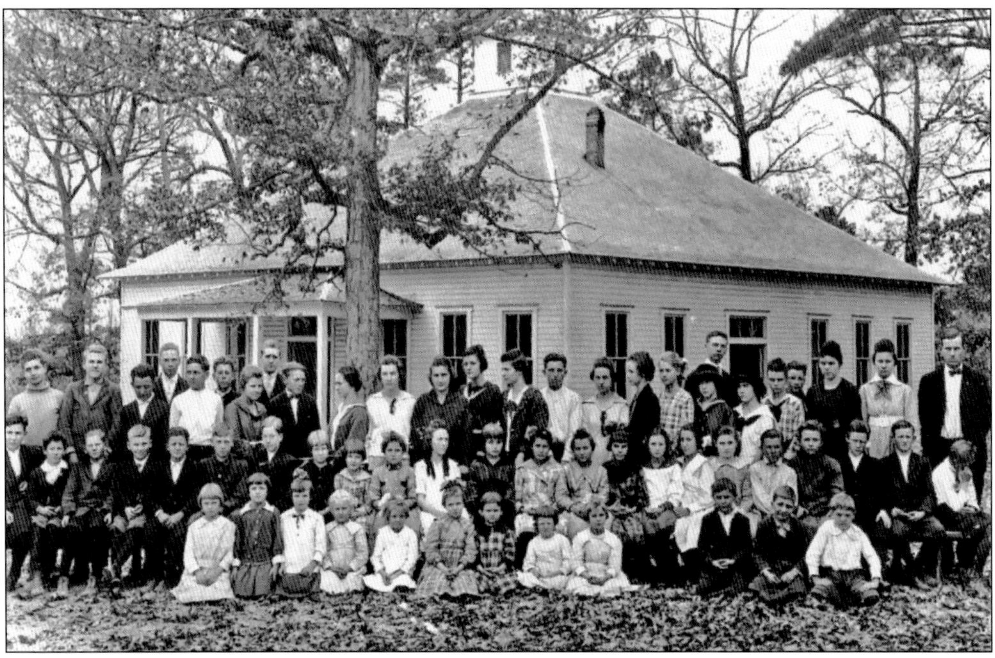

Set among the shading oaks, the new building for Summerfield School was opened in the fall of 1921. The first class to graduate from the new building received their diplomas in May 1922. The graduates were Carrie Dell Davidson, Millard Ledbetter, and Lucille Hightower. (Courtesy of Helen Campbell.)

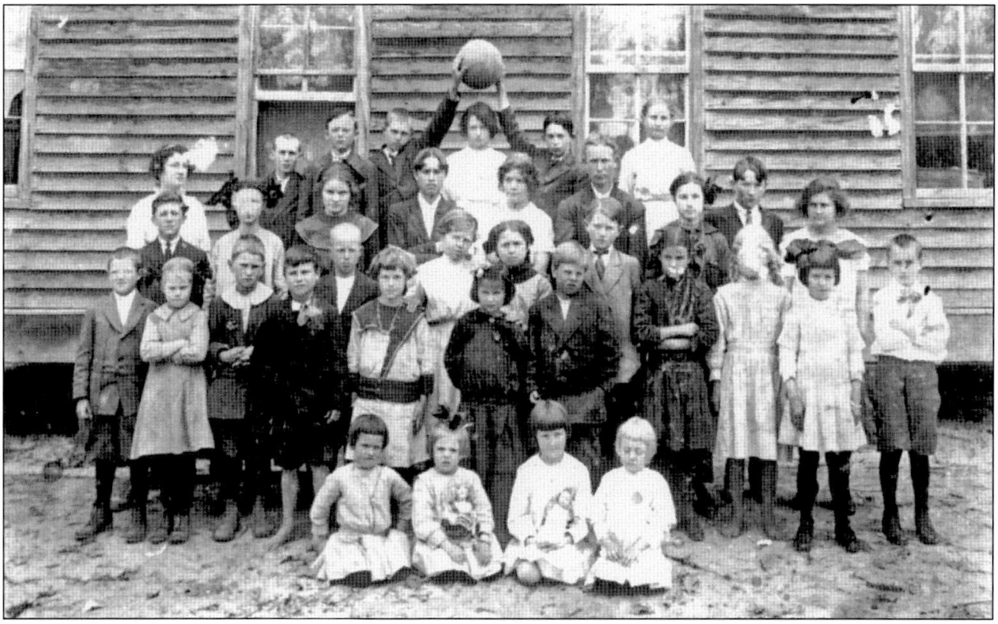

Walnut Grove School was established during the administration of school superintendent E. H. McClendon. These students were wearing their Sunday best when they posed for this photograph in 1915 with their teacher, Lucille Dawson (back row, left). Children often played with their own toys during recess. Note the dolls held by the girls in the first row and the basketball held by the boys in the top row. (Courtesy of Bill W. Hightower.)

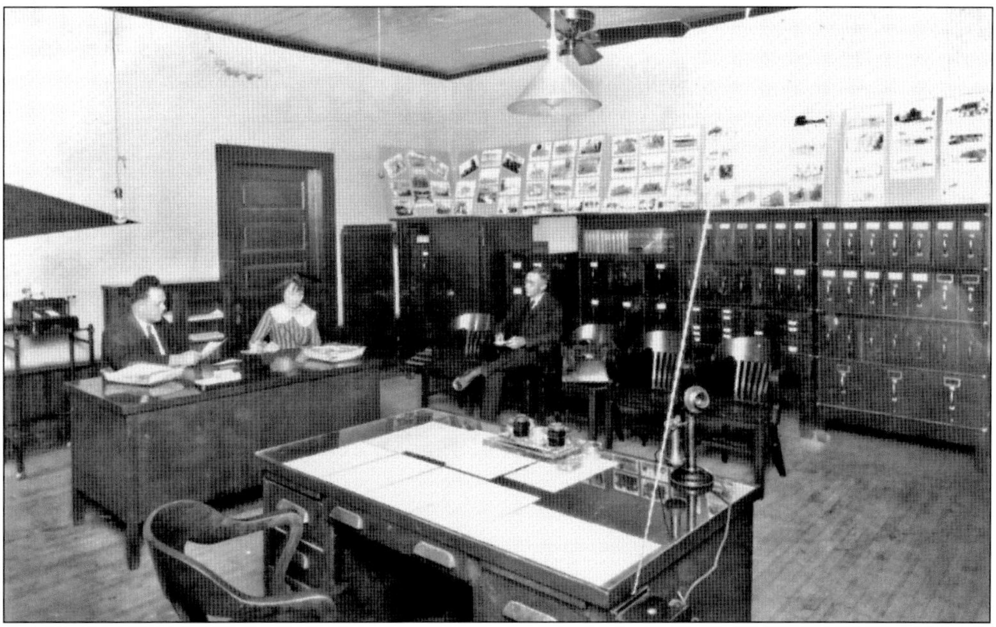

Many of the photographs in this chapter were made in the early 1920s for the Claiborne Parish School Board. Here some are shown being displayed above the file cabinets in Supt. John S. Patton's office. Patton served as superintendent of Claiborne Parish schools from 1920 until 1935. During his administration, many frame structures were replaced with new brick buildings. (Courtesy of the Claiborne Parish School Board.)

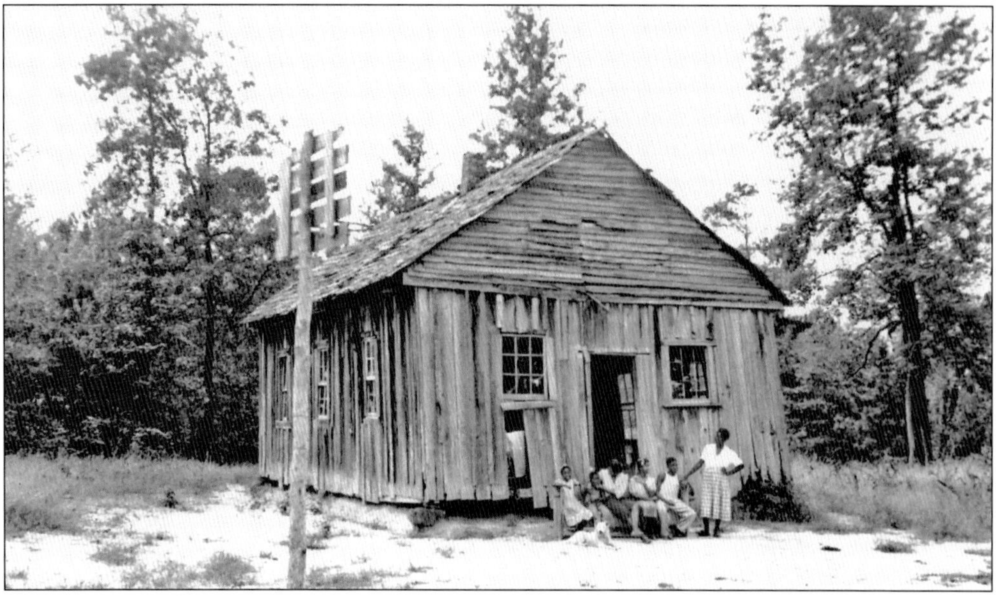

Wafer Chapel School was located approximately 6 miles east of Homer. At one time, there were 62 rural elementary schools and 4 high schools for black students in Claiborne Parish. Due to lack of funds, many school buildings were in a poor state of repair. It was left to the parents of the students to furnish the amenities needed to operate the schools. (Courtesy of A. D. Williams.)

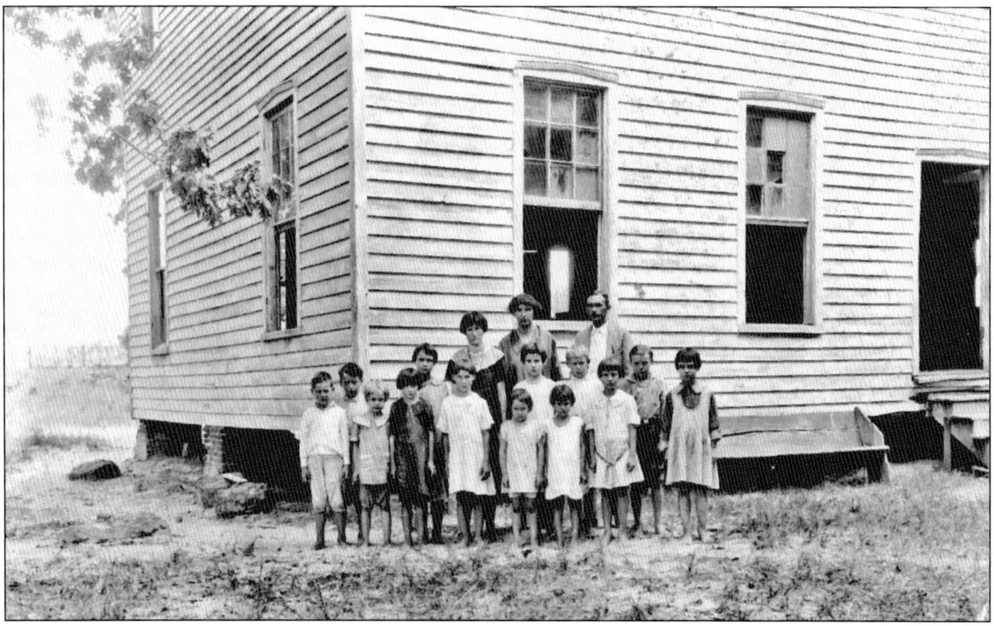

Founded in 1870 by Austin Harris and Col. J. W. Nicholson, the Arizona Academy soon became known for its academic excellence. A private school until 1910, it was deeded to the Claiborne Parish School Board and became Arizona Rural School. The school consolidated with Lisbon in 1928. The building was dismantled in 1946, and salvageable materials were donated to the Arizona Methodist Church. Barefoot students and their teacher stand beside the school in the early 1920s. (Courtesy of the Claiborne Parish School Board.)

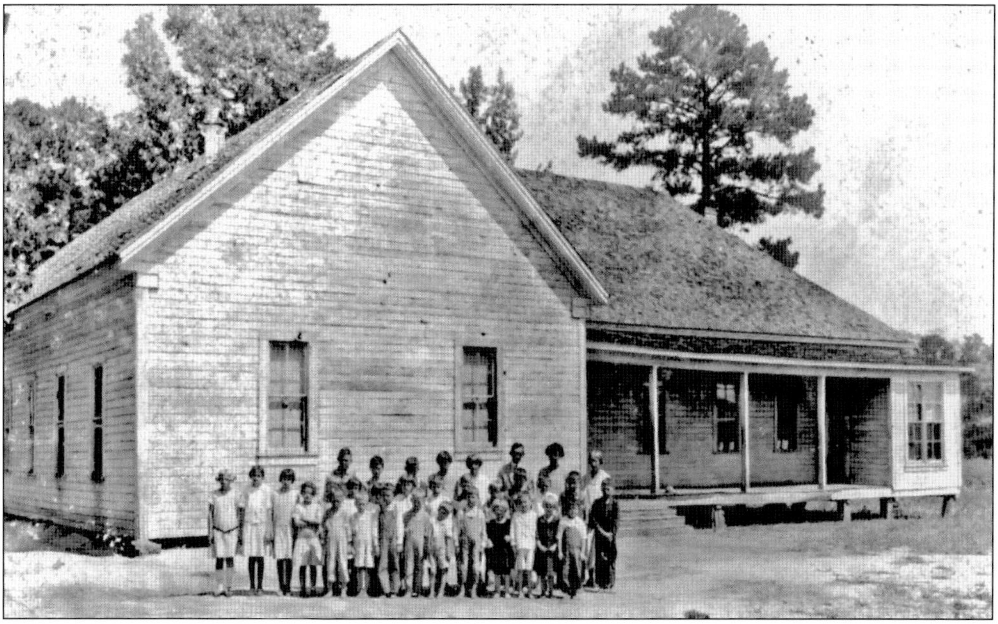

Rural schools once dotted the landscape of Claiborne Parish. The length of school terms varied with the planting and harvesting of crops. Most children walked to school, making it necessary that schools be located within walking distance. This photograph shows Thurmon School, which served rural families in the Summerfield area. Thurmon School was consolidated with Summerfield School in the early 1920s. (Courtesy of the Claiborne Parish School Board.)

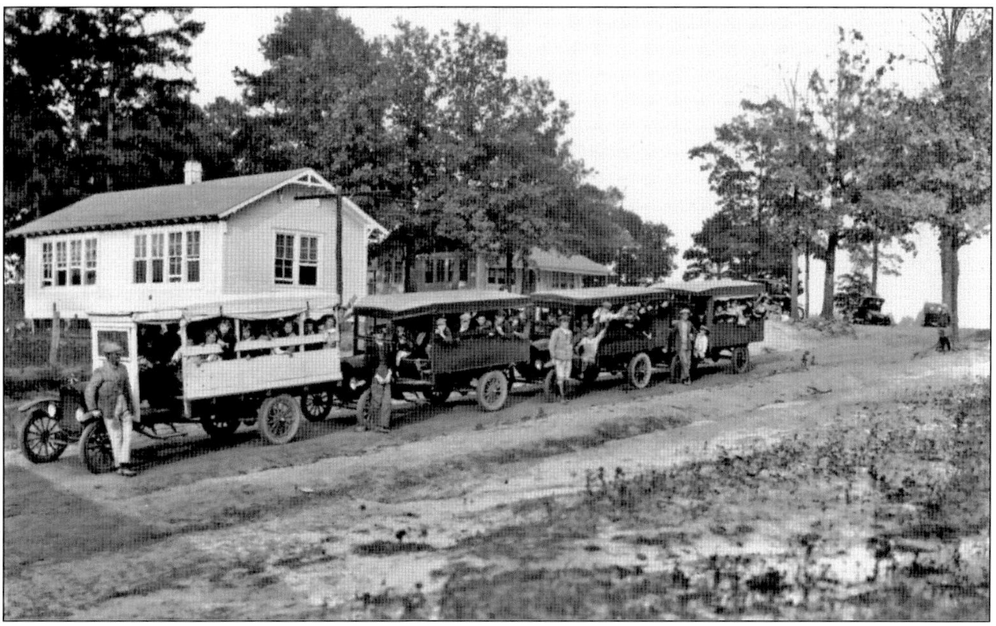

In this 1923 photograph, buses are shown picking up students at Athens School. Early school buses were converted trucks with two benches running the length of their beds. Canvas awnings suspended over the top could be rolled up or down to accommodate changes in the weather. The first school bus drivers were volunteers or even older students. (Courtesy of the Claiborne Parish School Board.)

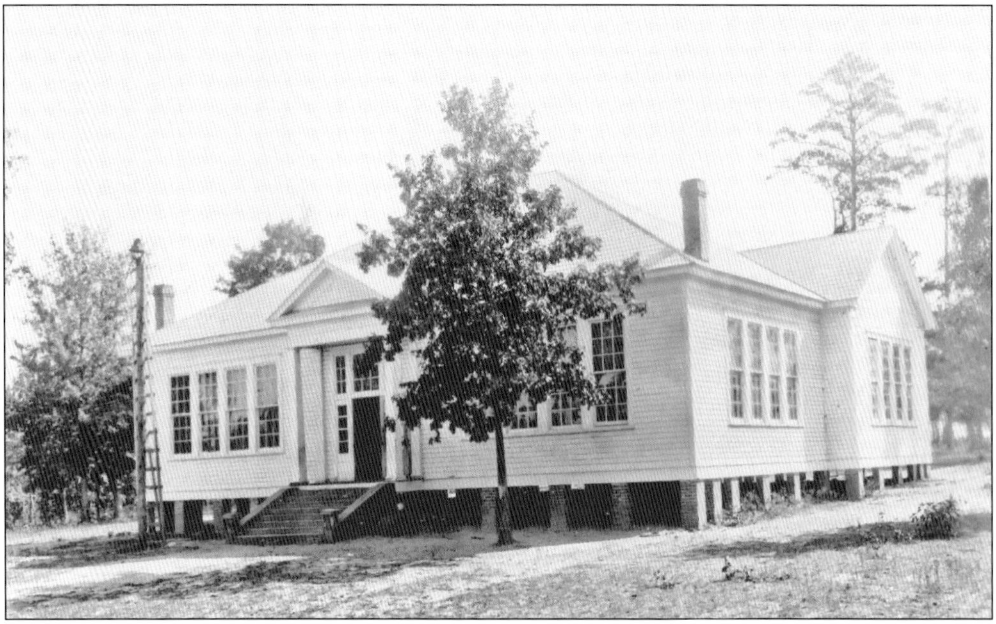

Younger children in the Hurricane community attended Hurricane Elementary School. Students of high school age attended Athens High School. A memorable event for the 50 students and four teachers at the Hurricane school was the occasion when, in 1924, the USS *Shenandoah*, a navy blimp, passed directly over the building. (Courtesy of the Claiborne Parish School Board.)

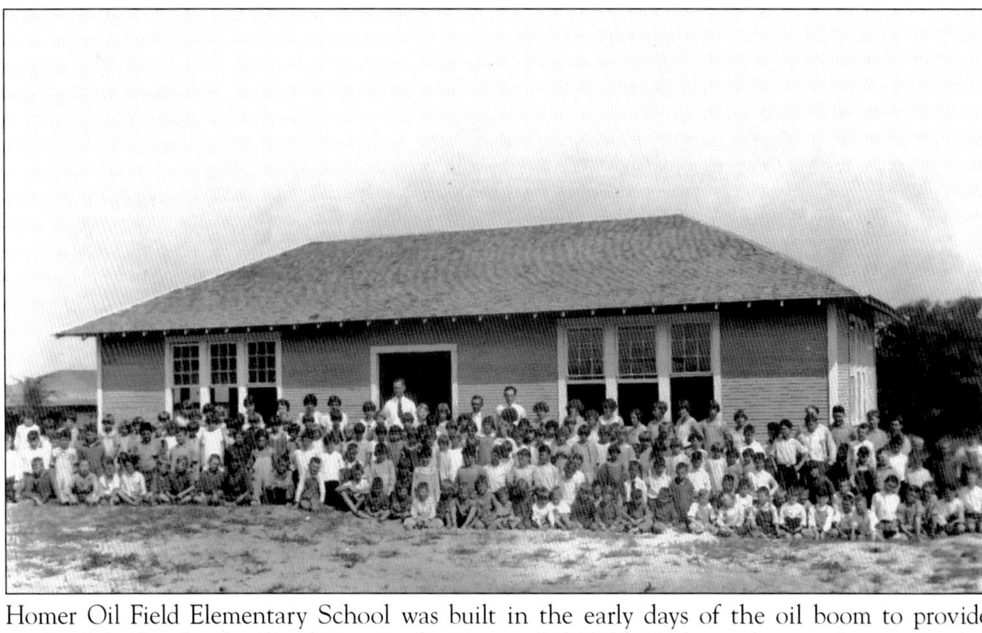

Homer Oil Field Elementary School was built in the early days of the oil boom to provide a school facility for families living in the Homer Oil Field. Each teacher taught two grades. High school students were bused to Homer High School to continue their educations. L. R. Tanner served as the school's last principal before the school was closed in 1936. (Courtesy of the Claiborne Parish School Board.)

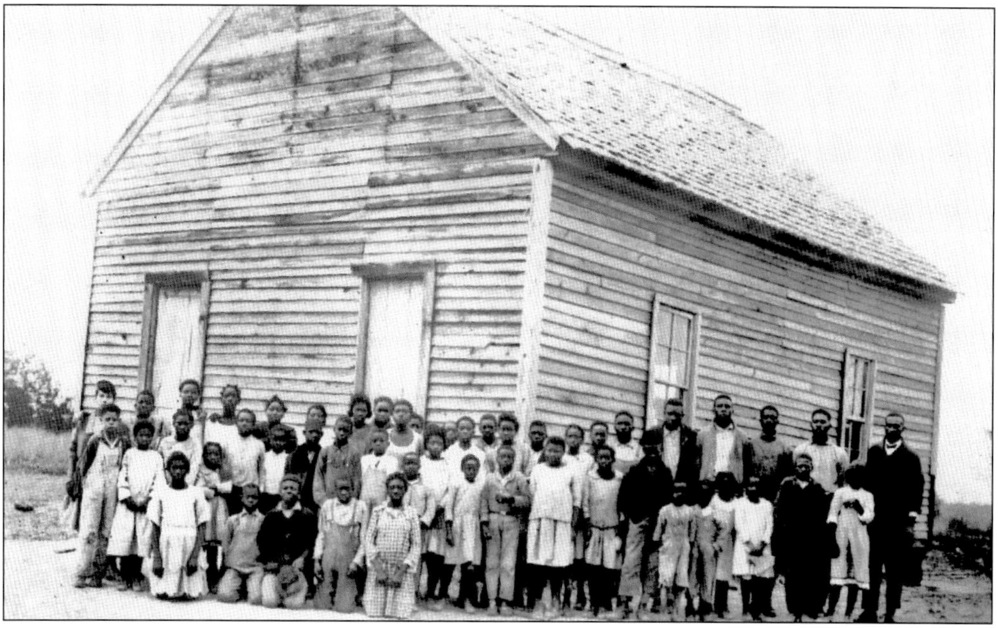

Schools for black children began appearing in rural Claiborne Parish in the early 1900s. In many cases, community churches were used as meeting places. Seats were benches made of rough wood, and textbooks were purchased by parents. Because children of most rural families were required to work in the fields during planting and harvesting times, these schools were in session only two or three months of the year. This unidentified rural school building is typical of early black schools. (Courtesy of A. D. Williams.)

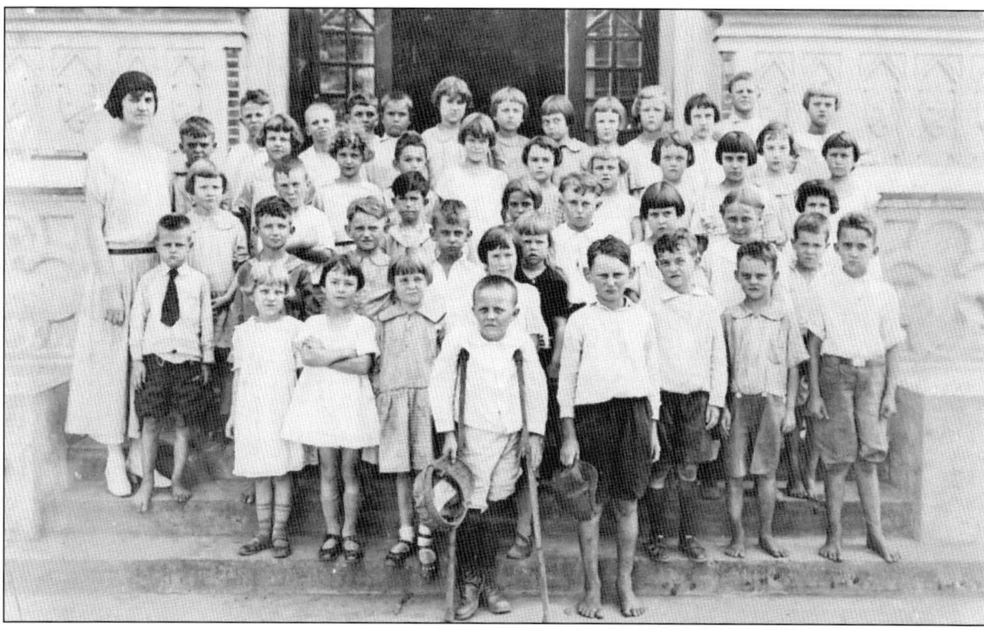

Because shoes were saved for special occasions, many children came to school with bare feet. Pictured on the steps of Homer Grammar School in the late 1920s, these students and their teacher pose for a class photograph. The building was torn down in 1949 after the present-day building for the elementary school was completed. (Courtesy of the Ford Museum.)

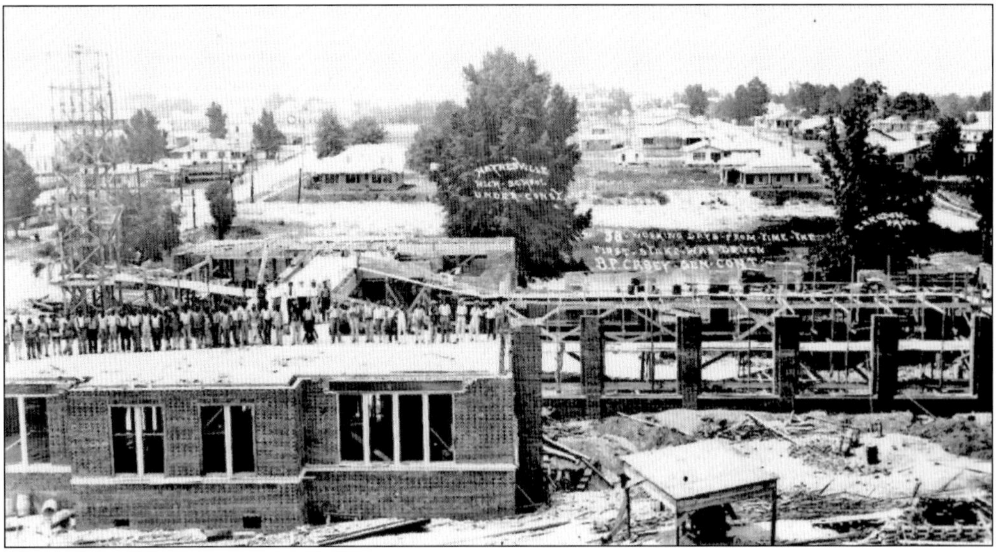

The first school at new Haynesville was built in 1899 and located on the site of Haynesville's present-day middle school building. Following the destruction of the building by fire on New Year's night 1904, another building was erected in time for graduation exercises for the senior class. During Haynesville's oil boom, the influx of new people created the need for a larger school, and in 1923, the oil-wealthy community was able to fund the construction of new brick school buildings. This photograph, taken 58 days after the first stake was driven, shows construction underway on the first building. A second building (below) and a principal's home were added in 1924, and a third building was completed in 1929. (Both courtesy of the Claiborne Parish School Board.)

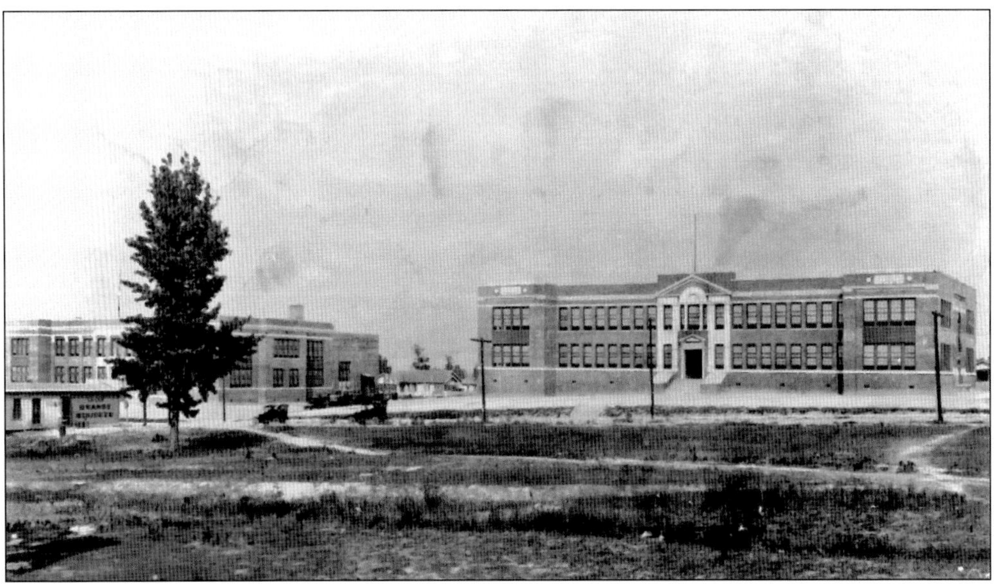

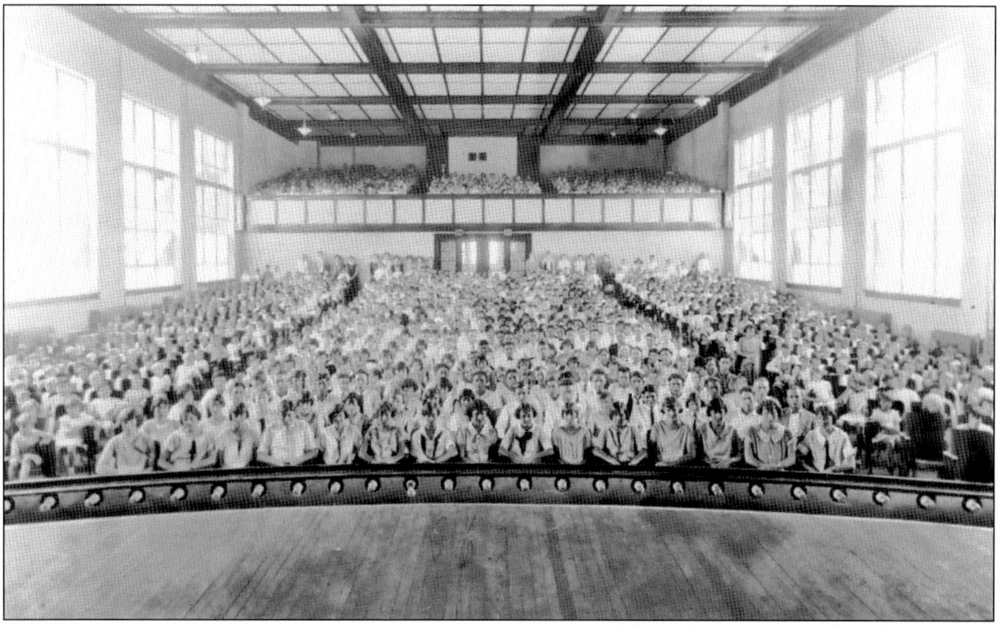

No vacant seats can be seen in this 1924 photograph of Haynesville's student body seated in the auditorium of their new building. According to building specifications, the seating capacity of the auditorium was 1,200 persons. Overcrowding continued to be a problem, especially when several rural schools were consolidated with Haynesville in 1929. (Courtesy of the Claiborne Parish School Board.)

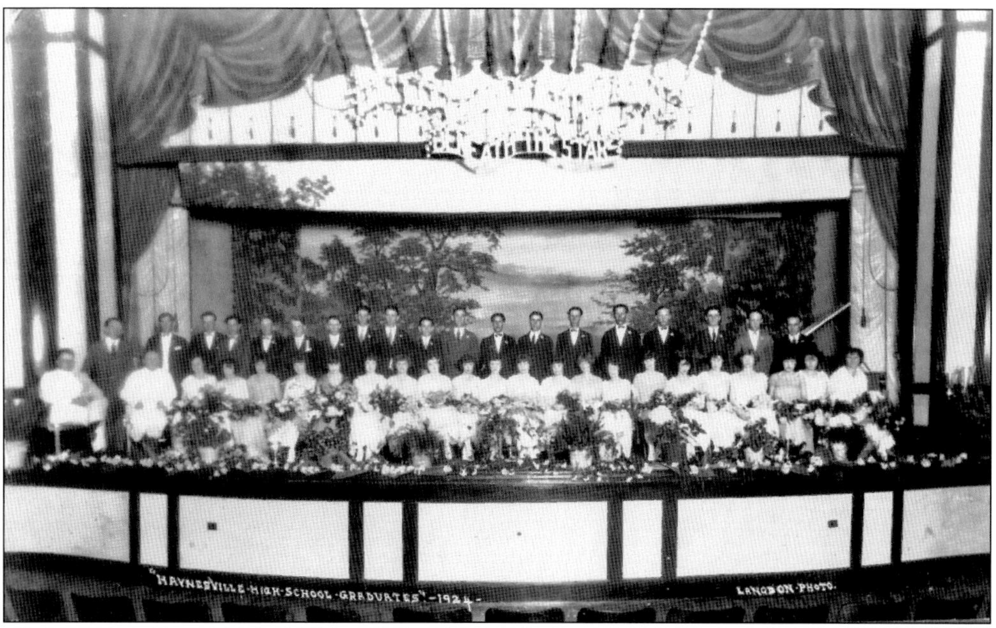

Claiborne Parish seniors looked forward to the Sunday baccalaureate services and commencement exercises held in May of each year. In this photograph, Haynesville's senior class of 1924 appears on the stage of the school auditorium. (Courtesy of the Claiborne Parish School Board.)

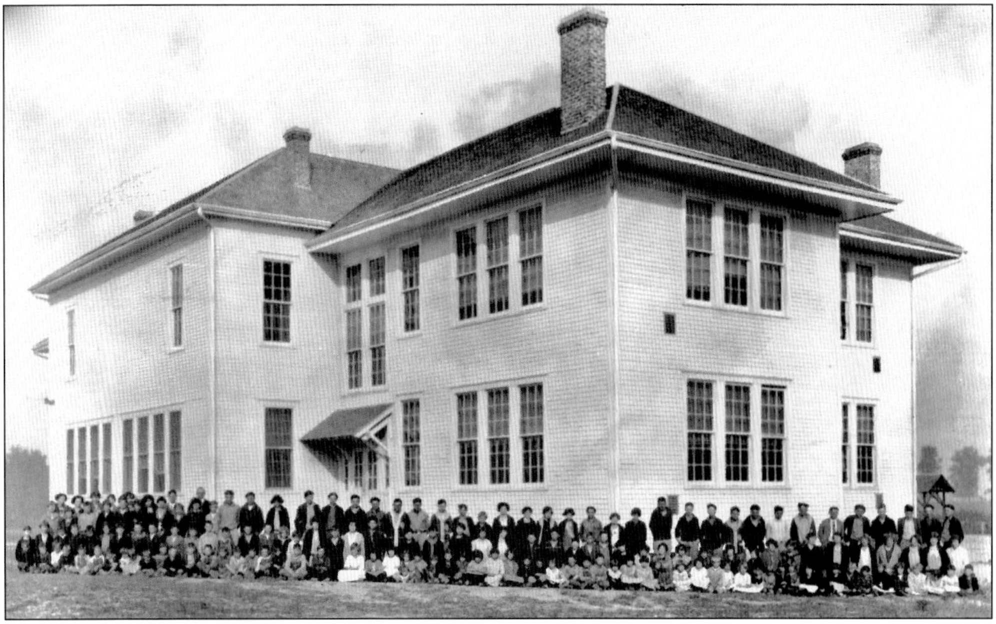

Blackburn, Ruple, and Bridgeman Schools were consolidated in 1922 to form a student body for the new Ruple School. L. L. Killgore and Albert G. McKee each served four-year terms as principal. The building burned in the spring of 1930, just one week before final exams. Students took their tests in the Ruple Baptist Church, on school buses, or on the grounds near the charred remains of the school building. (Courtesy of the Claiborne Parish School Board.)

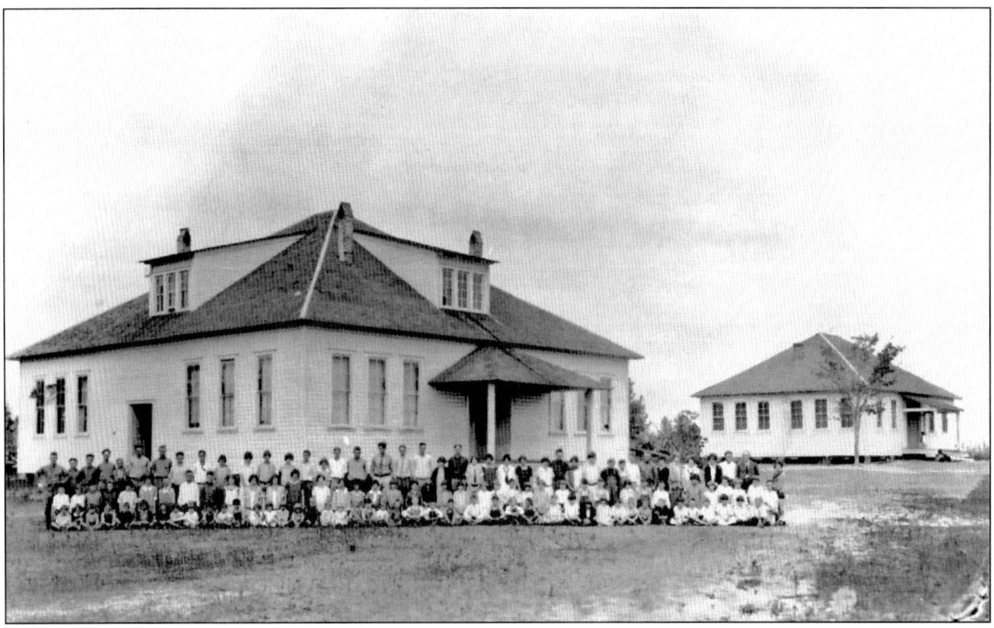

The Weldon community was first known as the Alabama Camp Ground, where great revival meetings were held each year. The school in the Weldon community was established in the early 1920s. In this 1923 photograph, students and faculty of the school are posed near the front entrance of one of the campus buildings. Weldon School was consolidated with Summerfield in 1926. (Courtesy of the Claiborne Parish School Board.)

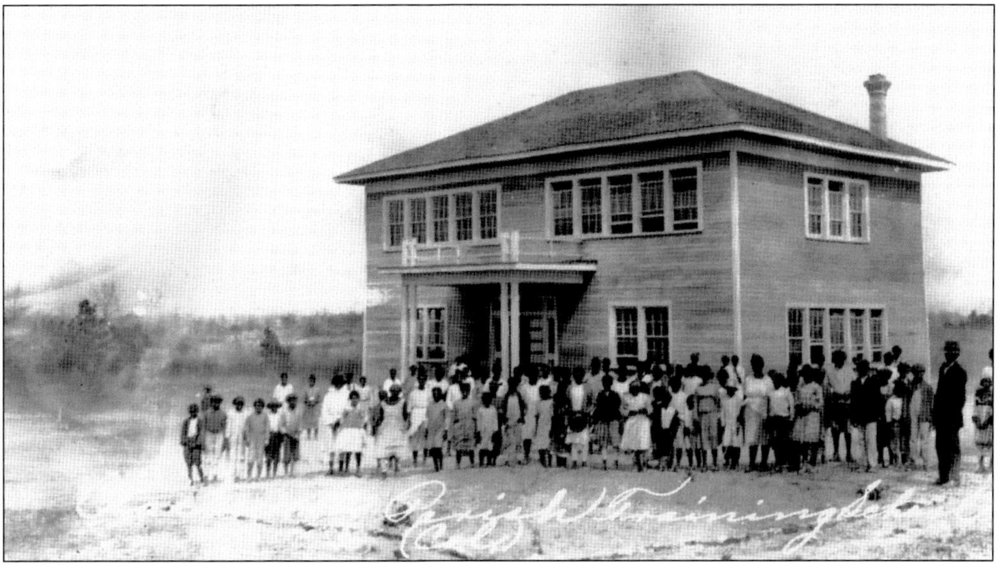

Claiborne Parish's first high school for blacks was St. John School. With the help of Rosenwald funds, construction was begun in 1916. Residents of the community donated logs to be milled for lumber to construct the school building and teachers' home. St. John School later became known as the Claiborne Parish Training School, where, under the administration of John S. Davis Sr., it was known as a leading training school for black teachers. The Claiborne Parish Training School was consolidated with Homer Colored High School in 1945. (Courtesy of A. D. Williams.)

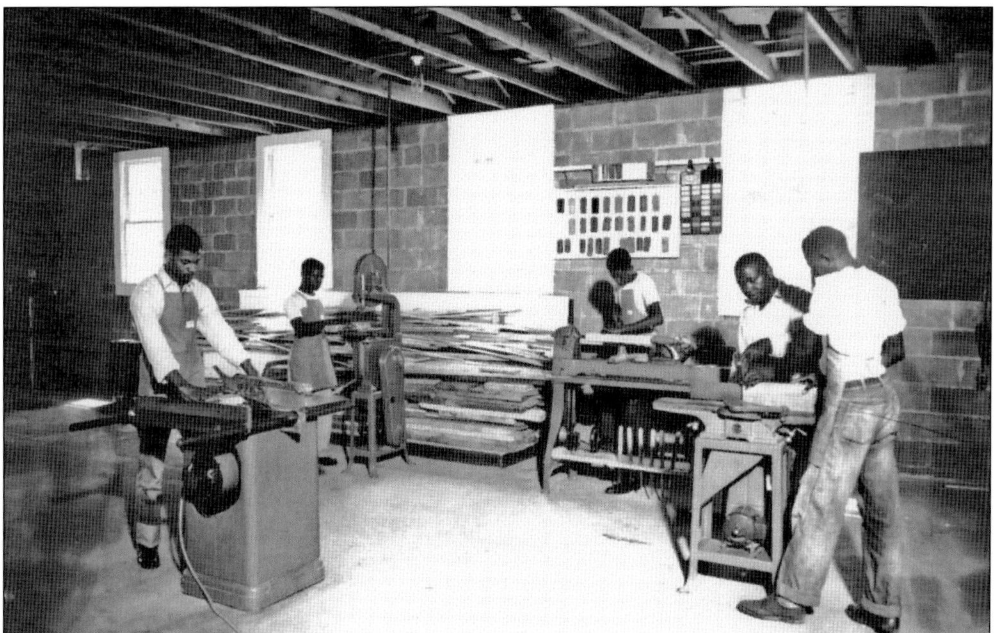

During the administration of Supt. F. C. Haley, 1945–1969, the Claiborne Parish School Board began broadening the vocational curriculum at its black high schools. At both Homer's Mayfield High School and Haynesville's Woodson High School, the board introduced courses in industrial arts, home economics, business, and music. (Courtesy of the Claiborne Parish School Board.)

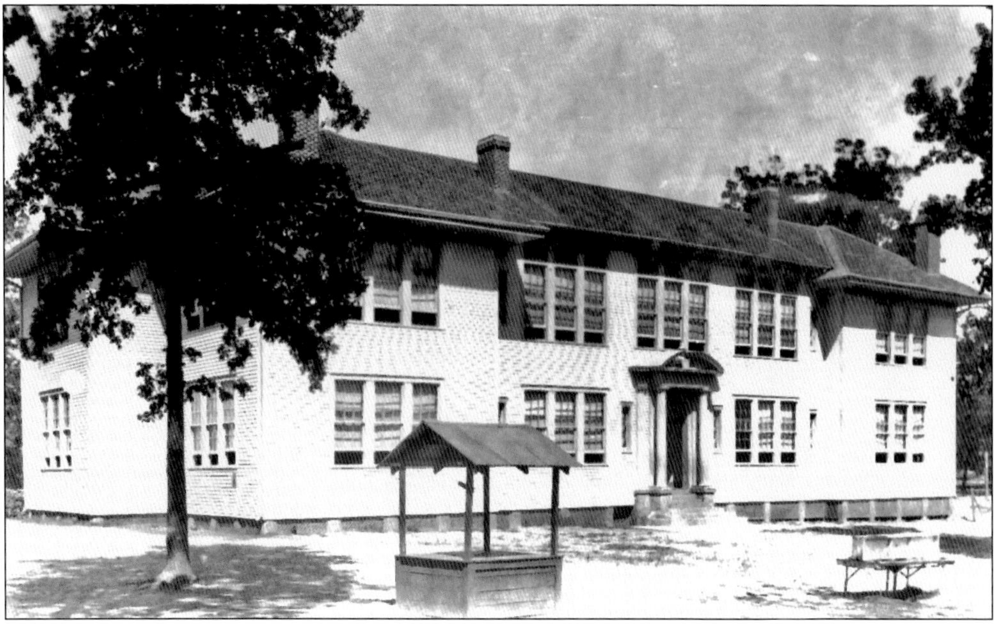

The campus of Lisbon School was eventually comprised of five buildings. The building shown here was constructed in the 1920s when Sharon, Antioch, and Arizona Schools were consolidated with Lisbon. The discovery of oil in the Lisbon Field in 1936 brought many new families into the community, and additional buildings were constructed to accommodate the increasing number of students. Lisbon School was consolidated with the Homer schools in 1970. (Courtesy of the Claiborne Parish School Board.)

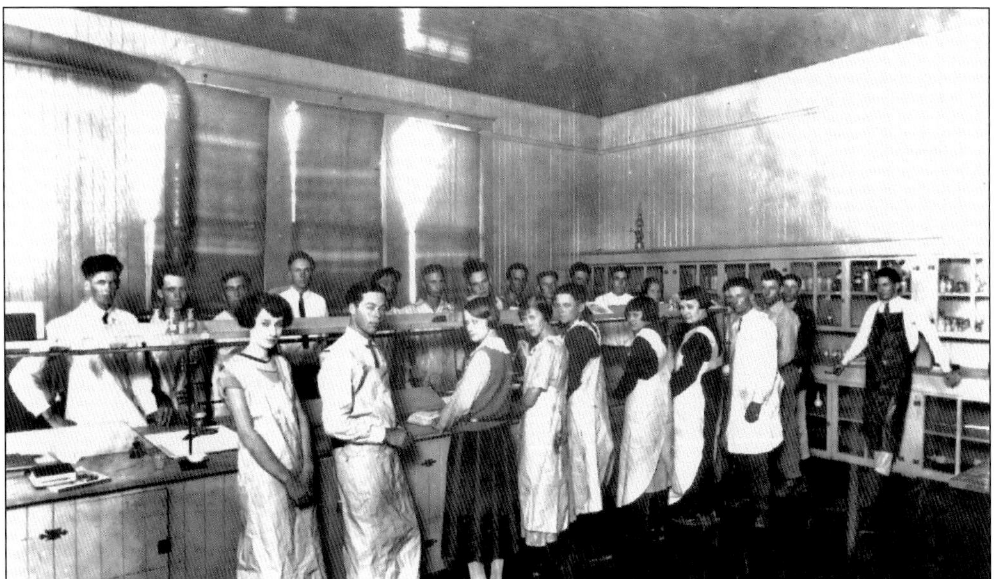

Students at Lisbon School received many academic and athletic honors. During the school's existence, Lisbon won the Class B State Literary Trophy more often than any other Louisiana school. According to a state survey, 75 percent of Lisbon's graduates went on to college. In this 1924 photograph, a chemistry class is completing an assignment in the school's well-equipped laboratory. (Courtesy of the Claiborne Parish School Board.)

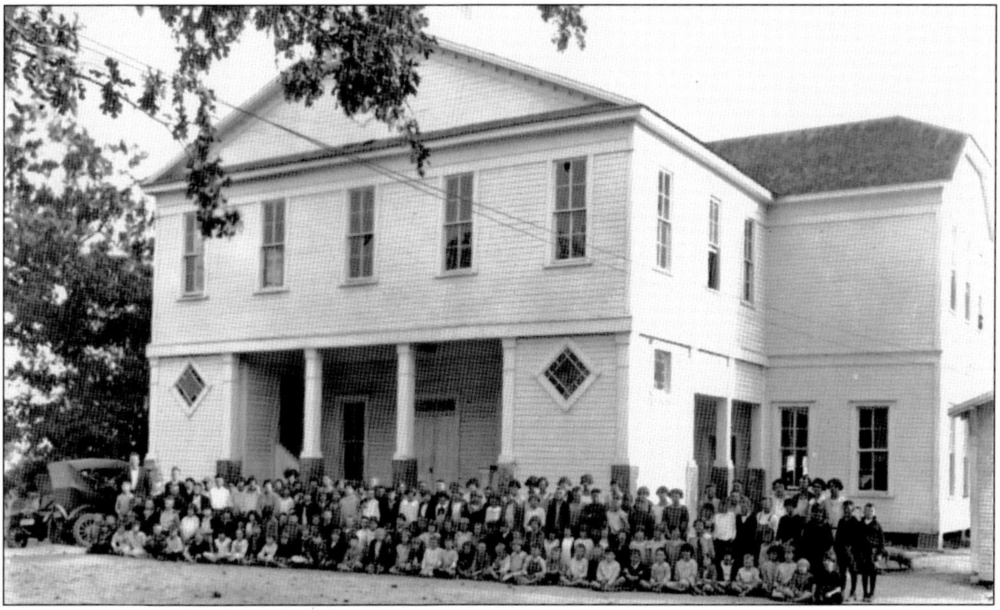

Unusual windows flanked the front entrance of Athens School, built in 1910. Livestock was allowed to range freely during this time, and family pets often followed the children to school. The pig, in the far right corner of this 1923 photograph, seems content no matter how he arrived. During a school program on May 6, 1929, people noticed the electric lights flickering, and near midnight, the school building burned. (Courtesy of the Claiborne Parish School Board.)

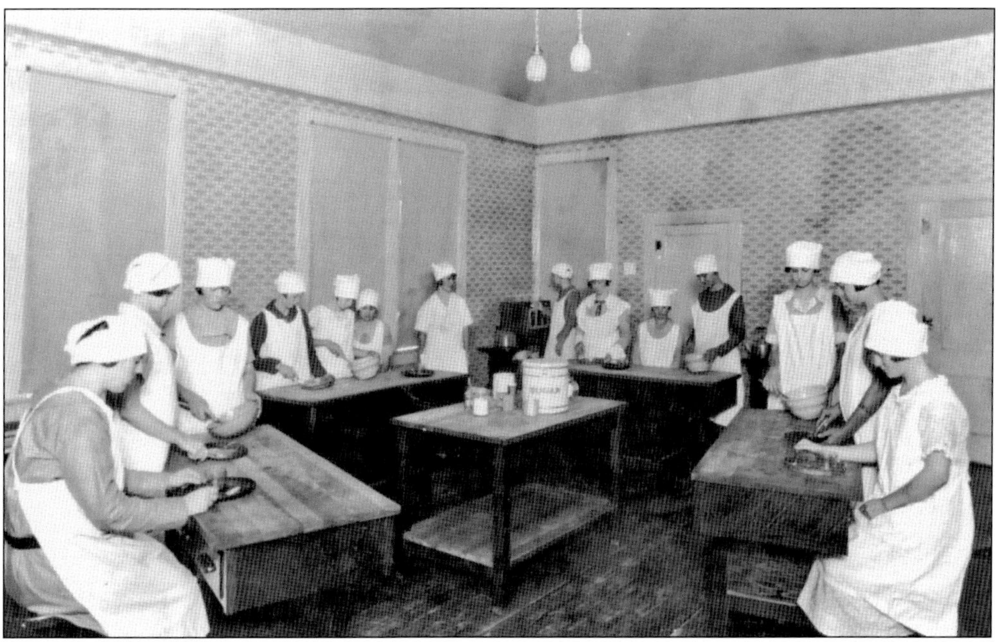

These young women have donned white caps and aprons to participate in a food preparation class at Summerfield High School. Their classroom was equipped with a single kerosene stove and preparation centers made of rough boards. Classes in home economics were introduced in Claiborne Parish schools in the 1920s. (Courtesy of the Claiborne Parish School Board.)

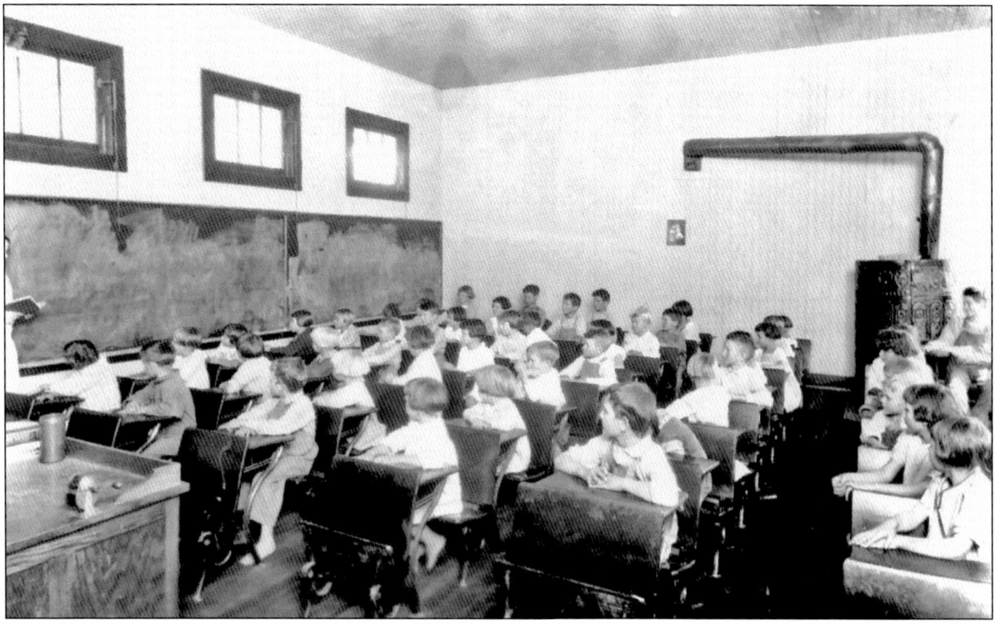

The Harris School, opened in 1922, was named in honor of T. H. Harris, a Claiborne Parish native and long-term state superintendent of education. By its second term, enrollment at the Harris School had reached 200 students. V. M. Robert served as the school's first principal. Harris School was consolidated with the Homer schools in 1957. Above, a grammar school class listens attentively to the lesson. (Courtesy of the Claiborne Parish School Board.)

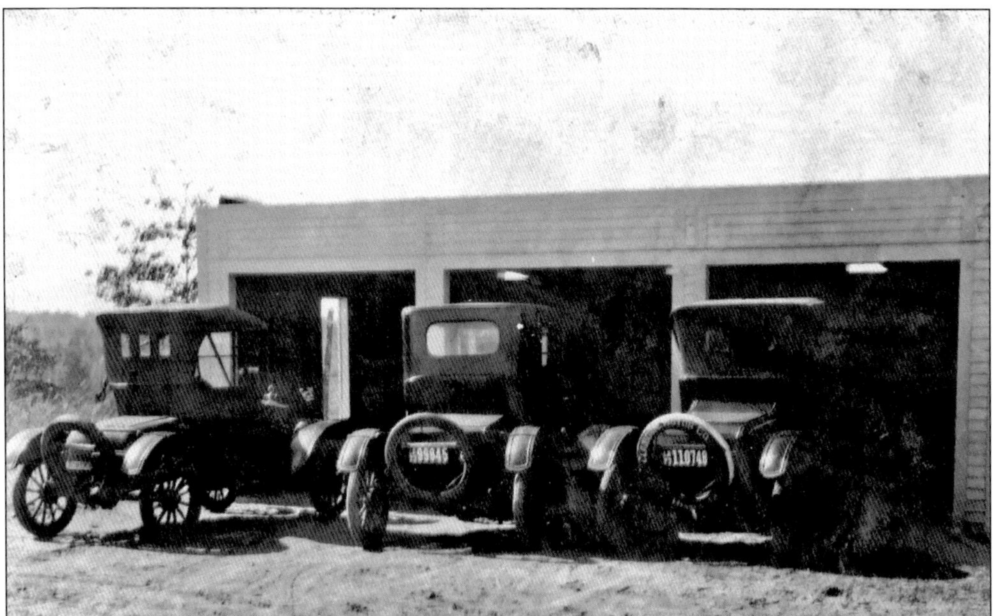

In this 1923 photograph, three automobiles are shown parked in a garage at the Harris School. Although it was still a challenge to travel over the poor roads, automobiles were seen more and more frequently in Claiborne Parish. Some schools converted their horse sheds or carriage houses into garages to accommodate automobiles. (Courtesy of the Claiborne Parish School Board.)

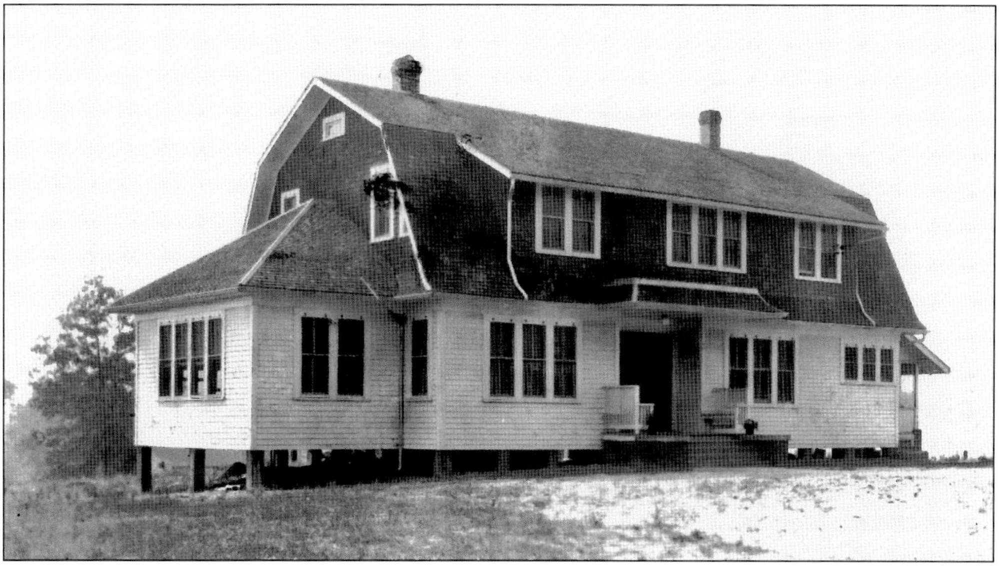

As population increased, more teachers were needed throughout the parish. Dirt roads and unreliable automobiles made travel difficult, so many teachers boarded with students' families during the school year. Homes for teachers and principals were built in some communities. Shown above is the well-equipped teacherage at the Harris School, which provided comfortable living quarters for some school personnel. (Courtesy of the Claiborne Parish School Board.)

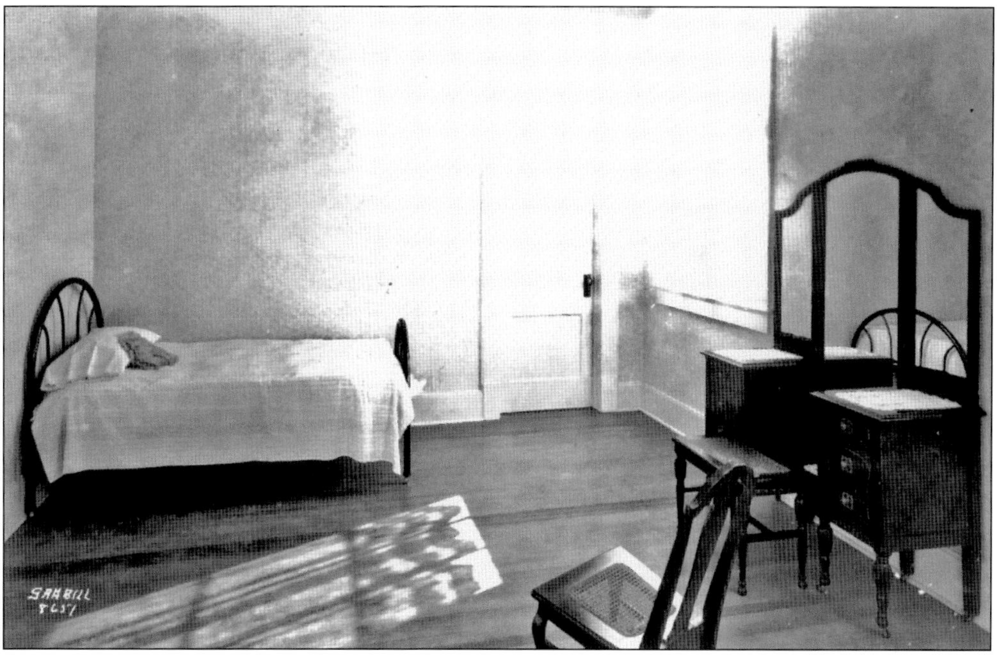

Although rooms in teachers' homes were often sparsely furnished, the availability of housing provided an incentive for teachers to accept positions. Meals and the services of a housekeeper were usually provided. The school board set certain standards for unmarried female teachers living in the teachers' homes. They were required to attend Sunday church services, forbidden to partake of alcohol or tobacco, and not allowed to have male visitors unless a chaperone was present. (Courtesy of the Claiborne Parish School Board.)

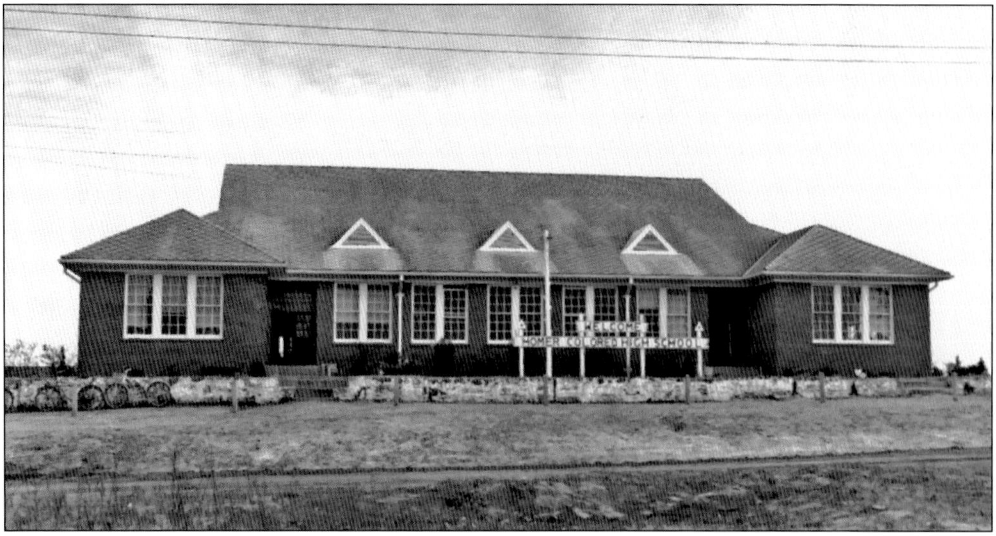

Homer Colored High School was an outgrowth of the Homer Normal Industrial and Bible Training School headed by Rev. Roy Mayfield in the early 1900s. Following the sale of the property in 1926 to the Claiborne Parish School Board, the school became Homer's first public high school for black students, with Allen Roy Rushing as the first principal. The school was renamed Mayfield High School in 1959. (Courtesy of the Claiborne Parish Library.)

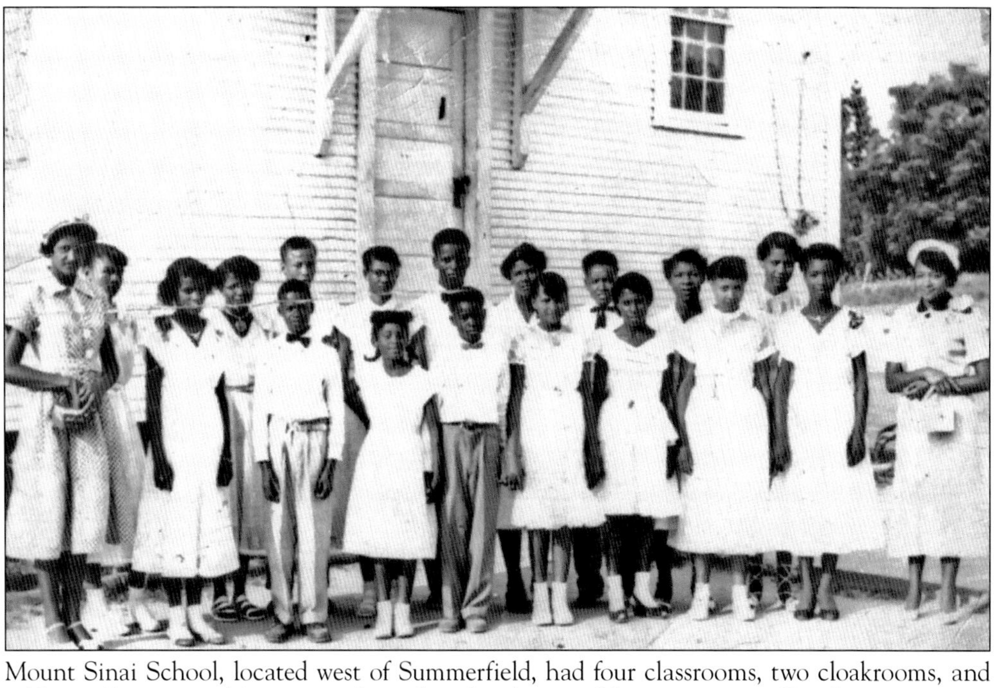

Mount Sinai School, located west of Summerfield, had four classrooms, two cloakrooms, and a library. Parents took turns supplying logs for the wood-burning stoves. Drinking water was drawn from the school well, and students drank from a shared gourd dipper. Students were, from left to right, (first row) Dorothy Brown, Florine Bell, Bobby Welch, Lou Bell, W. C. Birch, Esther Brown, Mattie Bell, Dionnie Lowery, Oddie Abbott, and Mildred James; (second row) Earnestine Meadows, Doris Bell, Raymond Walston, Theo Hay, Ferdinand Bell, Geneva Bell, Joseph James, Bernice Meadows, and Jean Bell. (Courtesy of Jean Bell Kendrick.)

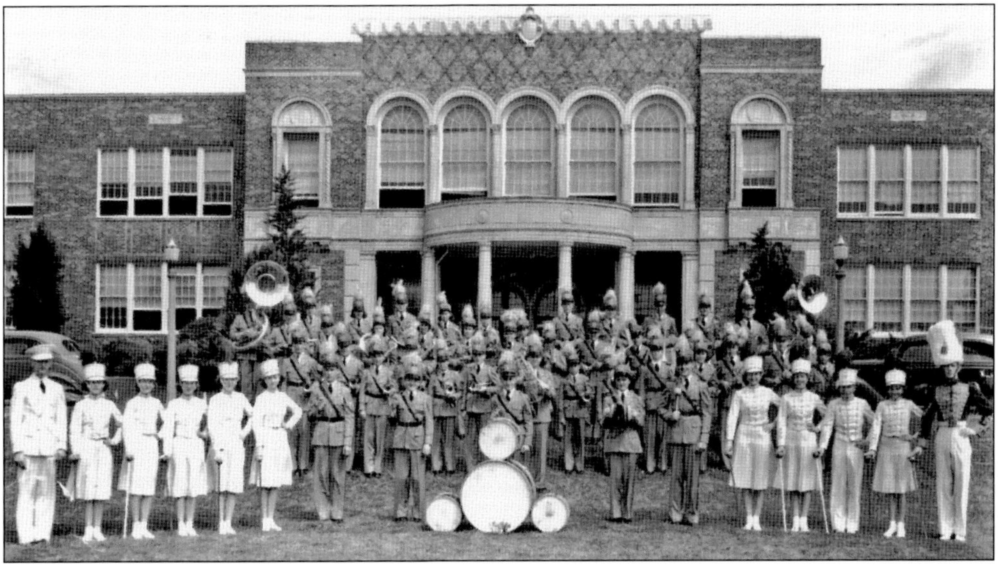

The first high school band in North Louisiana, comprised of 15 boys, was organized at Homer in 1924. The larger schools in the parish later offered band as part of the curriculum. Pictured above is the Homer High School marching band, directed for many years by Phillip Kendall (far left). During Kendall's long tenure, the Homer High School band received many honors, including being invited to march in the 1957 Orange Bowl Parade. (Courtesy of the Ford Museum.)

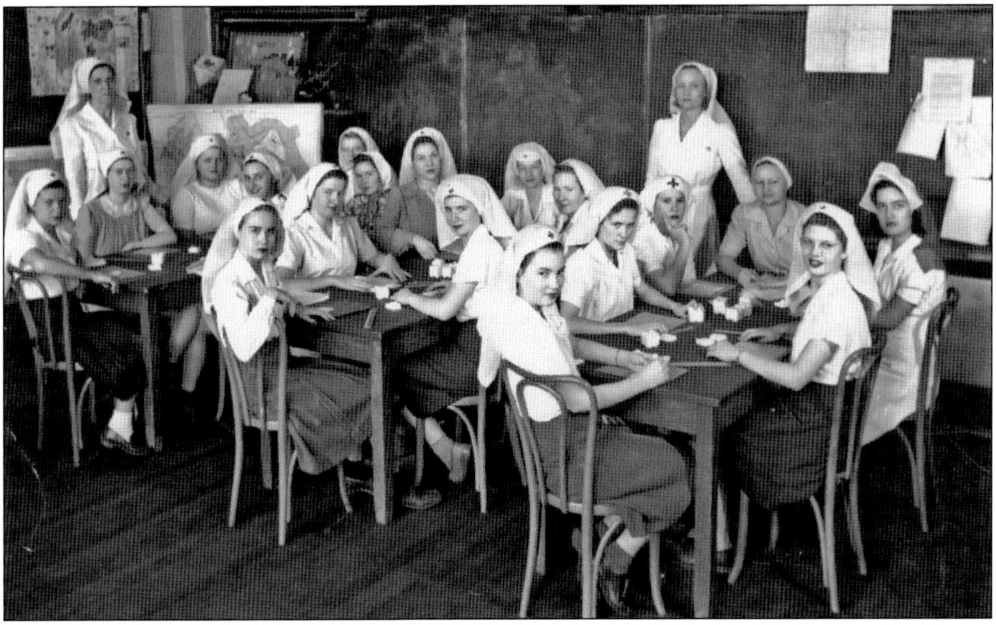

During World War II, the first aid class at Homer High School wrapped bandages for the war effort. From left to right are (first table) Maxie Billingsley, Imogene Thompson, Sally Thomson, Diane King, LeVon Bridgeman, and Mary Kerlin; (second table) Anna Laura Harkness, Betty Ann Gladney, Martha Kerlin, Hazel Bush, Catherine Sale, and Joanne Kendrick; (third table) Patsy Fomby, Phyllis Westall, Gwendolyn Tanner, unidentified, Kathleen Thomas, and Mary Elizabeth Walthall. Standing from left to right are instructors Charlotte R. Wilson and Lummye Seals. (Courtesy of Maxie Garrett.)

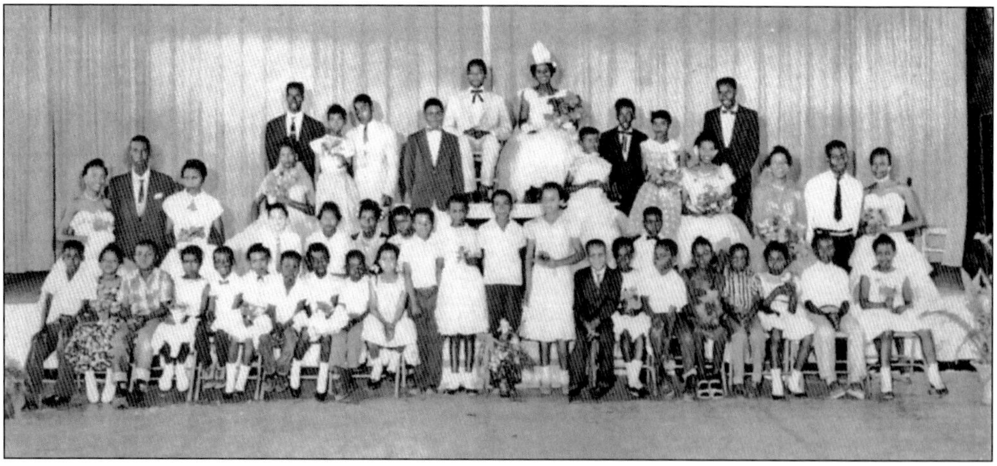

May Day celebrations, once held in all the parish schools, provided a fun day of outdoor games and contests. The maypole was wrapped, and the May king and queen were chosen. In this early-1950s photograph, students at Hillcrest School in Athens are shown posing in the school auditorium with their May Day king and queen. (Courtesy of Beth Malray.)

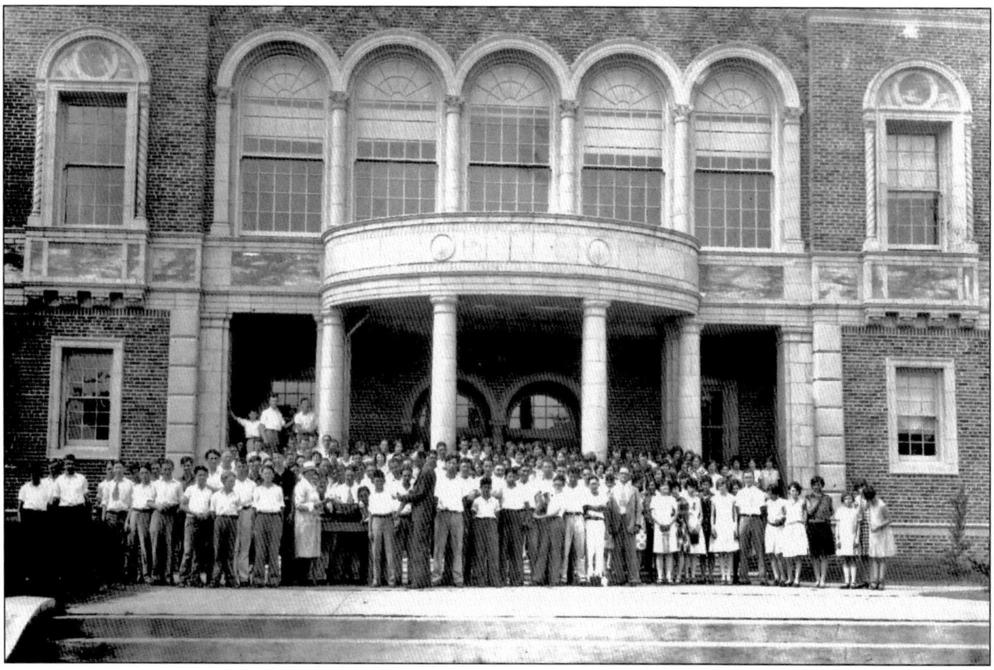

During the early 1930s, the Homer High School student body received smallpox vaccinations from public health officials in the parish. P. C. Rogers was principal at that time. In May 1980, the World Health Organization announced that smallpox had essentially been eliminated worldwide, and the practice of vaccination throughout the world was discontinued. (Courtesy of Frank and Jane Speer.)

Four

Go! Fight! Win!

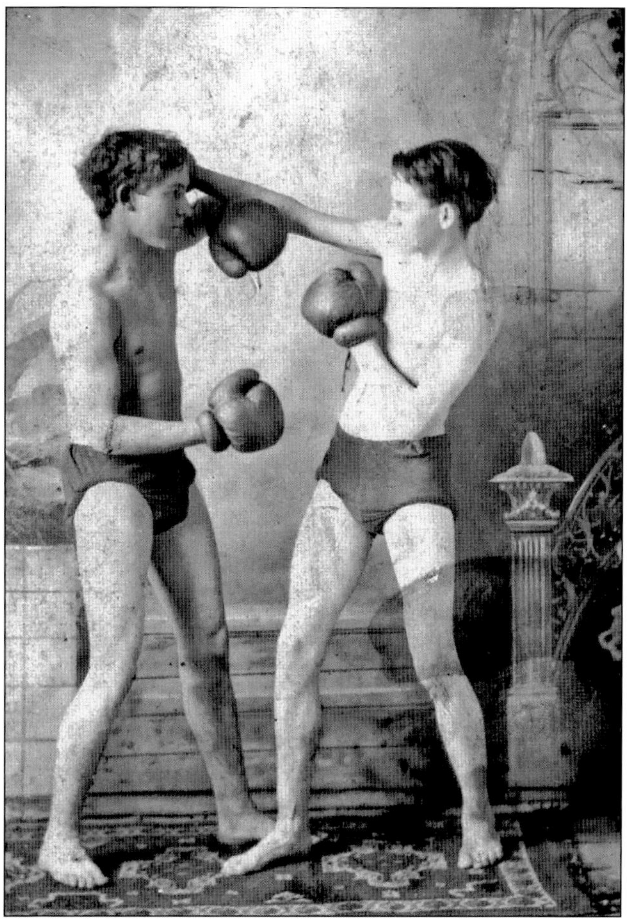

A competitive spirit became evident early on in the communities of Claiborne Parish. Sports events gave citizens a chance to visit with each other and cheer for their favorite athletes. These pugilists, shown about 1910, are Herbert Ford (left), founder of the Ford Museum, and his cousin Desmore Nelson (right). Nelson furthered his education at the U.S. Military Academy, graduating in 1913. (Courtesy of the Ford Museum.)

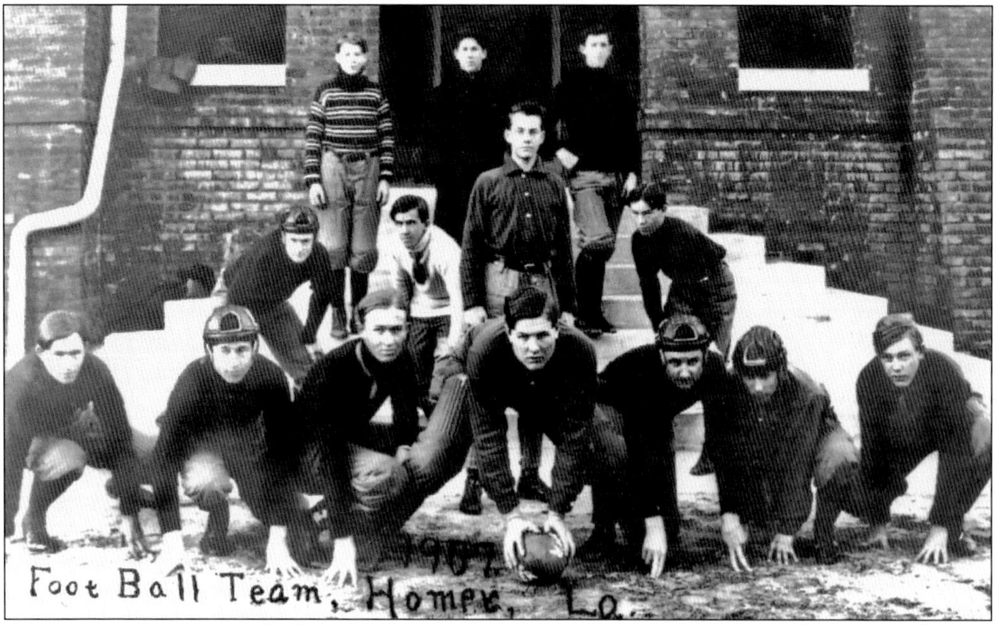

The first match between the Homer and Haynesville football teams took place in 1907. Here Homer's team is pictured just before they boarded wagons to travel to Haynesville to play the rematch game. Team members are, from left to right, (first row) Sam Kerlin, John DeLoach, Hugh Wilder, Charlie Kirkpatrick, Yandell Wideman, Atwood Gibson, and Carl Cameron; (second row) Harry Fortson, Enos McClendon, Era DeLoach, and Desmore Nelson; (third row) Joe Kirkpatrick, Herbert Ford, and James McClendon. Each team won at home: Homer 10-5 and Haynesville 5-0. (Courtesy of the Ford Museum.)

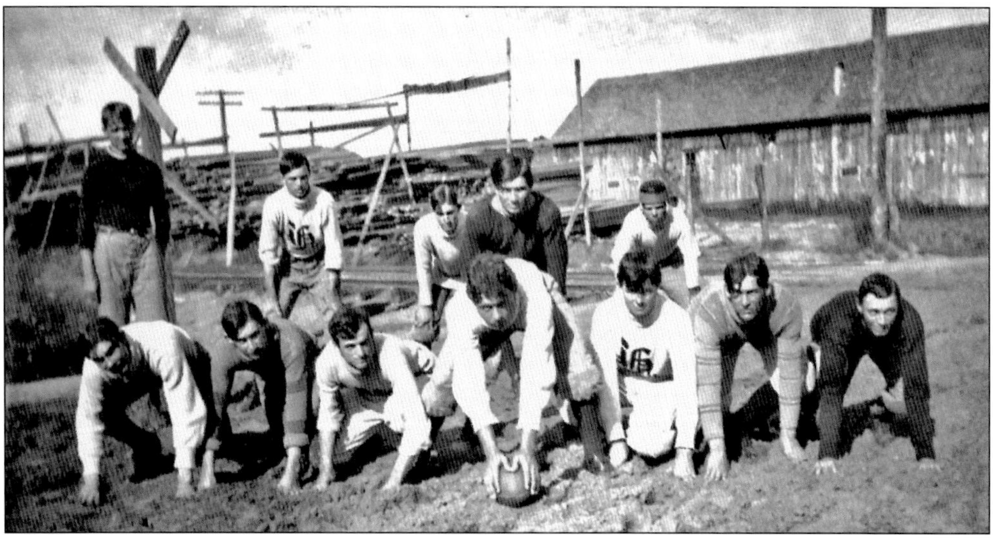

In 1907, Haynesville's first football team had 18 players. Shown here are some members of the original team: Bill Dawson, Stanley Phipps, Jim Garrett, Dade Sale, Ardis Sims, C. E. Miller, Claude Beene, M. M. Morelock, A. T. Bevill, G. H. Sherman, C. M. Brown, Webb Smith, and O. H. Dawson. The Homer-Haynesville competition is the longest standing football rivalry in Louisiana. Beginning in 1923, and for many years thereafter, the game was played on Thanksgiving afternoon. (Courtesy of Monte Banks.)

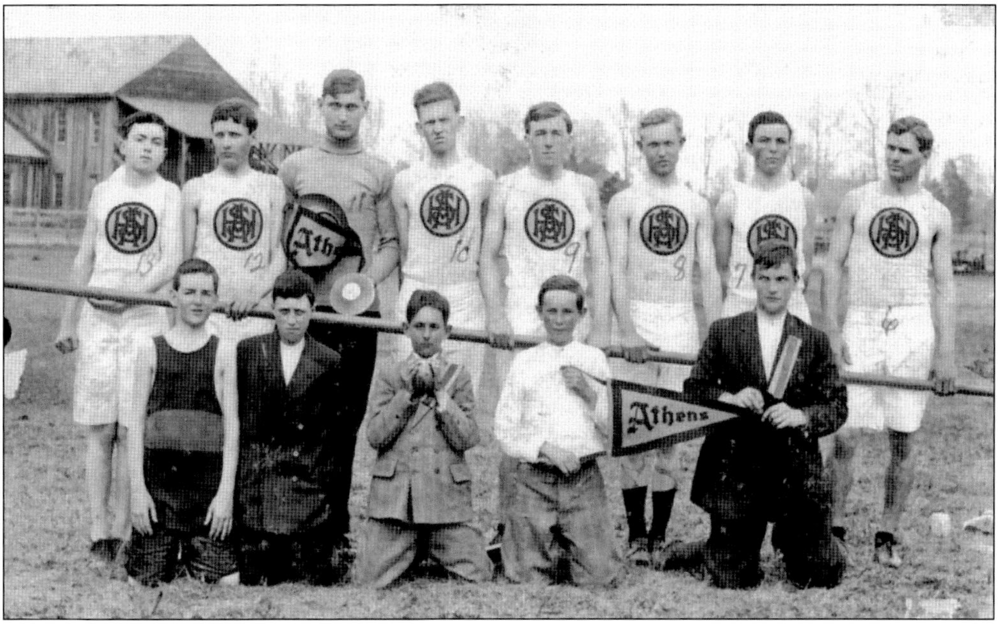

Holding a wooden vaulting pole and shot put, members of the Athens High track team posed for this c. 1920 photograph. Team members are, from left to right, (first row) Drew Bridges, Joe Marsalis, Wideman Watson, Dewey Watson, and unidentified; (second row) four unidentified, Walton McKee, Ab Atkins, unidentified, and Aub Atkins. (Courtesy of the Ford Museum.)

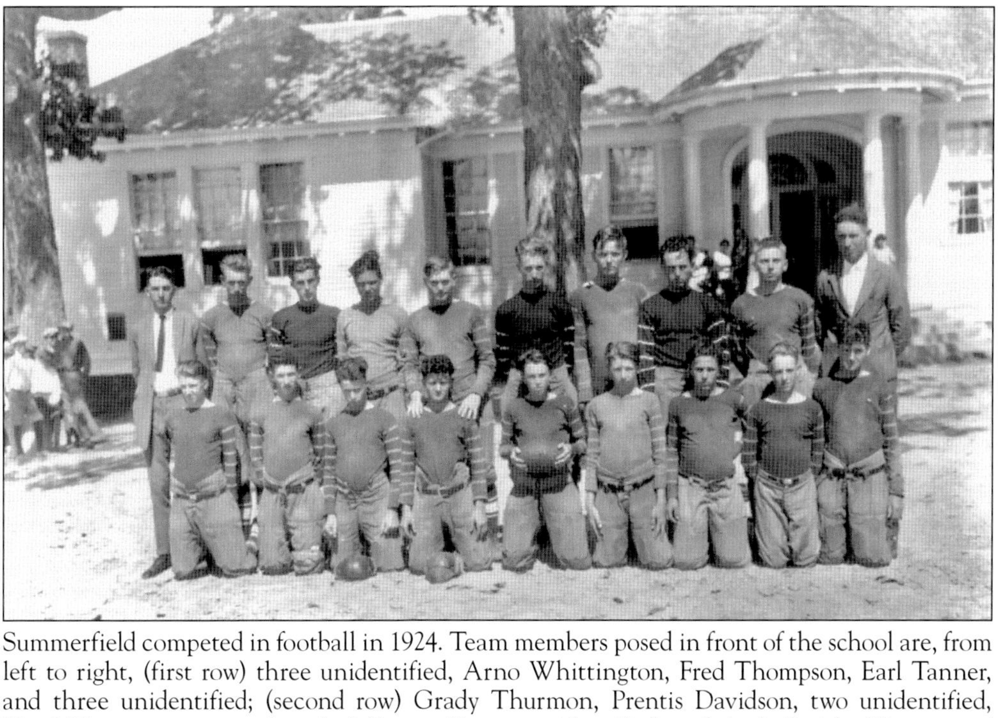

Summerfield competed in football in 1924. Team members posed in front of the school are, from left to right, (first row) three unidentified, Arno Whittington, Fred Thompson, Earl Tanner, and three unidentified; (second row) Grady Thurmon, Prentis Davidson, two unidentified, Floyd Thurmon, two unidentified, Rupert Barger, unidentified, and A. A. Smith. (Courtesy of the Claiborne Parish School Board.)

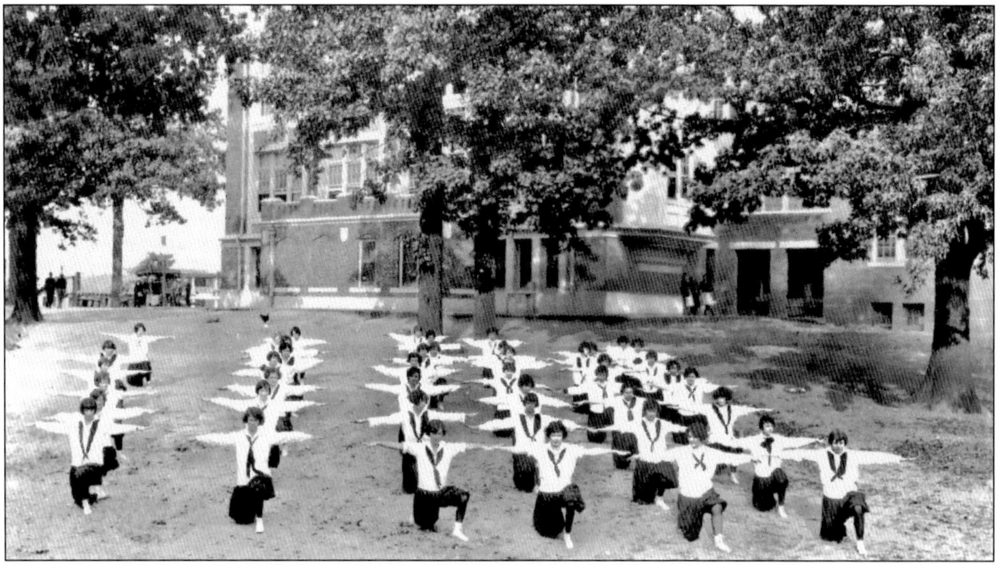

The uniforms worn by the girls in Homer High's physical training class consisted of long-sleeved middy blouses, knee-length bloomers, black knit stockings, and white shoes. During the 1920s, public schools were required to offer physical education classes to all students over the age of eight years. (Courtesy of the Claiborne Parish School Board.)

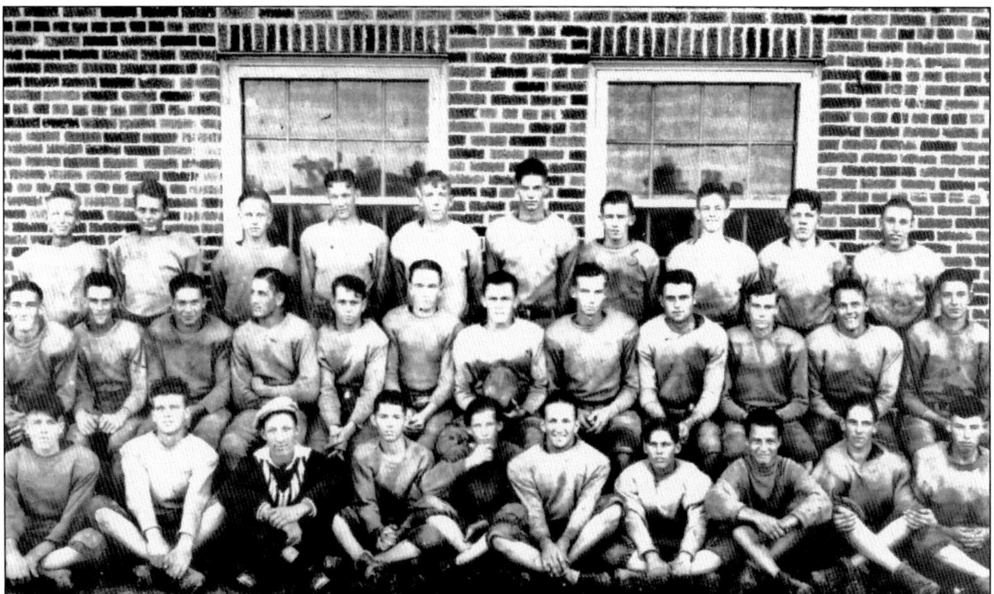

Homer High's 1928 football team, coached by T. F. Wilbanks, went 12-0, beating Warren Easton 26-12 for Homer's first state title. Four hundred fans paid a reduced fare offered by the L&NW to attend the championship game in Alexandria. Players are, from left to right, (first row) B. Garr, G. Robinson, B. Tompkins, H. Moffet, E. Smith, J. Auld, G. Carroll, A. Adkins, F. Tindall, and P. Fincher; (second row) K. Gentry, H. Cameron, R. Camp, E. Tompkins, C. Bass, H. Brock, B. Cameron, T. Bickham, C. Kendrick, B. McMurry, E. Higgins, and C. Knox; (third row) S. Abercrombie, L. Fulmer, J. Robertson, E. McClung, F. Williams, E. Adams, E. McKenzie, J. Cameron, L. Thompson, and C. Adkins. (Courtesy of the Ford Museum.)

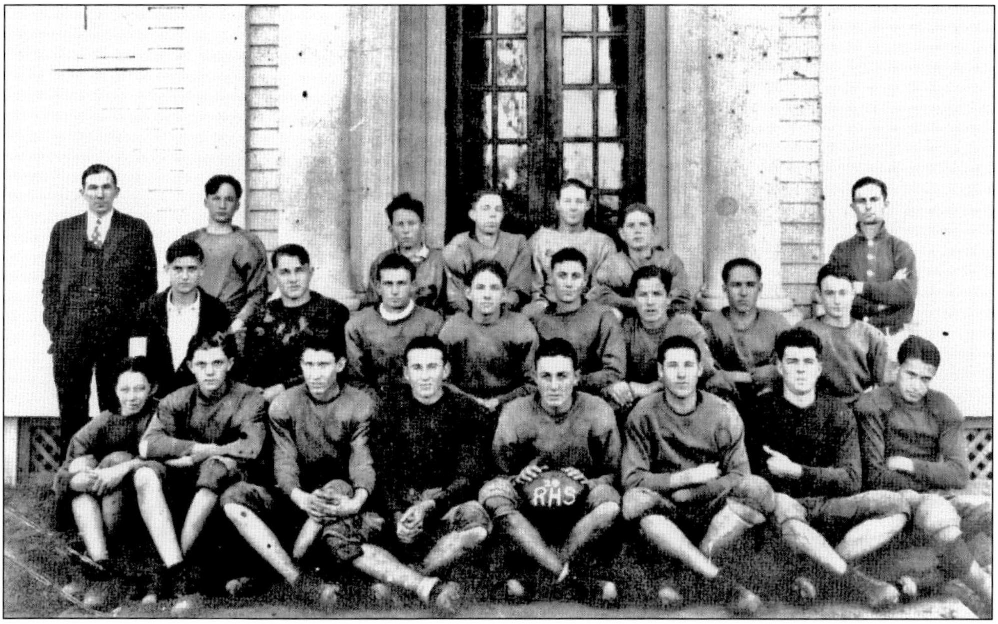

The 1929 Ruple Hornets advanced to the state playoffs, only to lose to Rayville in a second-round playoff game. Players provided all their equipment except cleats. Students purchased shoes at the Ruple store, removed the heels, and attached the cleats to the soles. Team members are, from left to right, (first row) G. Tinsley, R. Hollenshead, B. Polk, L. Camp, G. Heard, R. Elmore, B. Ruple, and D. Tinsley; (second row) C. Hollenshead, C. Manry, B. Walker, C. Thomas, M. Heard, B. Robinson, D. Elmore, and O. Fletcher; (third row) Principal A. McKee, L. Bates, T. Camp, O. Land, M. Thomas, H. Hollenshead, and coach M. Durham. (Courtesy of the Ford Museum.)

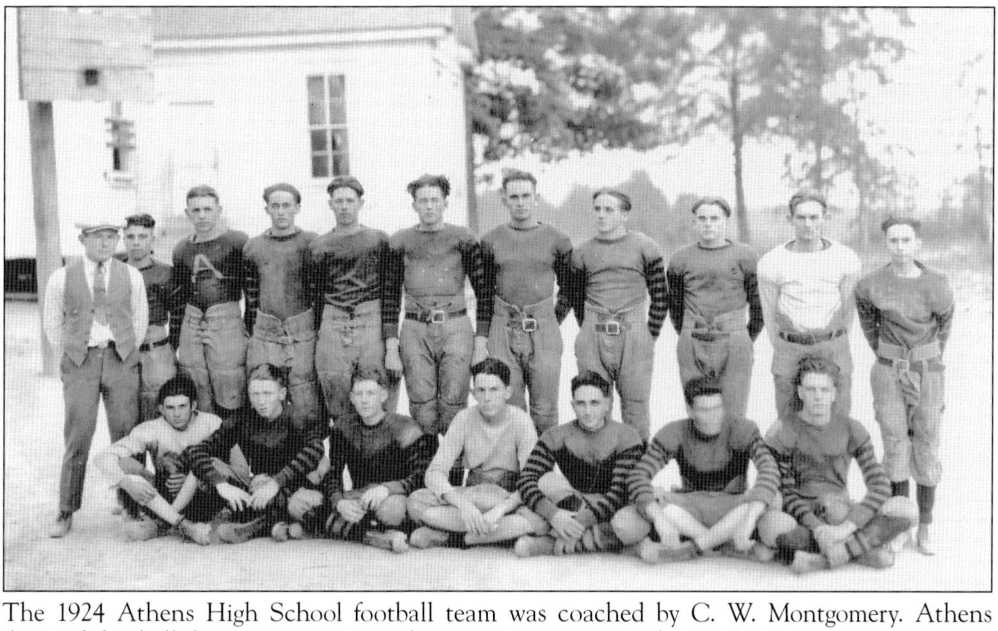

The 1924 Athens High School football team was coached by C. W. Montgomery. Athens dropped football from its extracurricular activities in 1929 after a player was paralyzed from injuries received while playing in a game against Gibsland. (Courtesy of the Claiborne Parish School Board.)

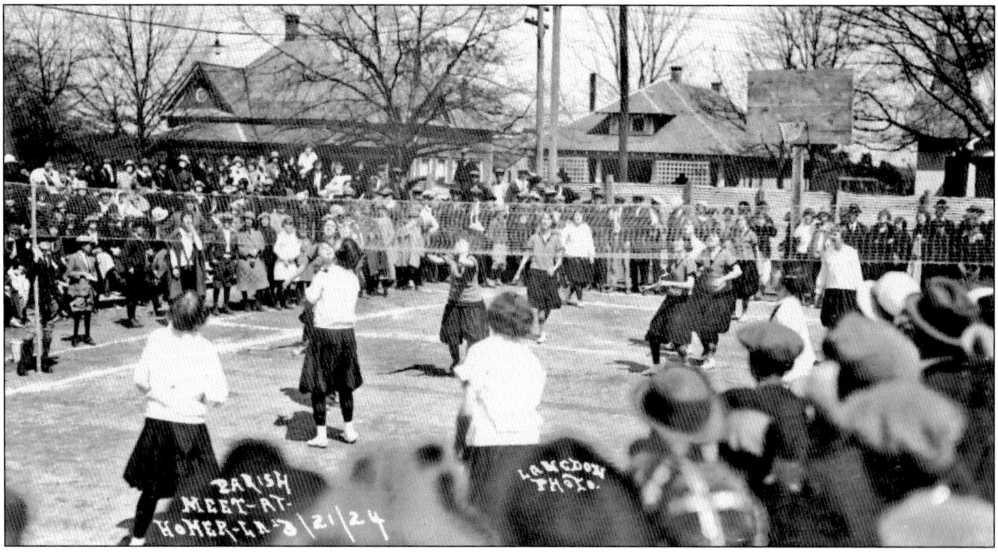

Large crowds gathered at Haynesville on March 21, 1924, to cheer for their favorite school teams in the Claiborne Parish Athletic Rally. The rally, a very competitive event, determined the parish champions in each sport. Local newspapers provided full coverage of the Claiborne Parish Rally, listing the results of each competition. The basketball court was easily converted into a volleyball court for the girls' championship game. (Courtesy of the Claiborne Parish School Board.)

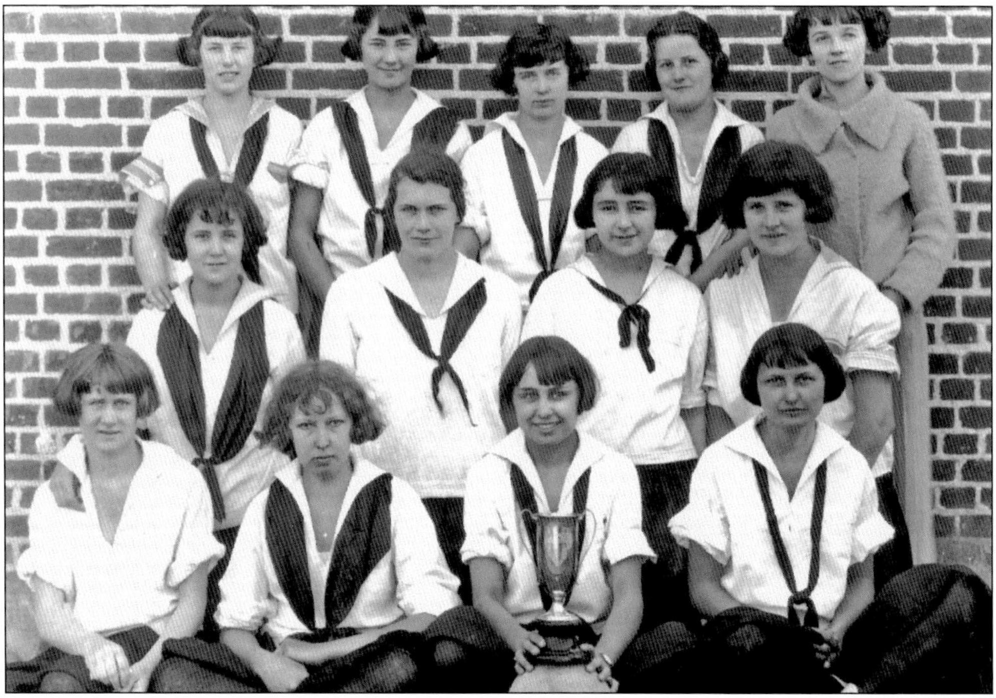

Girls' volleyball was a popular physical education activity during the 1920s. Belle Atkins coached Haynesville's winning team in the 1923–1924 Claiborne Parish Girls' Volleyball Championship tournament held in Haynesville at the parish rally. (Courtesy of the Claiborne Parish School Board.)

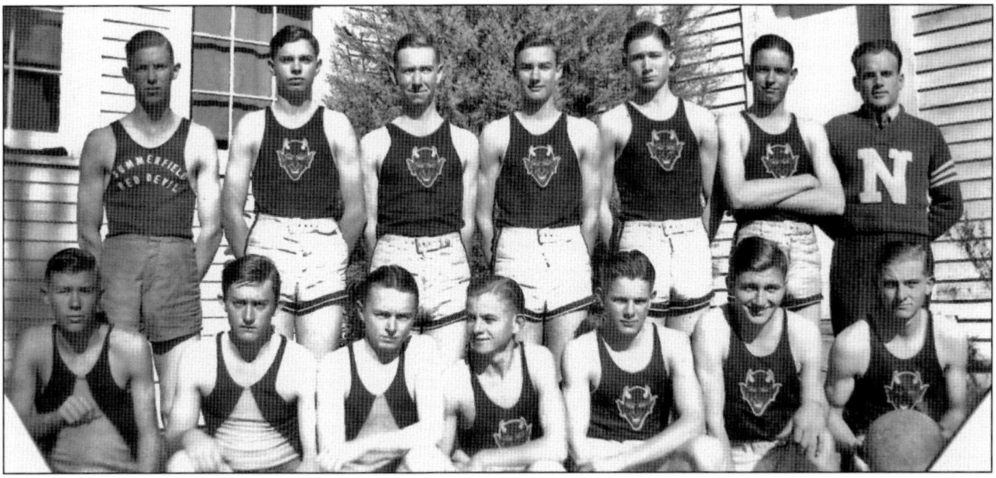

The members of Summerfield's 1936 basketball team are, from left to right, (first row) unidentified, B. Murry, C. Gully Jr., ? Sayers, T. Tanner, E. Hightower, and ? Sayers; (second row) J. Smith, B. Brown, W. Hightower, E. Mitchum, J. Lee, J. Burley, and coach Buck Sims. During the administration of Principal A. C. Adkins, the name of Summerfield's athletic teams was changed from the Red Devils to the Rebels. (Courtesy of Carole Sims Tabor.)

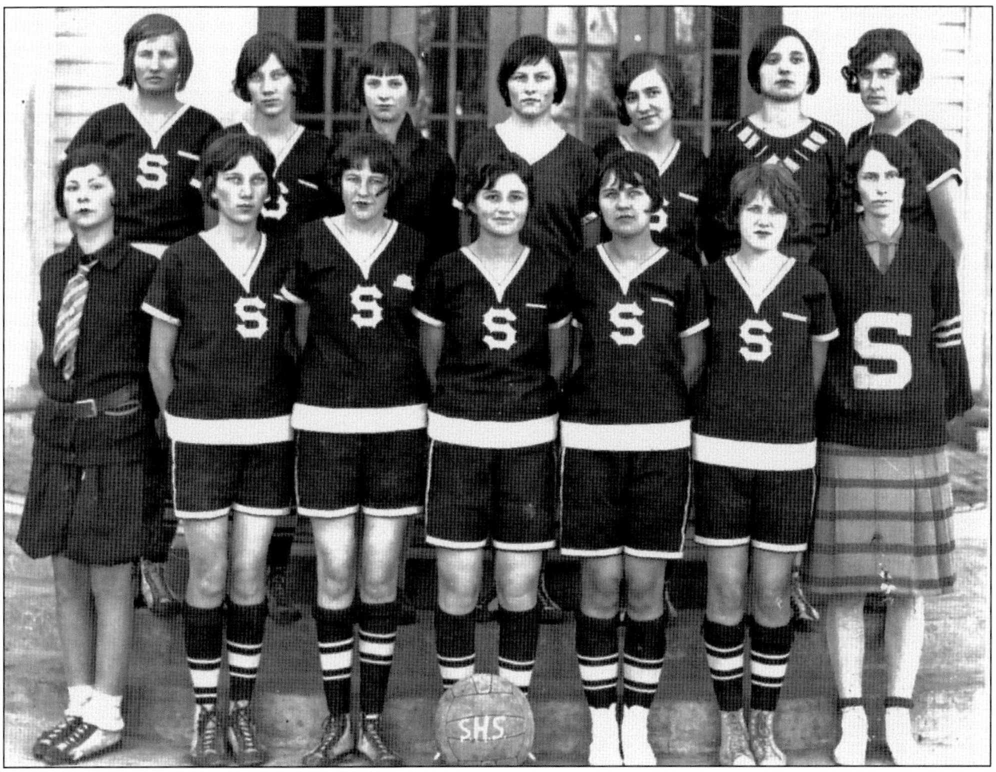

Summerfield became well known for its championship girls' basketball teams. Members of the 1930 team are, from left to right, (first row) Hazel Shirey, Inez Foust, Lucille Thompson, Inez Barber, Wilma Shirey, Estelle Strahan, and coach Minnie Fomby; (second row) Noreen Moss, Irene Foust, Martee Davidson, Marie Baker, Clotel Rasberry, Leloe Rogers, and Alibelle Raley. (Courtesy of Kate Sherman.)

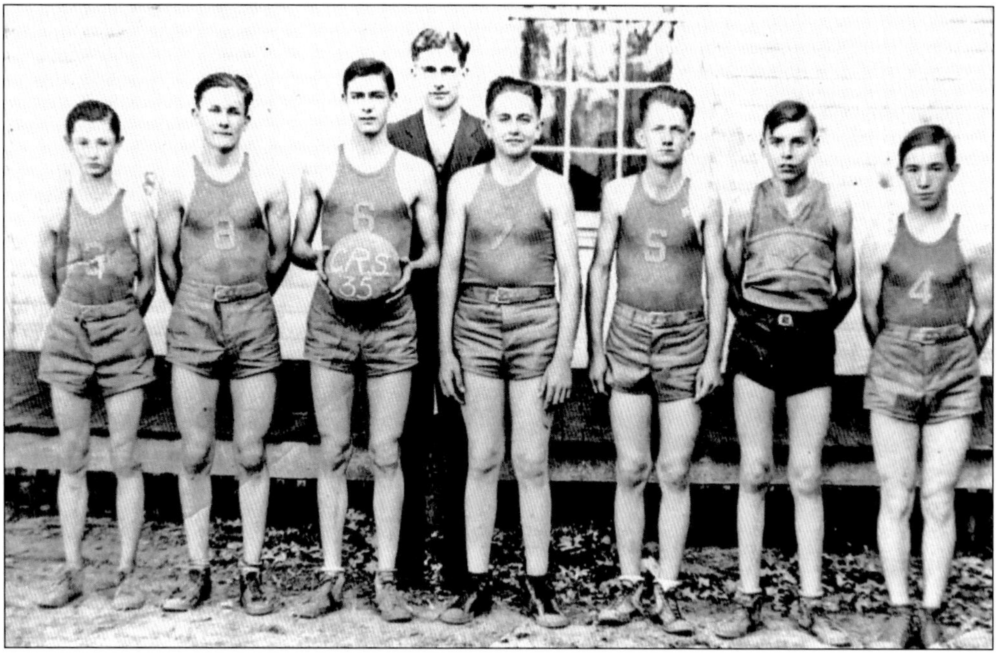

The Cross Roads basketball team competed with other schools until the school was consolidated with Athens. The teacher/coach of the 1935 team was Dale Lowery (back). Team members were, from left to right, Dale Watson, Sam Keen, Ardis Anderson, Bo Harmon, T. L. Gardner, Ovis White, and Harvey Caldwell. (Courtesy of the Ford Museum.)

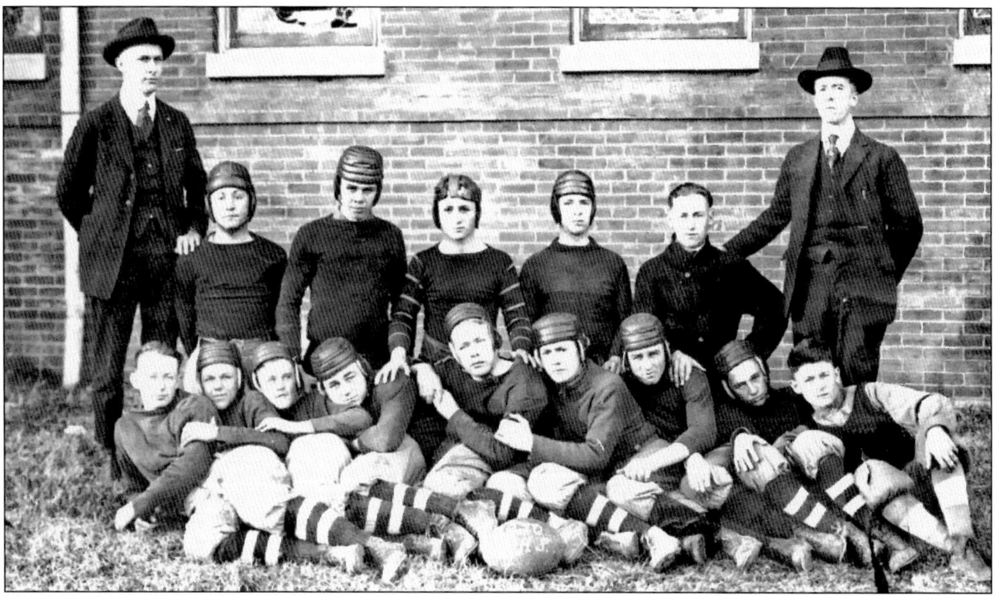

The 1920 Homer High School football team posed in front of the Homer Methodist Church for this photograph. Team members are, from left to right, (first row) Malcolm Menefee, Russell Smith, Jim Olive, Boyce O'Bannon, Ozzie McClung, Wilbur Moreland, Leslie Gill, Gaston Baucum, and Jack Ryan; (second row) Principal W. C. Boone, Albertus DeLoach, John Nick Brown, Edgar Osborn, Moses Robinson, Tom Baker, and coach John Moore. (Courtesy of the Ford Museum.)

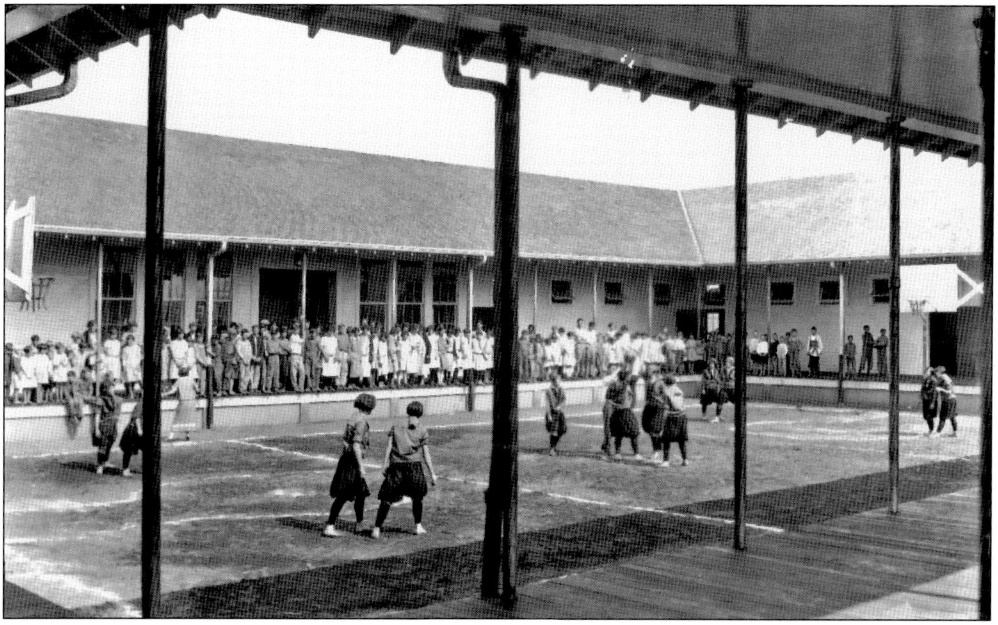

Harris School once had an open-air basketball court with a dirt floor. Classrooms surrounded the court, and spectators were protected from the elements by roof overhangs. In this photograph, the Harris girls' basketball team is shown in action. By 1930, the gymnasium had been roofed and floored. A three-mil, five-year tax was passed to pay for the renovations. (Courtesy of the Claiborne Parish School Board.)

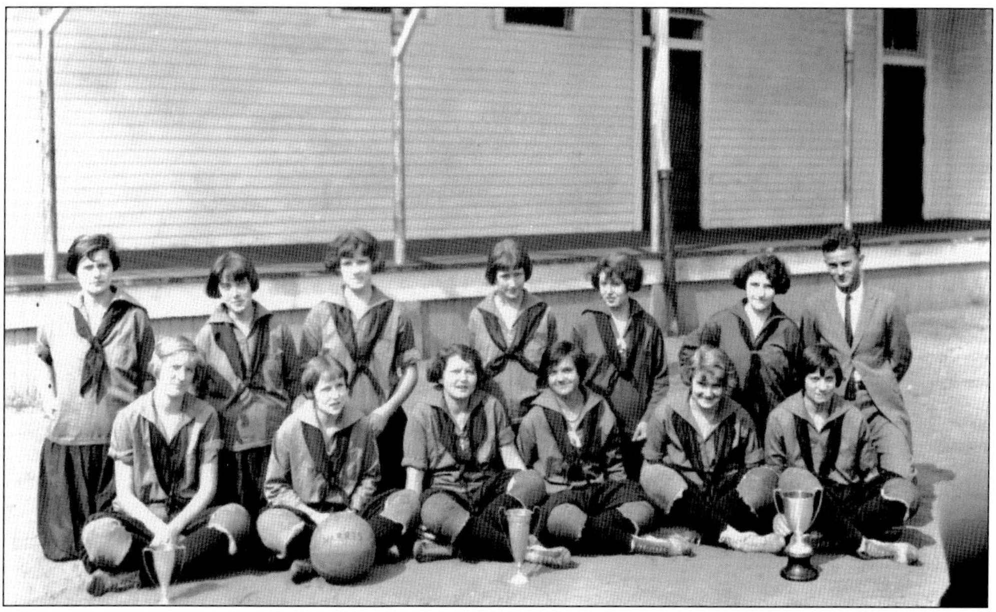

The 1923–1924 "Wonder Team" of Harris High School is shown here posing with the Claiborne Parish, North Louisiana, and State Championship trophies. Team members are, from left to right, (first row) Myrtle Wade, Maggie Camp, unidentified, Mabel Miller, Debet Crow, and Sybil O'Rear; (second row) Hazel Baugh, Hazel Smith, Opal Miller, Ima Knighten, unidentified, Velma Pierce, and coach V. M. Robert. (Courtesy of the Claiborne Parish School Board.)

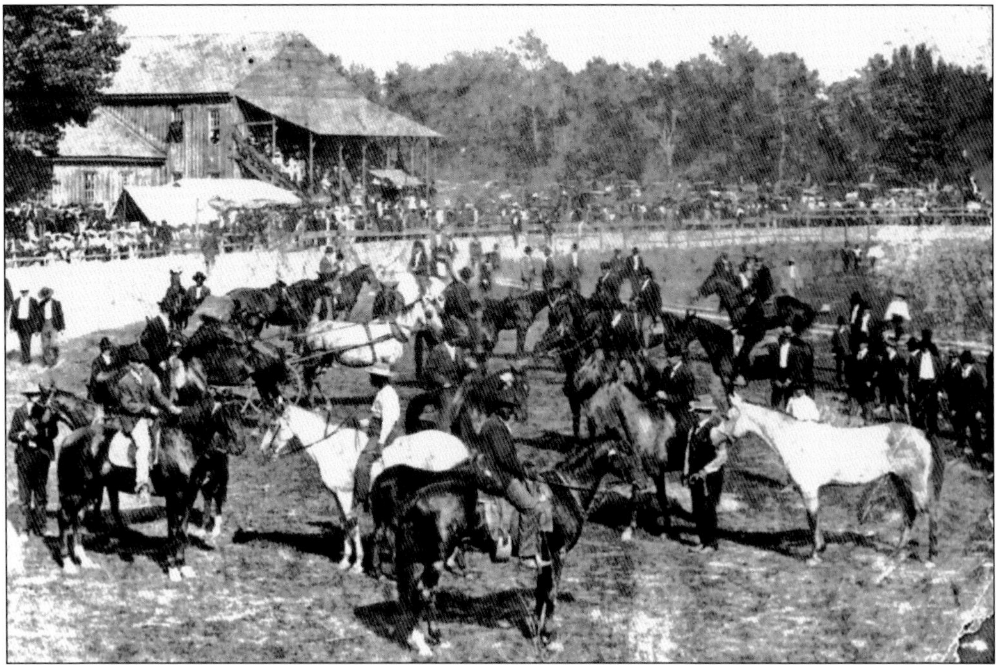

According to the July 28, 1889, edition of the *Louisiana-Weekly Journal*, the Claiborne Parish fairgrounds were located "on the railroad just south of Caney Creek, on the right hand side of the Minden road." The grounds featured a two-story exposition hall, a machinery hall, lunch houses, and a grandstand overlooking the racetrack. The track was considered to be one of the best in the state. Several fast horses were scheduled to race for the grand opening on October 21, 1890. (Courtesy of Edith K. Kirkpatrick.)

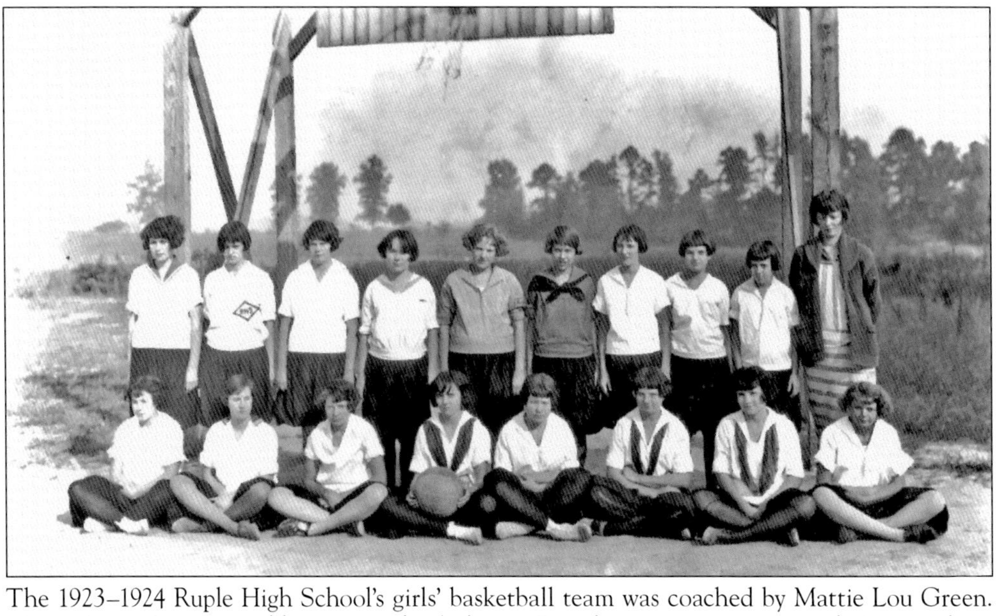

The 1923–1924 Ruple High School's girls' basketball team was coached by Mattie Lou Green. The girls' uniforms were bloomers with stockings. Bare legs were not permitted. Two or three games a week were played on the dirt courts in the afternoons after school. Note the wooden backboard in the background. (Courtesy of the Claiborne Parish School Board.)

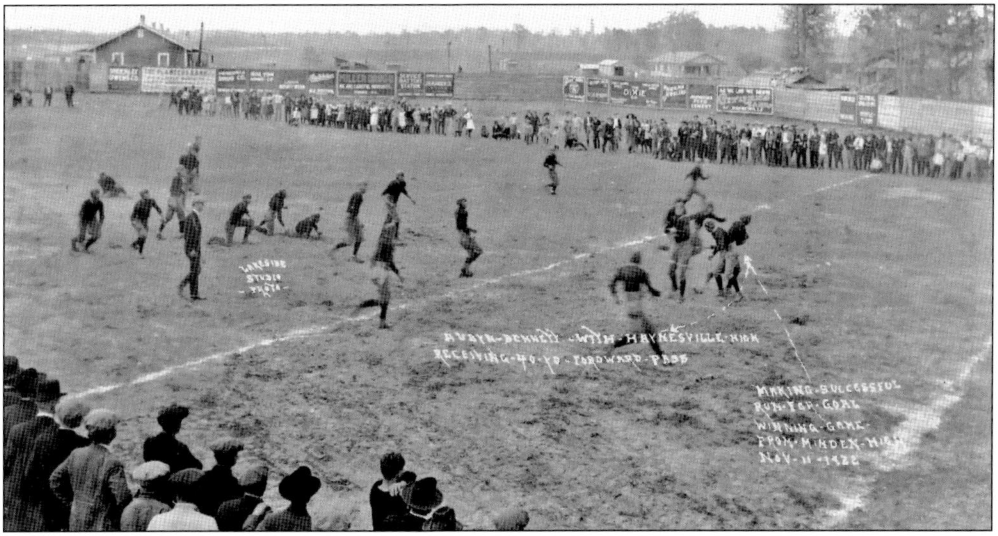

On November 11, 1922, Haynesville and Minden played their annual football competition at Haynesville. Aubyn Bennett scored Haynesville's winning touchdown on a 40-yard catch. Because the fields were not lighted, all games were played during the day. No bleachers had been constructed, so fans stood on the sidelines as they watched the game. Signs advertising Homer and Haynesville businesses appear on the tall plank fence surrounding the field. (Courtesy of the Claiborne Parish School Board.)

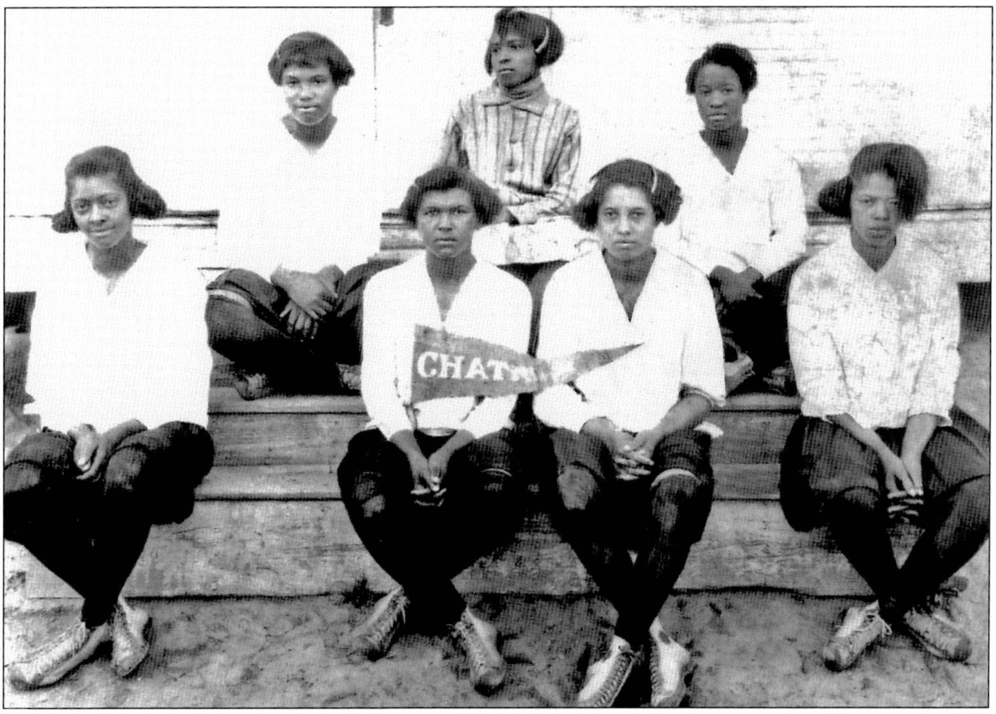

During the 1920s, Chatman School competed in basketball with teams from other black schools in the area. The Chatman girls' basketball team posed for this photograph on the steps of the school. Team members are Trudy Taylor, Hazel Lyons, Elizabeth Rhodes, coach Fannie Pickens, Lillie Mae Watts, Lillie Mae Jones, and Lucille Watts. (Courtesy of the William Chatman Estate.)

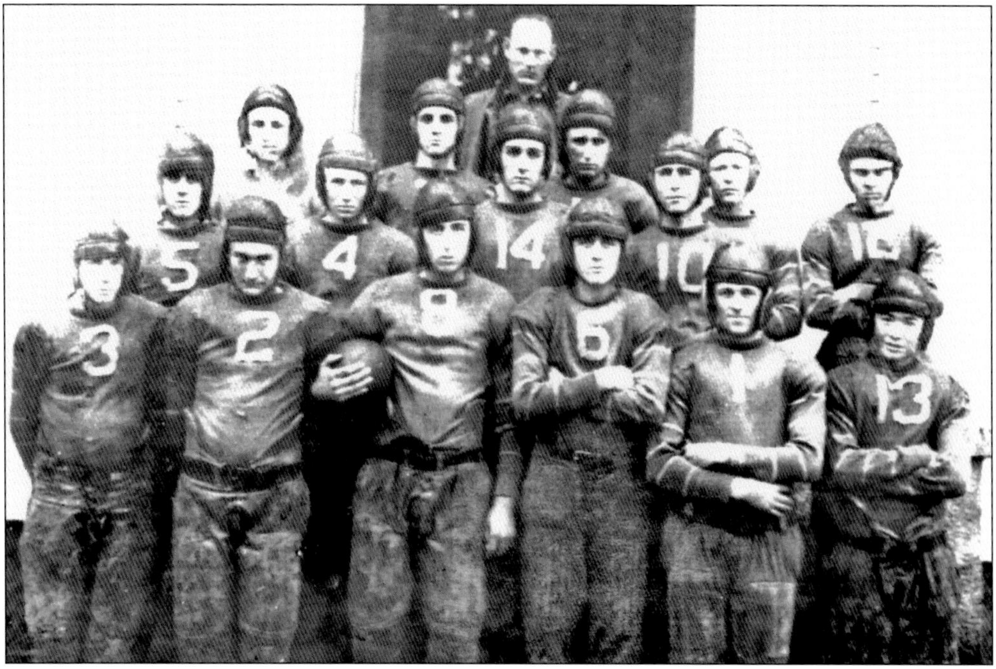

Members of the 1925–1926 Lisbon football team are, from left to right, (first row) Lynn Heard, Dewey Jackson, Paul Aycock, Alton Martin, George Allen White, and L. D. Pendergrass; (second row) James Kimbell, Leonard Swint, Ray Aycock, Herbert Lowery, and Winston Squyres; (third row) Cortez Lowery, Hillard Greer, Herbert Killgore, and James Fowler. Coach C. C. Campbell is standing in the back. (Courtesy of Don Aycock.)

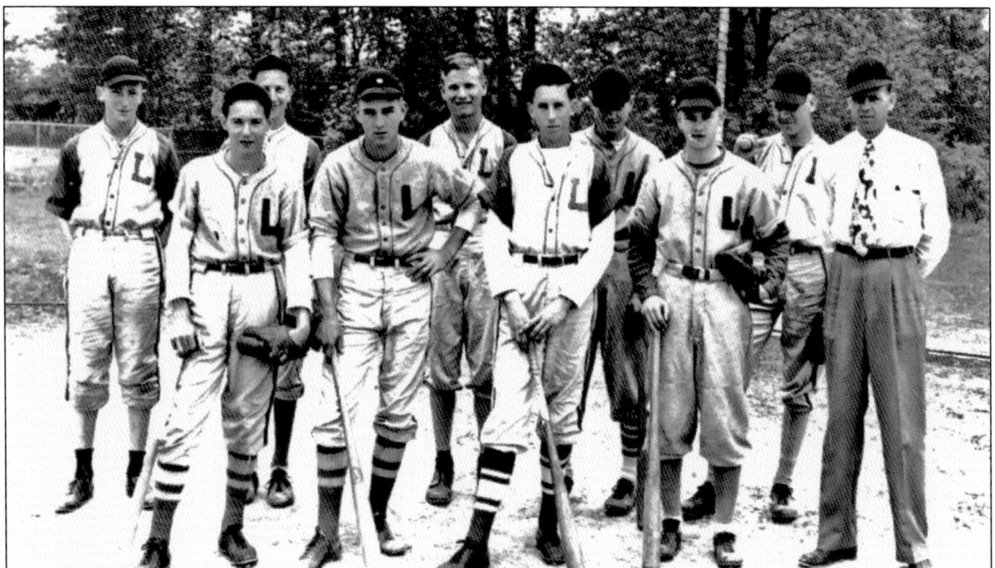

The record of the 1950 Lisbon Eagles took them to the state playoffs. Team members are, from left to right, (first row) James Allen McAdams, Don Aycock, David Kimbell, Don Haynes, and coach Grady Saulters; (second row) Melton Wilson, Travis Tanner, Bobby Cook, Olen Aycock, and Joe Richardson. (Courtesy of Don Aycock.)

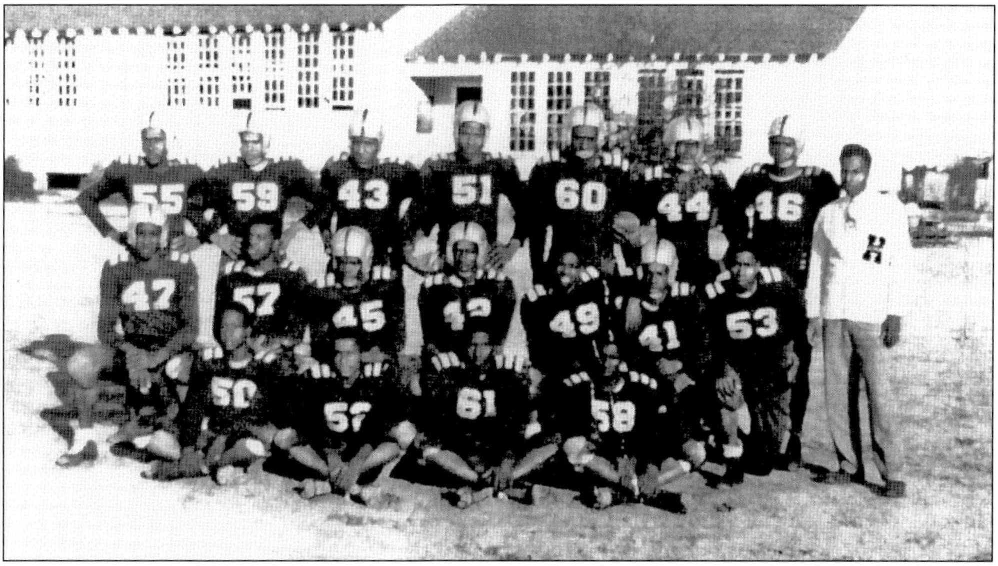

The Haynesville Colored High School football team posed for this photograph in front of the school in 1952. The school building was built in 1927 on 12 acres of land donated by Verge White. In 1960, the school was renamed Woodson High School in honor of Carter B. Woodson, a nationally known educator and historian. A total of 753 students were graduated from this school. (Courtesy of Sherman Brown.)

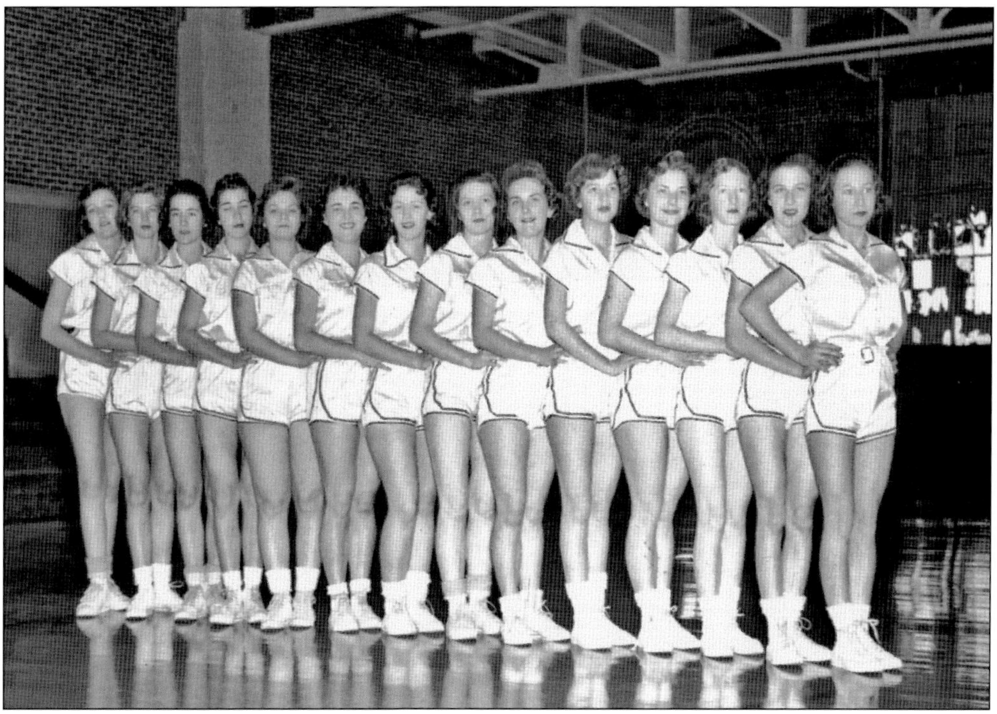

Members of the 1957 Homer High girls' basketball team are, from left to right, Nelwyn Dobbins, Glynda Tuggle, Etta Faye Caskey, Carolyn Wasson, Patsy Byrd, Millie Hawthorne, Linda Mizell, Polly Pair, Martha Oden, Carrie Hollenshead, Alice Harmon, Earline Batton, Katie Ruple, and June McDonald. The girls finished third in 1-AA play. (Courtesy of the *Guardian-Journal*.)

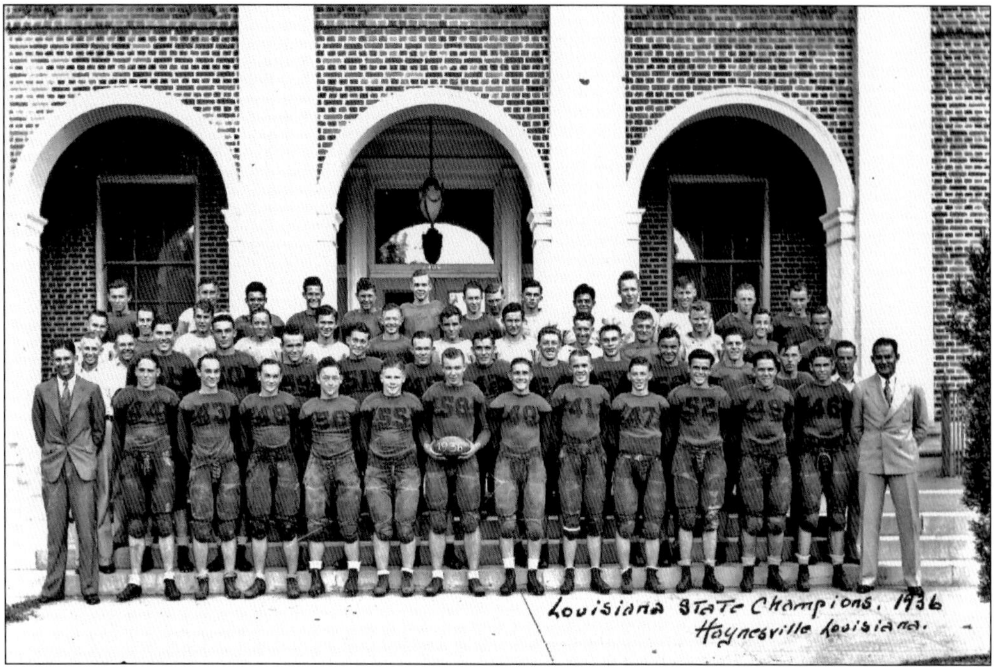

Haynesville High won its third Louisiana High School State Championship in 1936 with a perfect 12-0 record. The team scored 344 points, giving up only 19 points. Cecil Crowley was coach from 1936 to 1938. Since that time, Haynesville has won 11 more state championships. (Courtesy of the Ford Museum.)

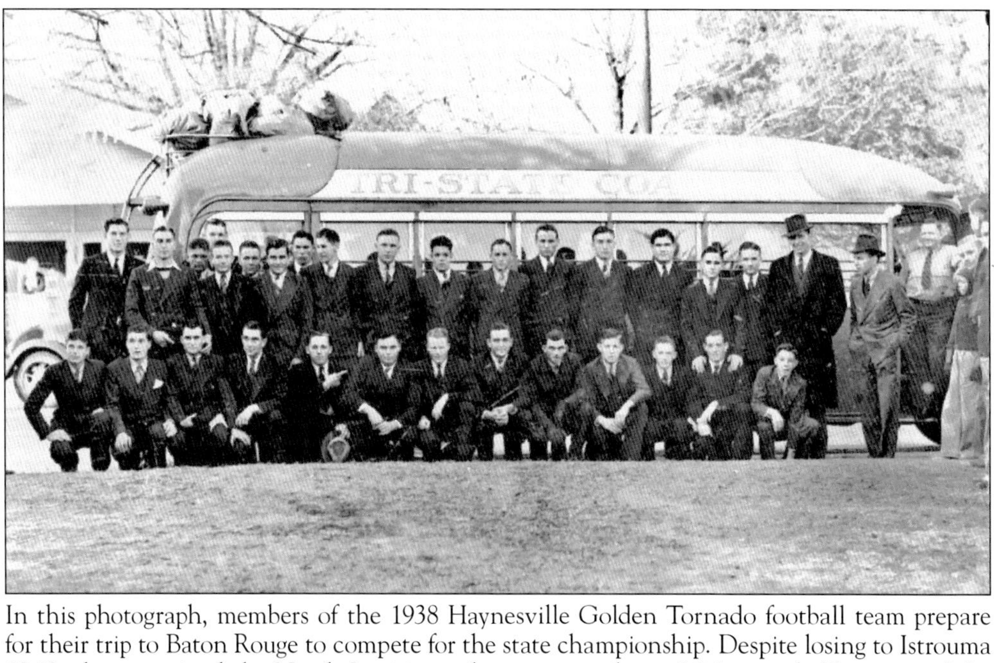

In this photograph, members of the 1938 Haynesville Golden Tornado football team prepare for their trip to Baton Rouge to compete for the state championship. Despite losing to Istrouma 19-12, they remained the North Louisiana champions with an 8-3-1 record. (Courtesy of the Ford Museum.)

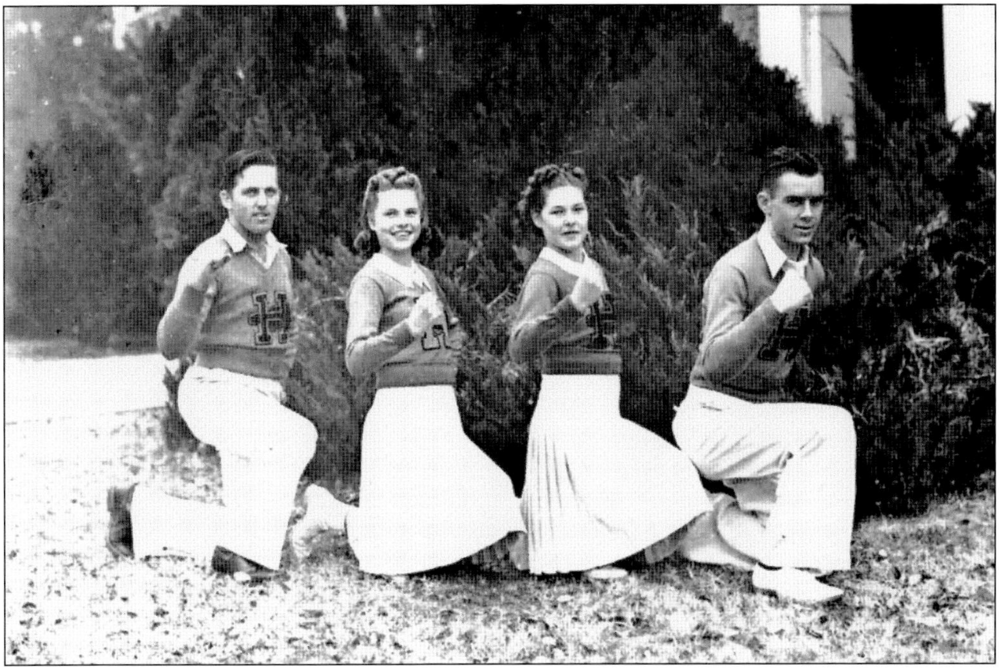

Leading cheers for the Haynesville Golden Tornado team in 1938 were, from left to right, Marvin Ray Elmore, Meredith Gibson, Billie Slaughter, and Dick Bond. (Courtesy of the Ford Museum.)

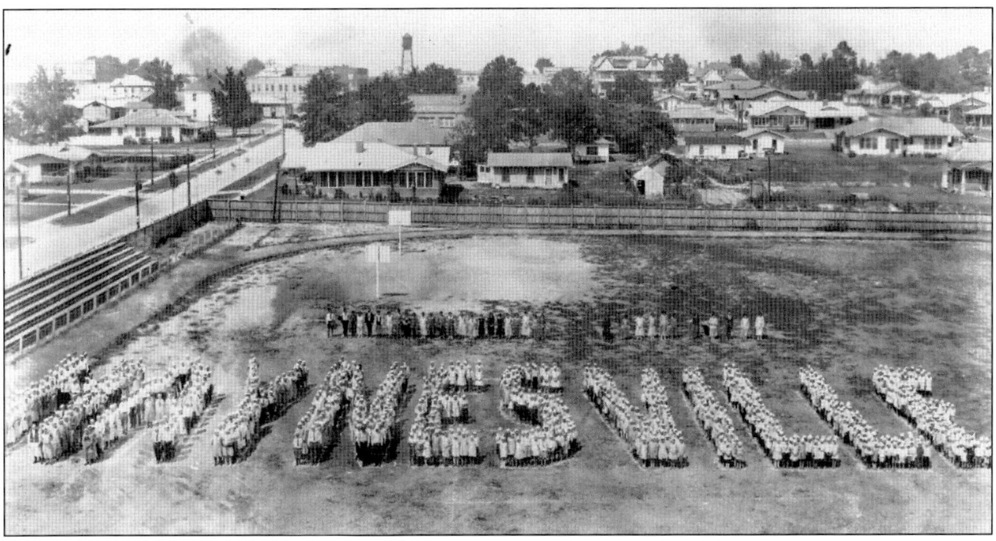

In 1923, there were enough students in the Haynesville school system to spell out the town's name on the vacant lot that was to become the site of the new high school. (Courtesy of the Claiborne Parish School Board.)

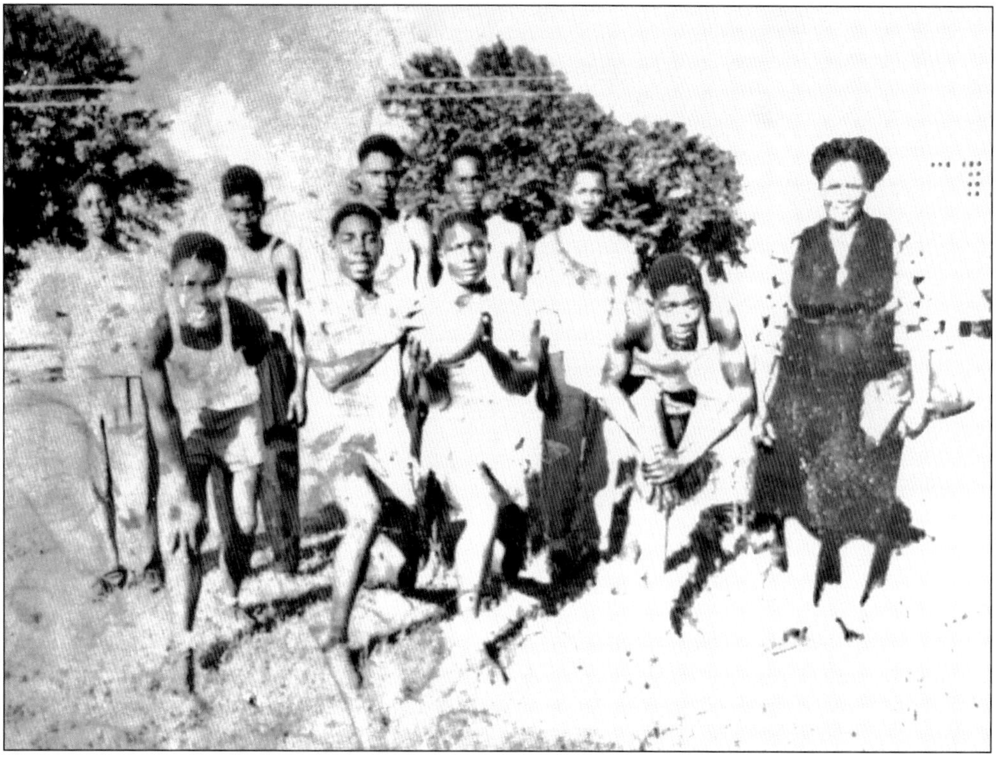

Members of the 1945 St. John basketball team are, from left to right, (first row) Marion E. Cooper Jr., J. E. Johnson, Charlie Jackson, and Guy Wells; (second row) Willie Knowles Jr., Wallace Weaver, Milo Kelly, Clayton Hall, and L. C. Wells. Annie Cooper (far right) is the teacher. St. John was the first high school for blacks in the parish. (Courtesy of the Ford Museum.)

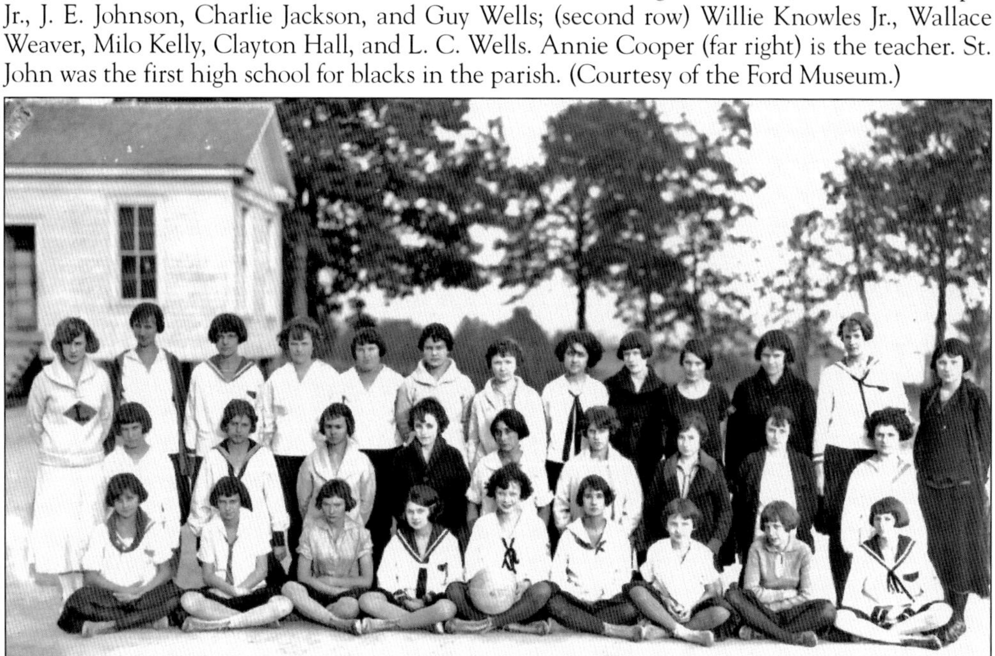

The 1924–1925 Athens High School girls' basketball team was coached by Margaret Postell. The popularity of girls' basketball was evident from the large number of girls participating in the sport. (Courtesy of the Claiborne Parish School Board.)

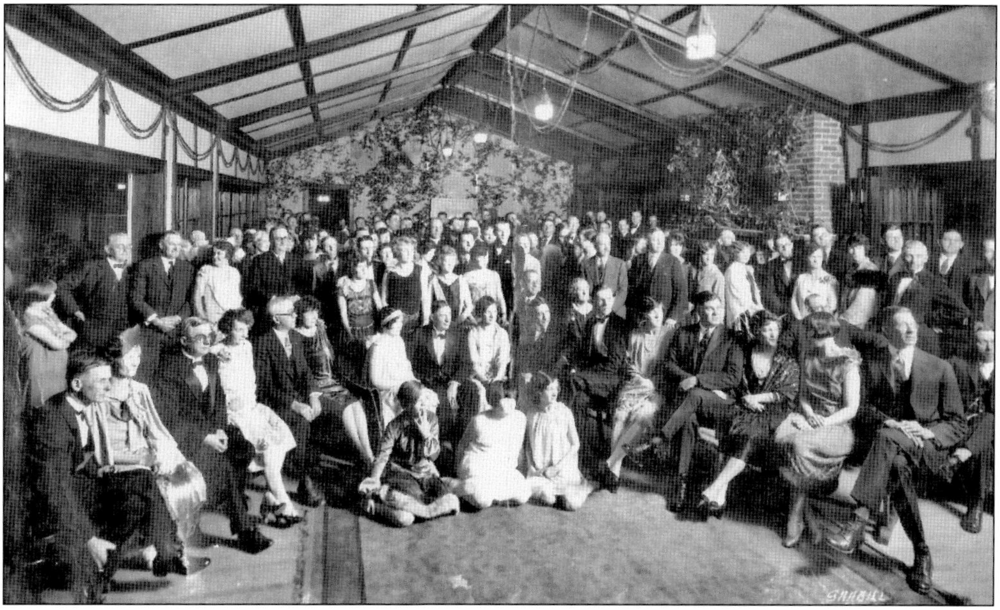

The Homer-Haynesville Country Club, built in 1926 by F. C. McClanahan, was located on Highway 79 midway between the two towns. In this photograph, club members have gathered to celebrate a festive occasion. (Courtesy of the Ford Museum.)

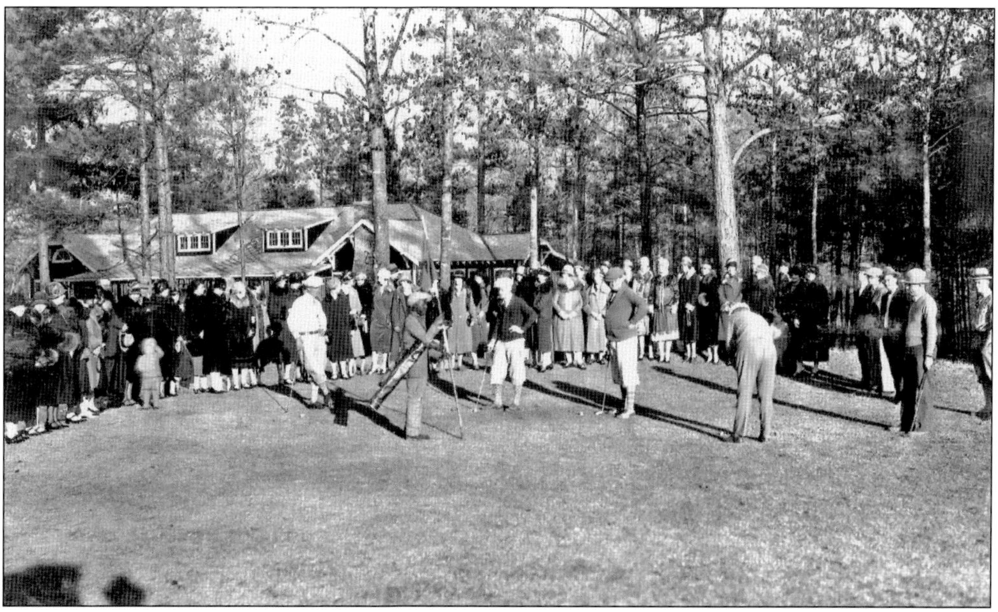

The Homer-Haynesville Country Club featured a nine-hole golf course. Black Kerlin aced the fourth hole in May 1928. In the 1950s, each town built its own facilities and, for a time, the club was used as a roller skating rink. The building was struck by lightning and burned in 1973. (Courtesy of Monte Banks.)

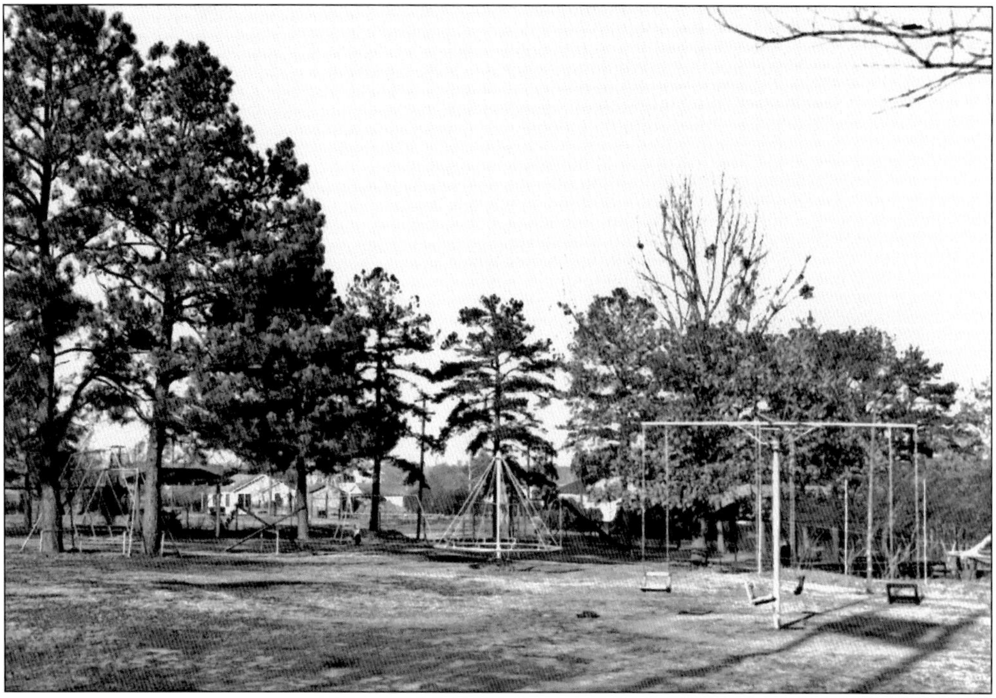

Homer's Coca-Cola Park provided recreation facilities enjoyed by many Homer residents from the 1940s until the early 1960s. It was the setting for many happy events as children played on the swings, seesaws, and other playground equipment placed throughout the park. The second floor of the Coca-Cola building was the location of "Teen Town," a large room featuring pool and Ping-Pong tables, a jukebox, dance floor, and concession counter. (Courtesy of the Claiborne Parish Library.)

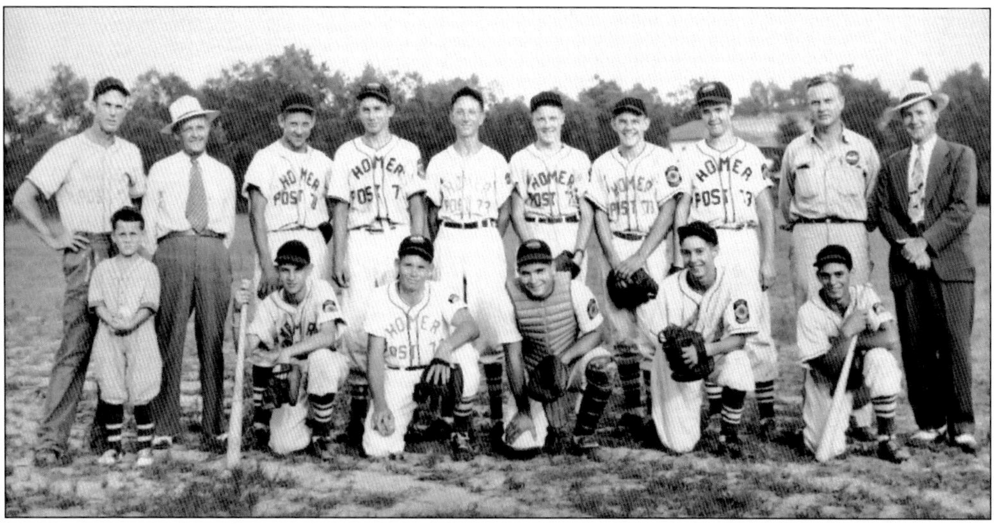

The Homer Coca-Cola Bottling Company sponsored Homer's American Legion Post No. 73 baseball team. Members of the 1948 team are, from left to right, (first row) Don Haynes, Al Doggett, Ray Rogers, James Allen McAdams, and Joe Manning; (second row) coach Howard Wall, batboy Bobby Ashley, Cecil Atkins, Joe Richardson, Doug Baker, Travis Tanner, Hall Nattin, Dennis Cook, L. E. Kirk, Joe Robertson, and Bud Meadors. (Courtesy of Gil Dowies family.)

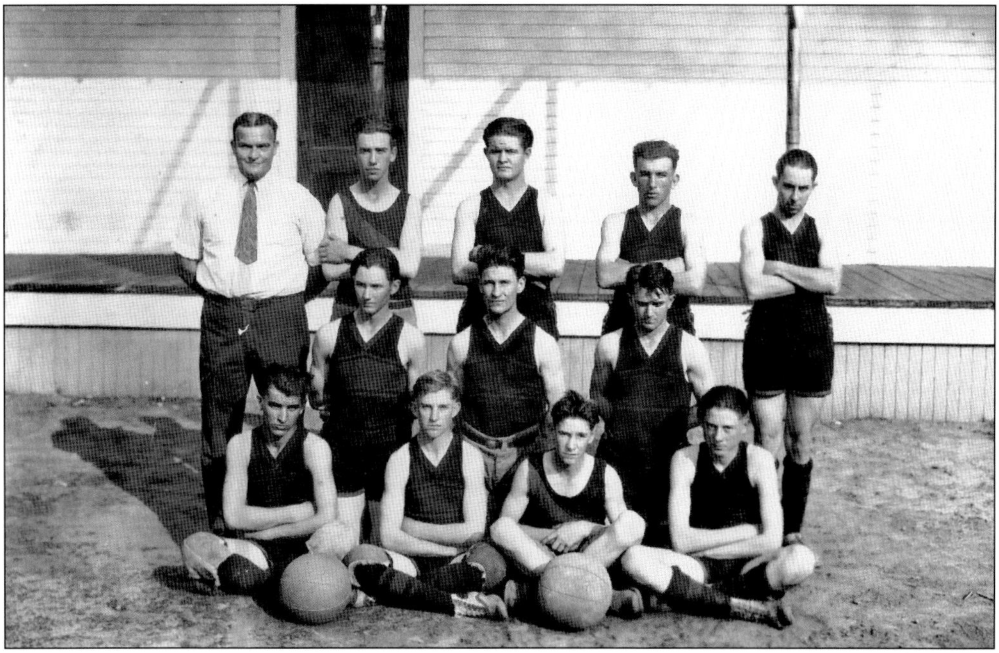

The Harris boys' basketball teams succeeded in winning a number of championships during the school's history. Some members of the 1923–1924 team were Pat Robert, Hayden Camp, Omar Knighten, L. P. Acklen, Curtis Hough, Tola Knighten, Fortson Kemp, and Leonard Frye. The team was coached by Howard Weston. (Courtesy of the Claiborne Parish School Board.)

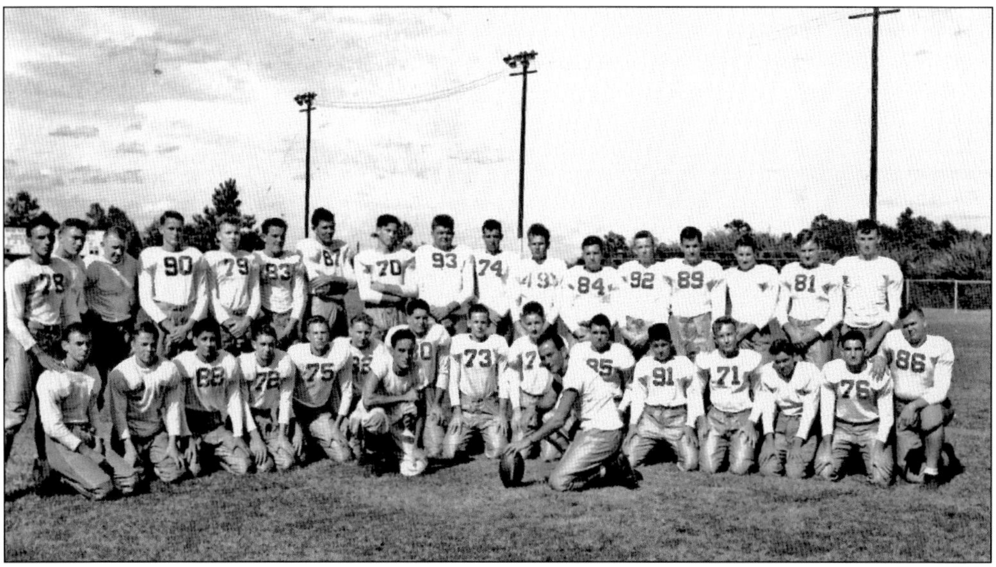

The 1945 Homer High football team was coached by Jimmy Karam (holding football) and Perry Angles (kneeling center front). Team members are, from left to right, (first row) B. Gentry, A. Atkins, E. Michael, H. Tanner, D. King, J. Woods, J. LeSage, C. Dickens, A. Fisher, B. Rowell, J. Michael, G. Meadors, J. Aubrey, H. Tabor, and G. Emerson; (second row) F. Ebarb, J. Robertson, B. Smith, J. Kimbell, F. Harkness, B. Hightower, O. Camp, W. Woods, L. Cook, H. Baker, D. Fortson, B. Hamil, J. R. Oakes, B. Simmons, D. Aubrey, S. Butler, and G. Loval. (Courtesy of Stuart Butler.)

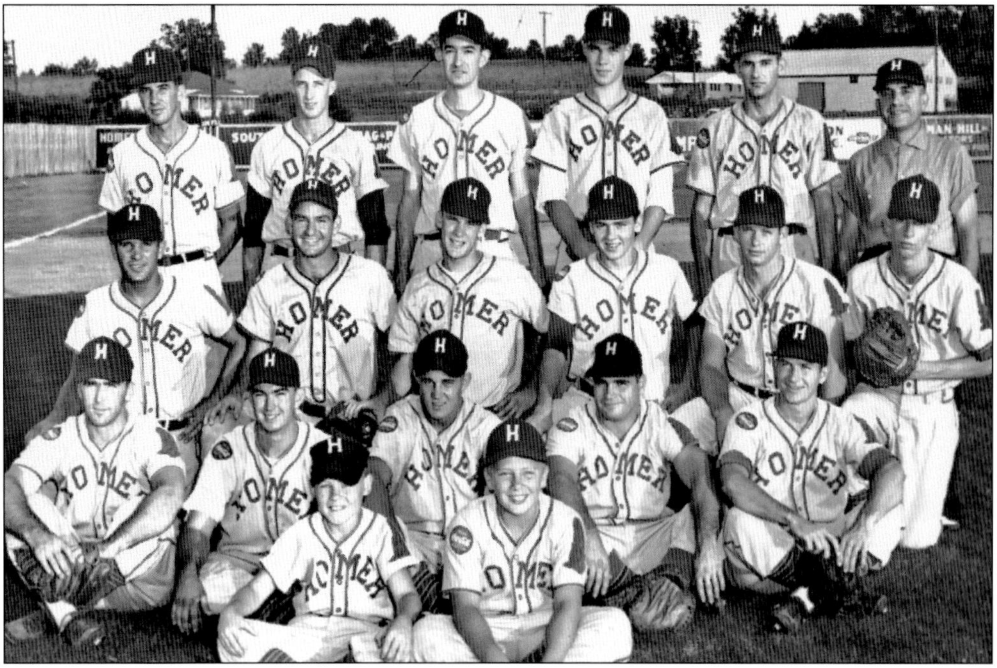

The semipro Homer Oilers played in the Big-8 League, winning the pennant in 1955. From left to right are (first row) batboys T. Townsend and D. Thomas; (second row) team members J. Pace, J. Bathea, G. Maxwell, R. Rogers, and C. Kimbro; (third row) team members T. Virgets, J. Goodwyn, D. Brown, B. Newton, A. Doggett, and B. R. Suggs; (fourth row) team members J. Barnette, J. C. Sells, B. McDonald, P. Dean, and C. Rugg, and manager P. Thomas. (Courtesy of the Ford Museum.)

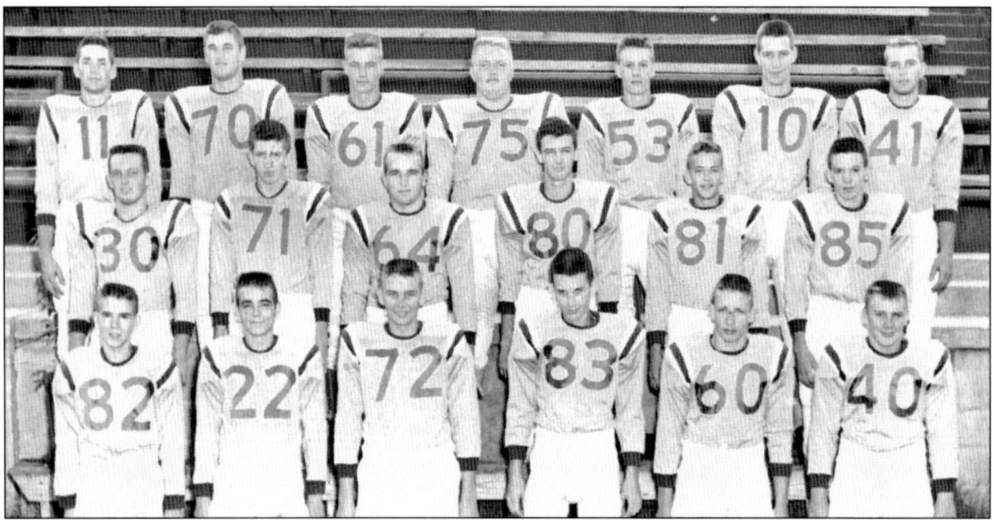

The 1957 "Iron Men" compiled an 11-2-1 record and were State AA Runners-Up. Twelve team members made All-District, five made All-State, one made All-Southern, and two made High School All-American. The "Men" had the leading scorer in District 1-AA, and their defense allowed only 71 points to be scored against them. Players are, from left to right, (first row) B. Thomas, D. Ackley, T. Owens, E. Pixley, B. Barker, and D. Thomas; (second row) G. W. Zachary, R. Perry, K. Hood, G. Davidson, J. Andrews, and C. Lewis; (third row) R. Wilkins, F. Miller, H. Coleman, J. W. Odom, R. Weaver, B. Flurry, and S. Camp. (Courtesy of the *Guardian-Journal*.)

Five

The Enduring Flame

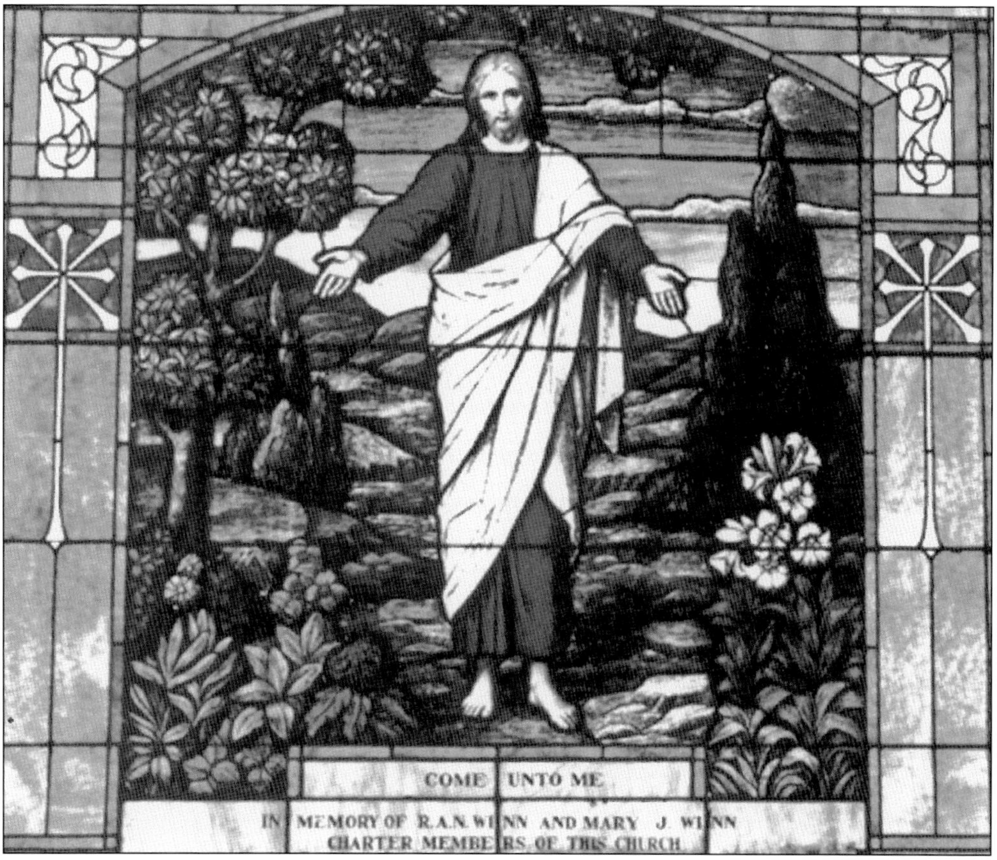

The beautiful sanctuary and stained-glass windows of Haynesville's United Methodist Church stand in sharp contrast to the rough brush arbors in which early congregations held their meetings. After building log homes for shelter, Claiborne Parish's settlers began to organize churches. A sustaining faith in God helped these sturdy settlers weather the trials of pioneer life and gave root to many Protestant churches. (Courtesy of the *Guardian-Journal.*)

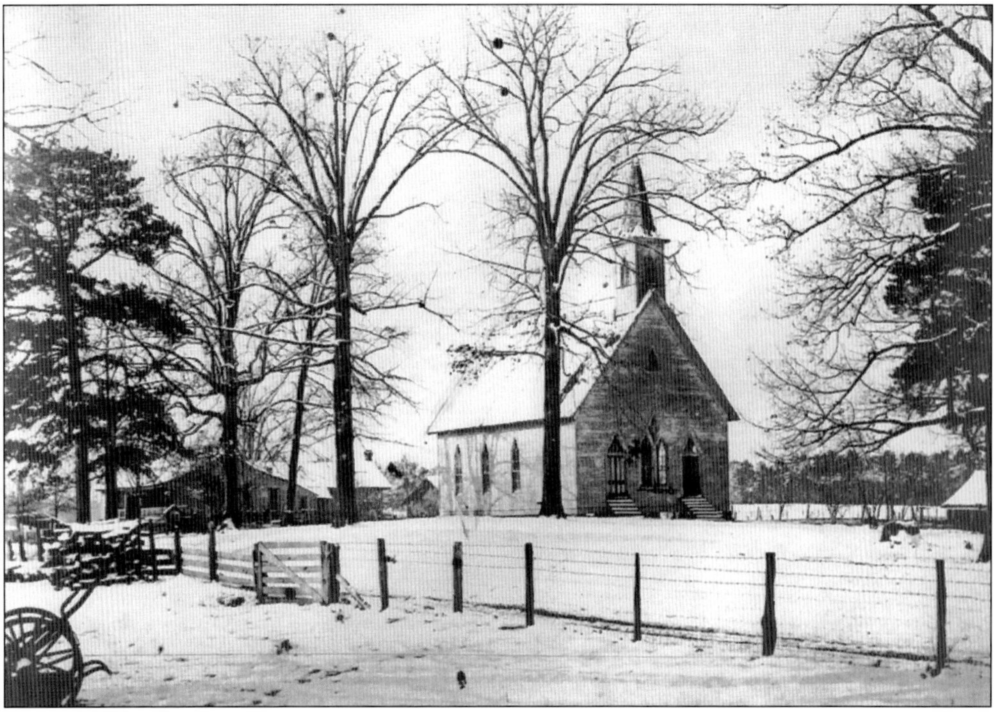

The first Methodist meetings in Claiborne Parish were camp meetings, where attendees camped for several days and met under crudely constructed tabernacles or brush arbors. The Summerfield Methodist Church had its beginnings at Corney Bluff (Scottsville) in 1845, with Rev. B. J. Hamilton as pastor. The congregation later moved to Summerfield and built the present structure in 1876. (Courtesy of Helen Campbell.)

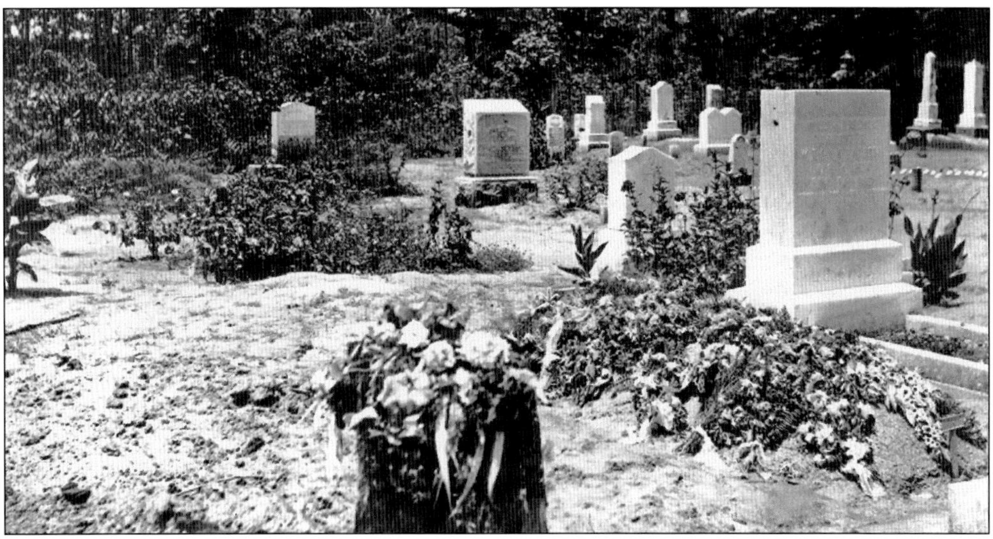

The Summerfield Cemetery serves as the final resting place for many early settlers in the surrounding community. The oldest legible marker is that of Jane R. Smith, who died on June 30, 1870. The Summerfield Cemetery is located adjacent to the Summerfield School on Louisiana Highway 9. This photograph of the cemetery was taken around 1925. (Courtesy of Helen Campbell.)

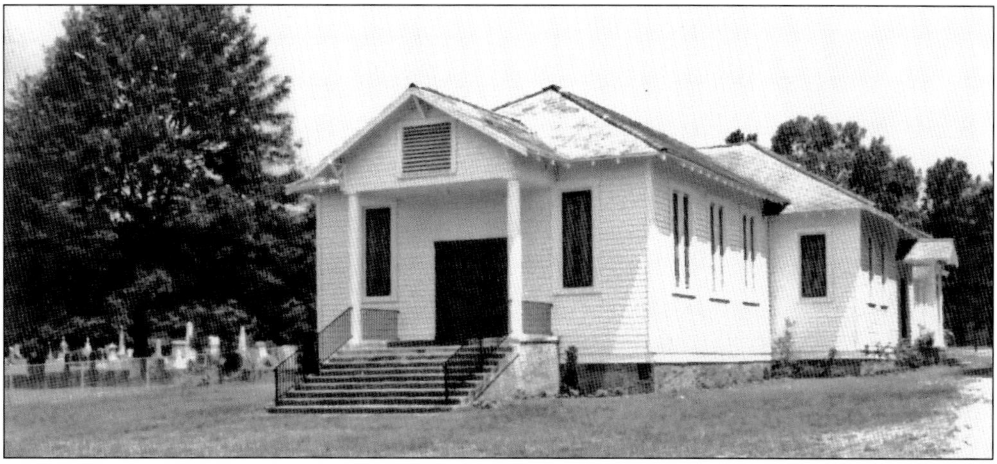

Originally named Providence Church, the Lisbon Methodist Church had its beginnings in 1850 with 57 white members and 9 black members. On July 21, 1850, Dr. Seth Tatum and Amanda Sherard were the first couple to be married in the church. The church currently occupies a 3-acre tract of land donated for a church and cemetery by James McClendon in 1871. In 1926, the church was moved, with mules and logs, several feet southeast to its present location. (Courtesy of Edith Kirkpatrick.)

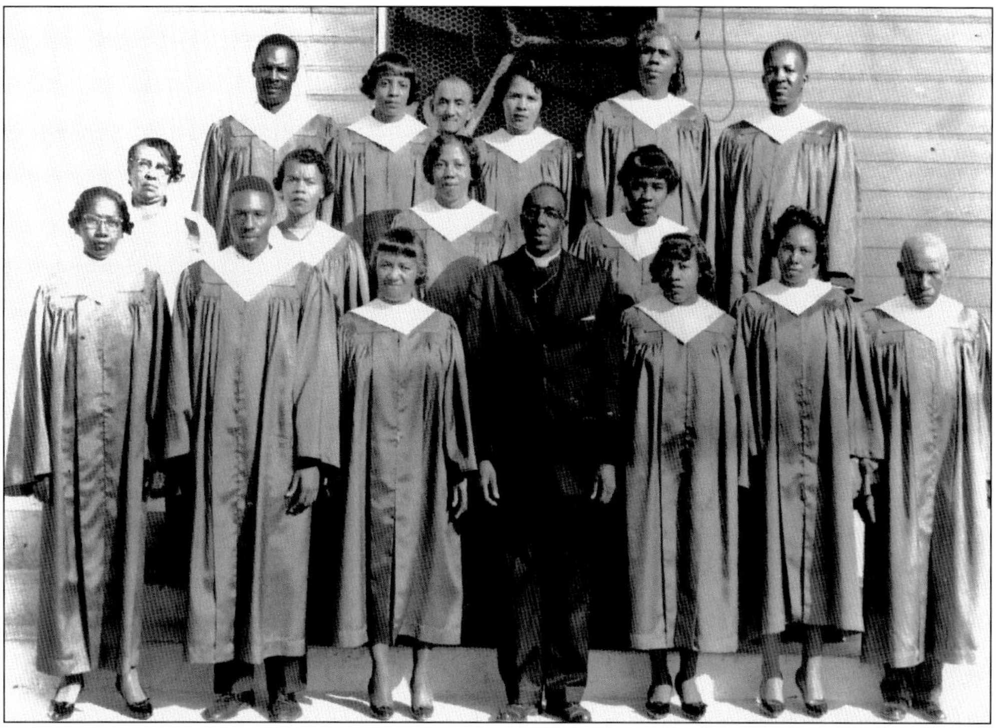

In 1866, after members of the Forest Grove Methodist Church had moved their church to the Arizona community, they donated their former building to the Forest Grove Colored Methodist Episcopal Church. Rev. Caesar Willis, the first pastor of the Forest Grove CME Church, walked several miles from Lisbon to conduct Sunday services. In 1887, a new building was constructed across the road from the original site. Here the Forest Grove choir is pictured in the late 1950s. (Courtesy of Juanita Hamilton.)

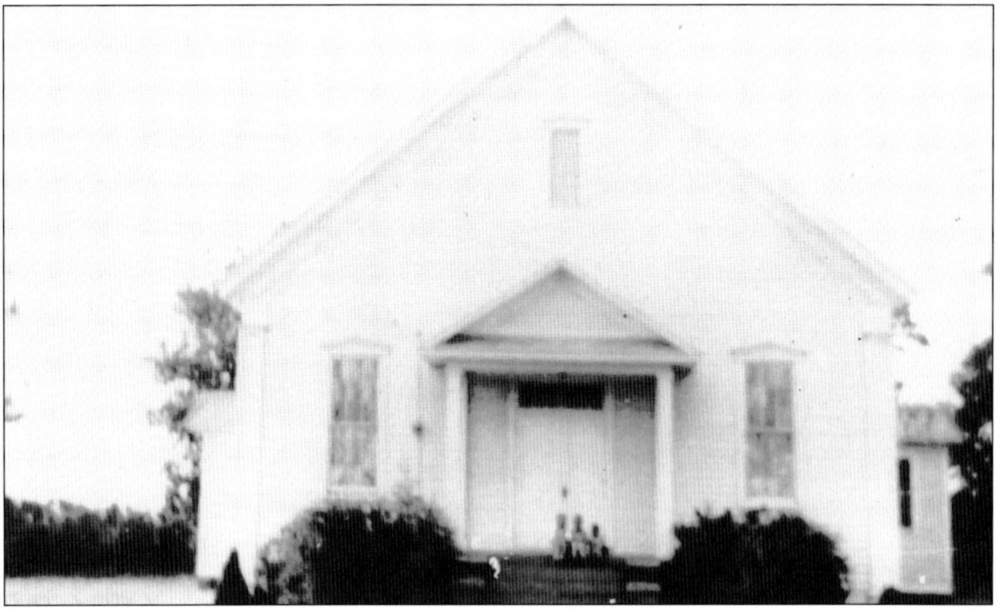

Rocky Springs Baptist Church was organized at Lisbon in 1845. The congregation met under a brush arbor until 1850, when a small church of hand-hewn boards was built. Following the tradition of that day, men sat on one side of the church while women and children sat on the other. The present building was completed in 1885 while Rev. J. W. Melton was pastor. (Courtesy of Edith K. Kirkpatrick.)

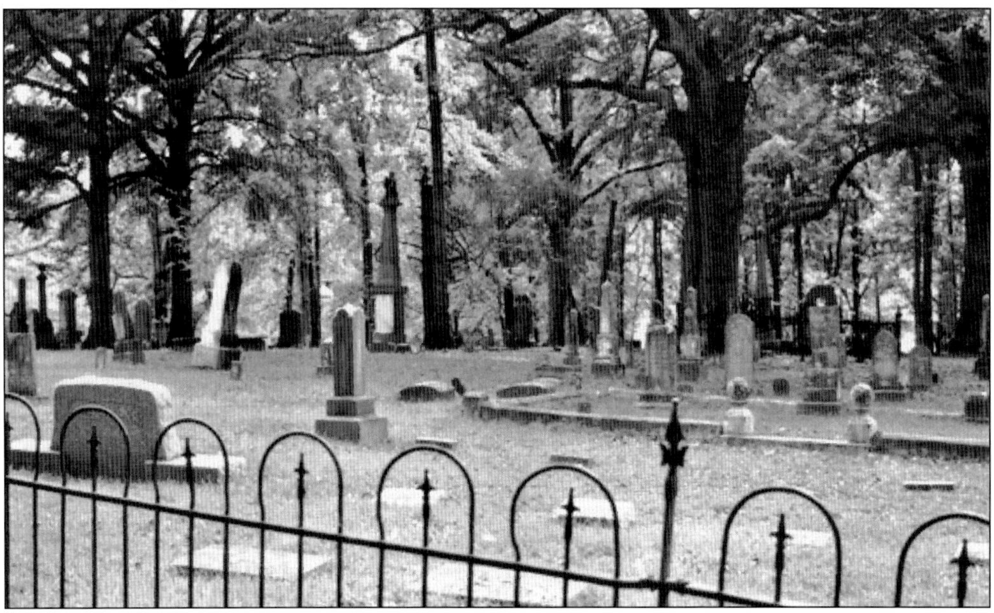

In 1850, the Claiborne Parish Police Jury set aside 5 acres on the outskirts of Homer to be used as a public burying ground. The first interment in the old Homer Cemetery was that of John A. Millican, an eight-year-old boy who died on March 17, 1850. Inscriptions on the older markers indicate that most of Homer's early settlers were born in Georgia or Alabama. One notable couple buried in the old Homer cemetery are John L. and Elizabeth Garrett, the parents of Pat Garrett, the federal marshal credited with killing Billy the Kid. (Courtesy of Kathryn H. Hightower.)

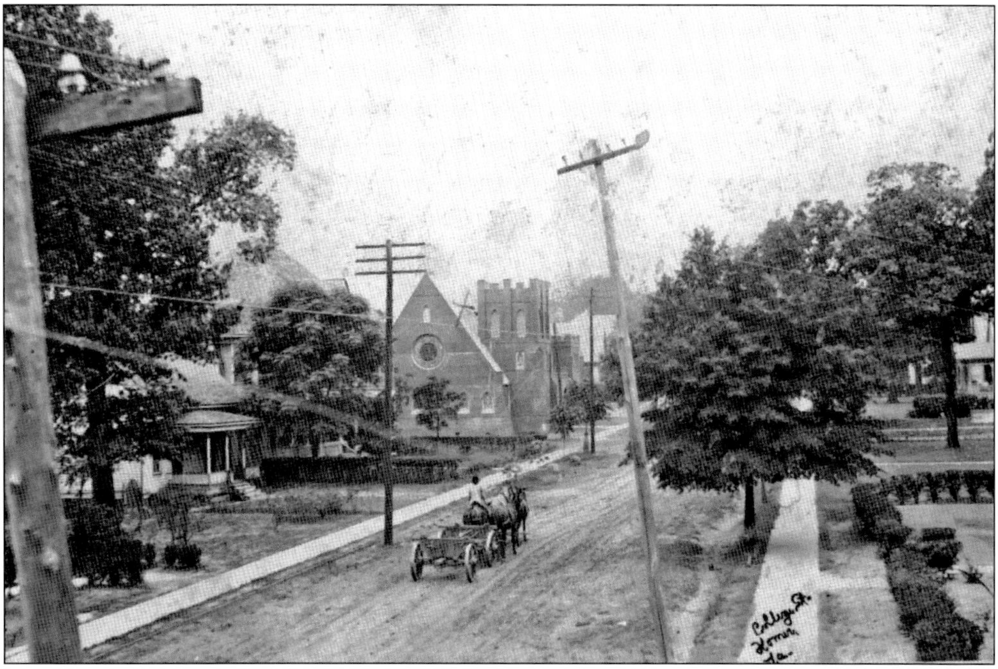

The *c.* 1906 building pictured here served as the meeting place for Homer's Methodist congregation until the present-day building was completed in 1924. Two round stained-glass windows were removed from the old structure and installed in the sanctuary of the new building on either side of the choir loft. (Courtesy of the Ford Museum.)

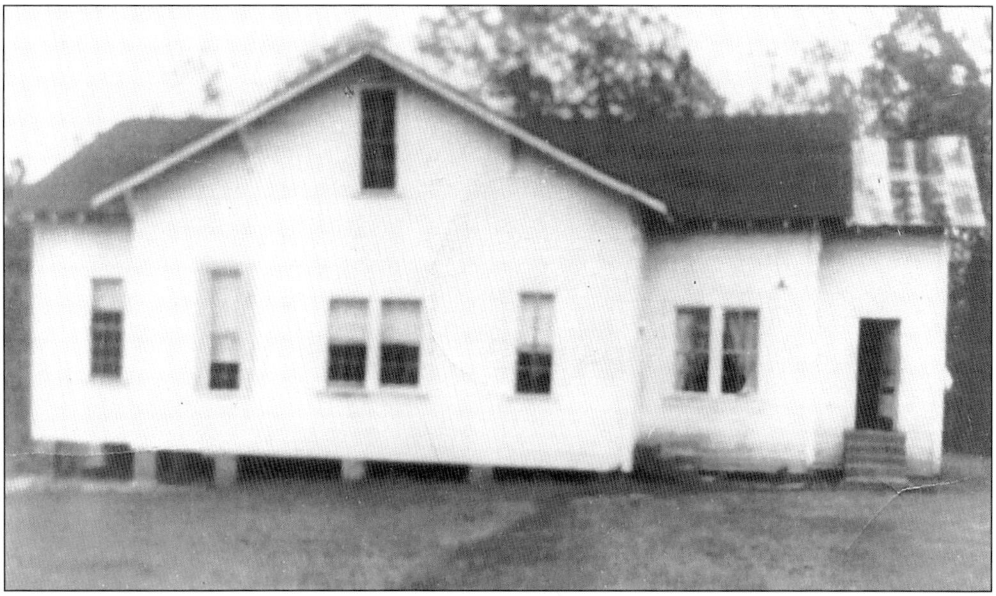

Deacon Ben Walker founded St. Luke Missionary Baptist Church in 1854. The St. Luke church is located in the southeast corner of Claiborne Parish near the Lincoln Parish line. The building shown here served as the church's meeting place from 1926 until 1968. A new building now occupies the site. (Courtesy of Trudy Walker Clark.)

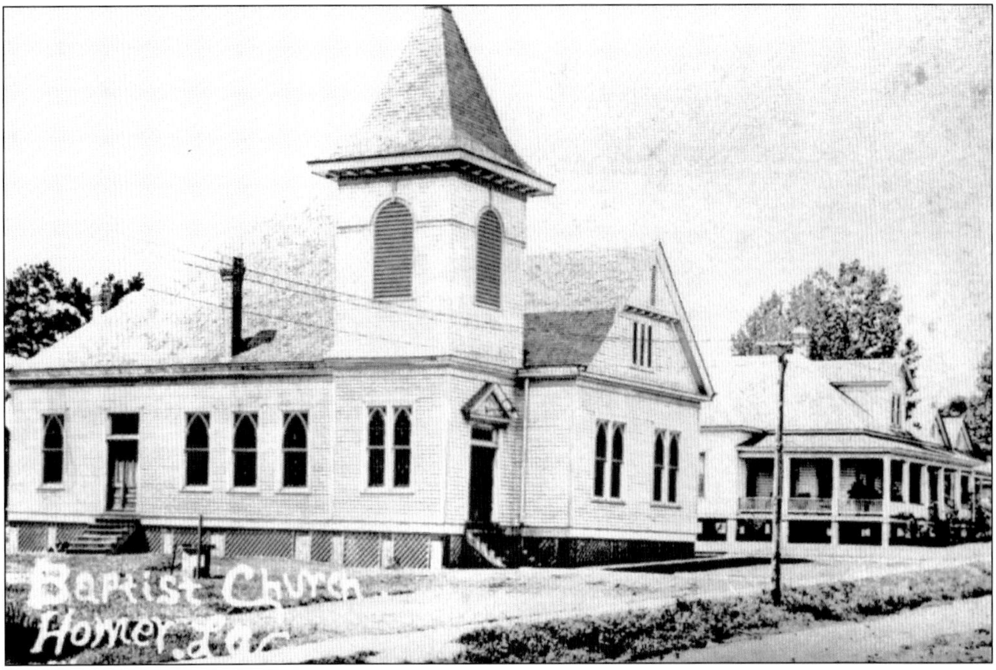

The First Baptist Church of Homer originated from the Ebenezer Baptist Church, organized around 1845. Church services were held once a month on Saturday and Sunday mornings. R. A. Hargis, the first pastor, received a salary of $100 a year. In 1905, the church erected a new building on South Main Street in Homer. Increased population resulting from Homer's oil boom led to the construction of the church's present-day building, completed in 1926. (Courtesy of the Ford Museum.)

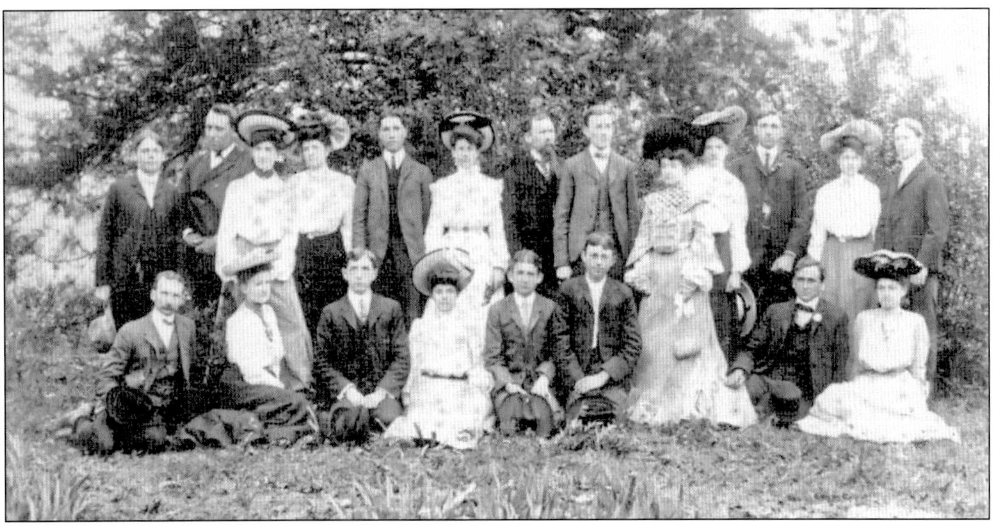

The members of a Young People's Sunday School class at the Homer Baptist Church in 1904 are, from left to right, (first row) Edgar Fortson, Grace McFarland, Charlie Fortson, Inez Aubrey, Dickson Shelton, Jim Oakes, ? Winston, and Dora Fortson; (second row) unidentified, Rev. H. M. Garnett, Bennie Kerlin, Jemmie Nelson, two unidentified, Thomas Nix, Dan Knighton, Sue Braden, Iris Kerlin, Will Dormon, Ada Mae Kimbell, and Aubyn Harris. (Courtesy of the Ford Museum.)

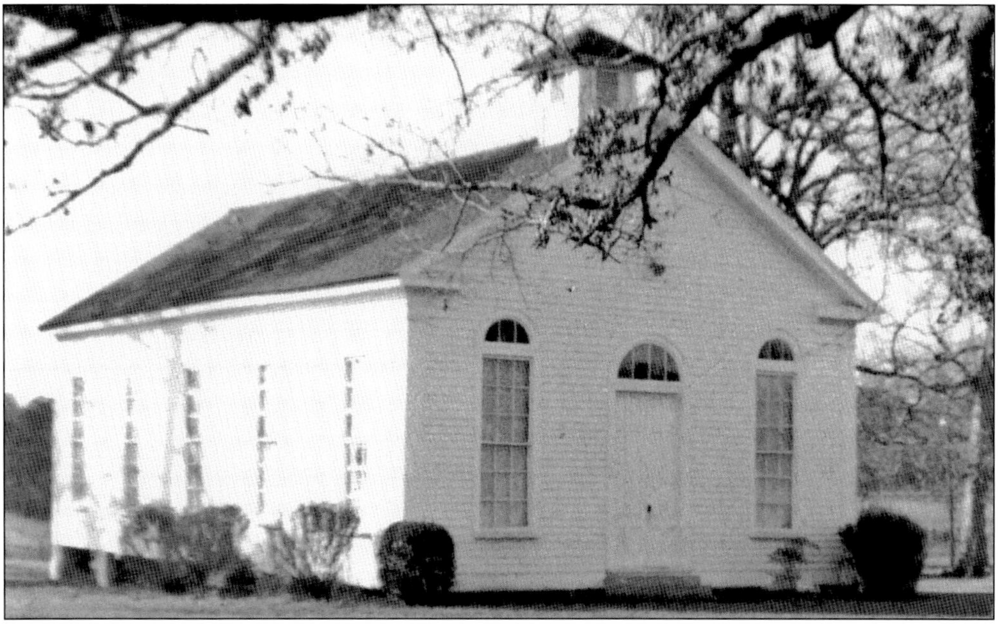

The Arizona United Methodist Church had its beginnings in the Forest Grove community. In 1866, the church was relocated from Forest Grove to the Arizona community. The present-day building, which is listed in the National Register of Historic Places, was completed around 1882 on land donated by Maj. Joshua Willis. (Courtesy of the Ford Museum.)

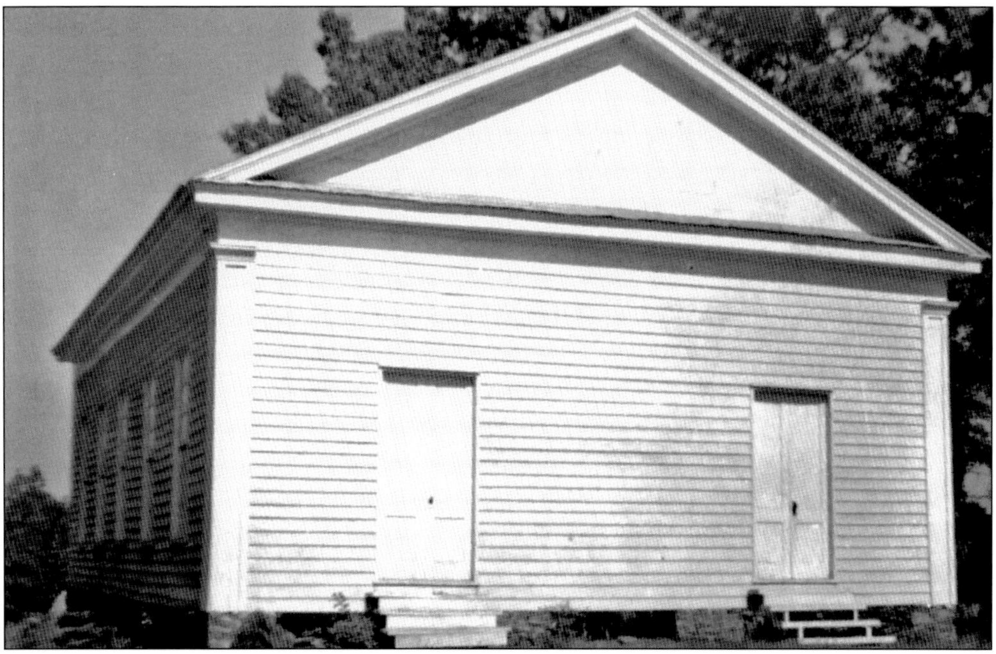

The Walnut Grove Church was organized near the Tulip community in 1847. In 1855, it was moved to Tulip and given the name Pisgah. The name was changed to Tulip Methodist Church in 1860. The present structure, which is listed in the National Register of Historic Places, dates from approximately 1872. A partition in the center of the pews separated male and female attendants. (Courtesy of the Ford Museum.)

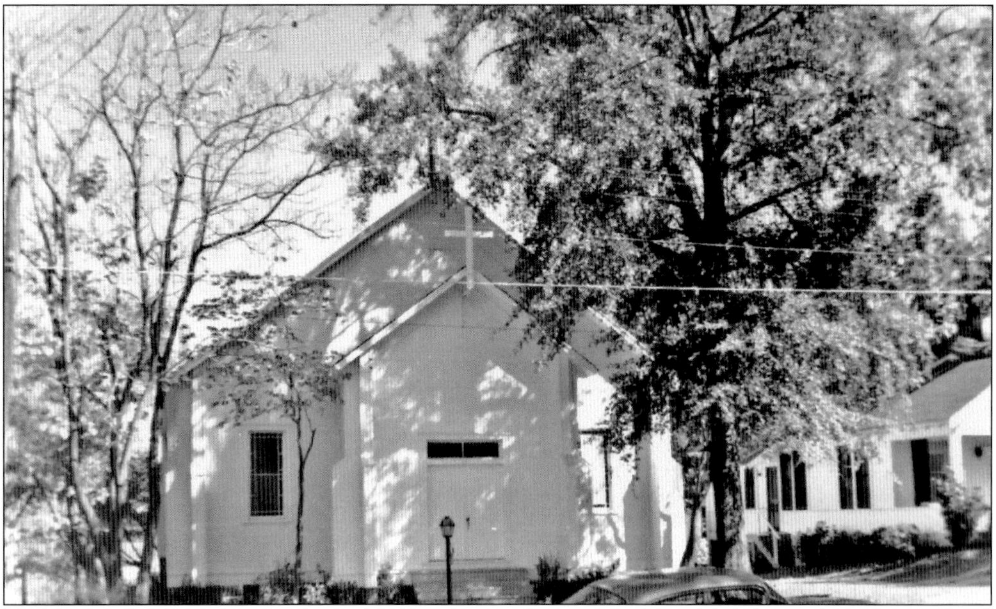

Employees of the L&NW Railroad Company founded Trinity Episcopal Church, dubbed "the Railroad Church," in 1909. Lumber was provided by the railroad and the various mills and companies it served. The church's first pastor was Rev. Sidney Lee Vail, who traveled by rail from Natchitoches twice monthly for Sunday services. The congregation of the Trinity Southern Methodist Church currently occupies the building. (Courtesy of Monte Banks.)

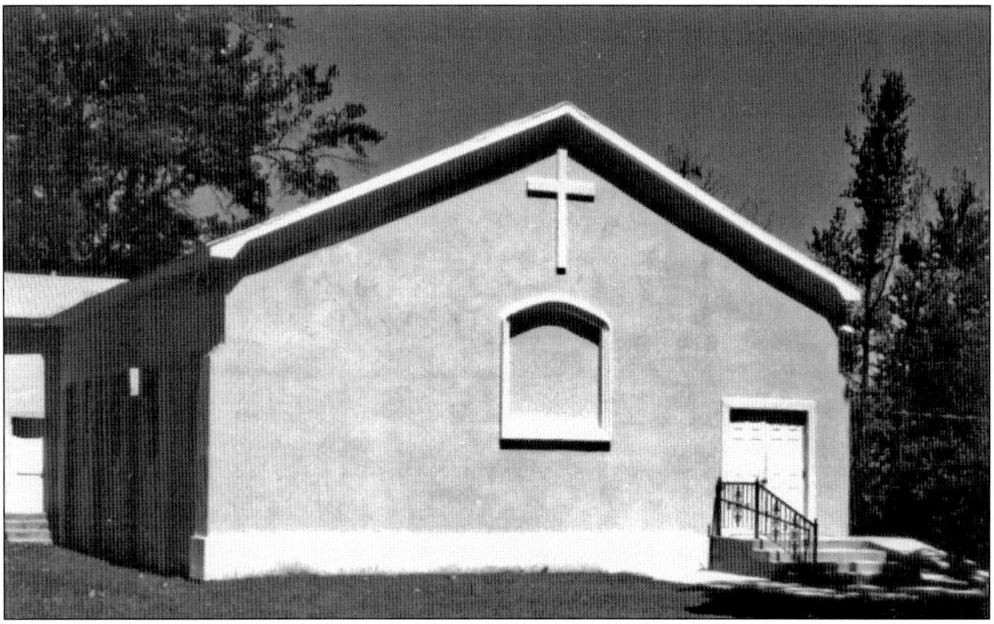

Construction began on the Center Springs CME Church in the summer of 1910. Land for the site was donated by Burrell Wafer. Lumber used in the construction came from trees that were cut and hauled by Louis Bailey to Billy Monk's mill. Many other church members donated goods and services that made completion of the project possible. (Courtesy of the *Guardian-Journal*.)

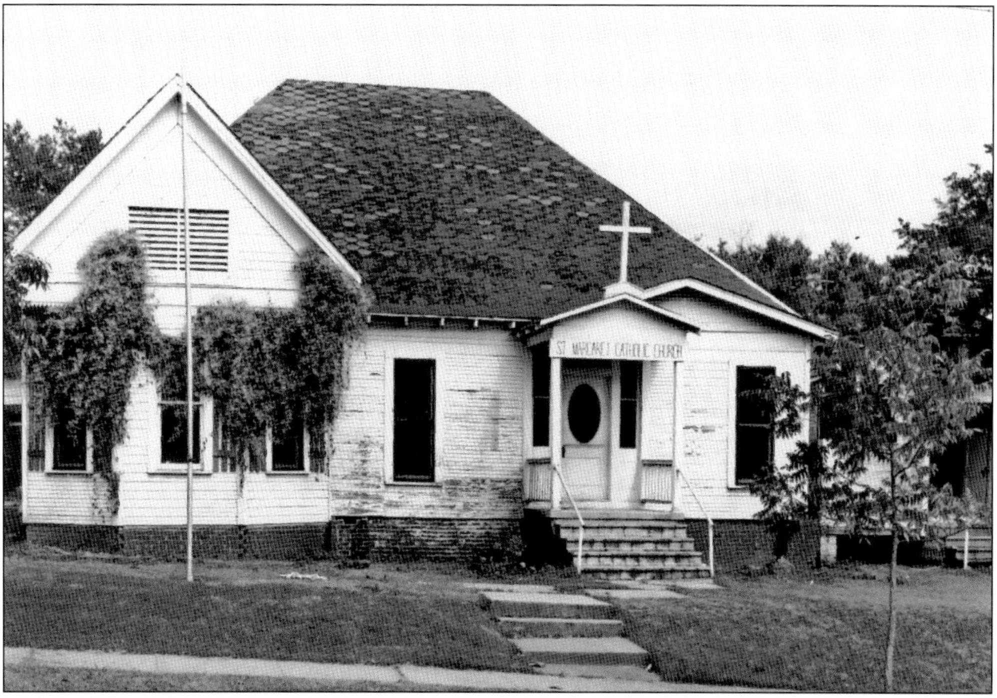

Although the population of Claiborne Parish was overwhelmingly Protestant, a few Catholic families also resided in the parish. Following the end of World War II, St. Margaret Catholic Church in Homer was established as a mission church. The church's first meeting place was a converted house located on the corner of North Main and East Second Streets. (Courtesy of Lucille Michael.)

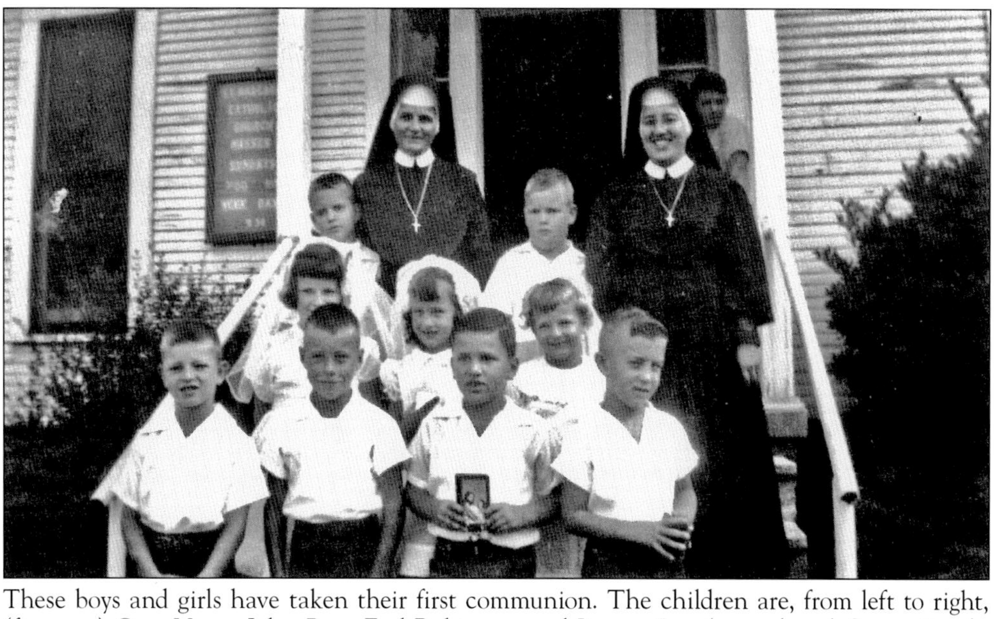

These boys and girls have taken their first communion. The children are, from left to right, (first row) Cam Vozar, John Poss, Earl Robinson, and Jimmy Zey; (second row) Susan Keogh, Joyce Zey, and Donna Vozar; (third row) Joe Hightower and Pat Hightower. (Courtesy of the F. T. Hightower family.)

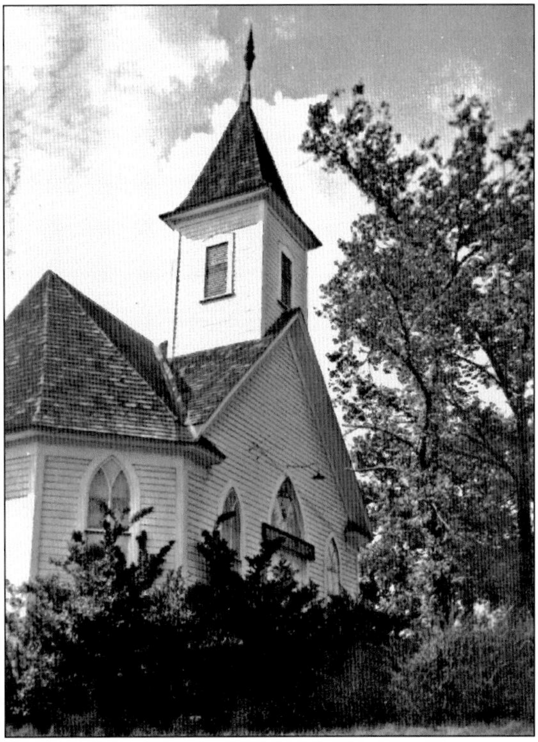

The Athens Presbyterian Church is the successor to an earlier church named Salem Presbyterian Church. Salem Presbyterian Church was situated across the road from the present-day Salem Cemetery in an area considered to be part of the Russellville community. After the new town of Athens developed, the church relocated to Athens. The present building dates from 1905. Salem Cemetery remains in active use today. (Courtesy of the Claiborne Parish Library.)

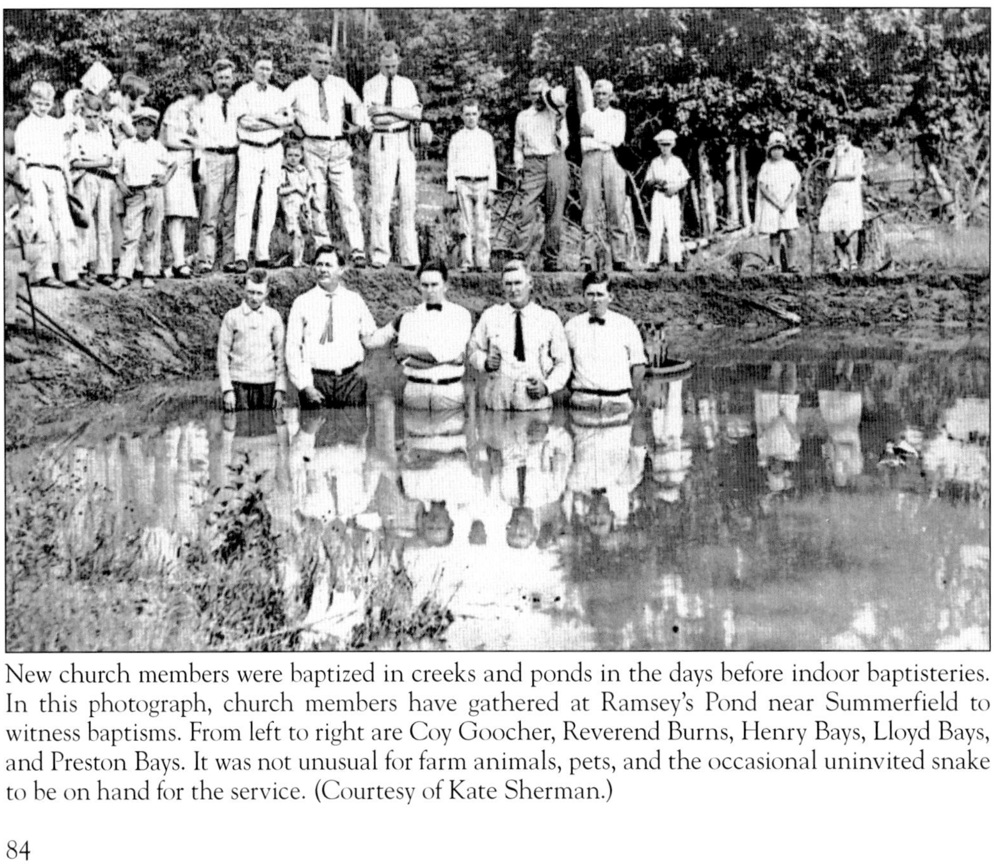

New church members were baptized in creeks and ponds in the days before indoor baptisteries. In this photograph, church members have gathered at Ramsey's Pond near Summerfield to witness baptisms. From left to right are Coy Goocher, Reverend Burns, Henry Bays, Lloyd Bays, and Preston Bays. It was not unusual for farm animals, pets, and the occasional uninvited snake to be on hand for the service. (Courtesy of Kate Sherman.)

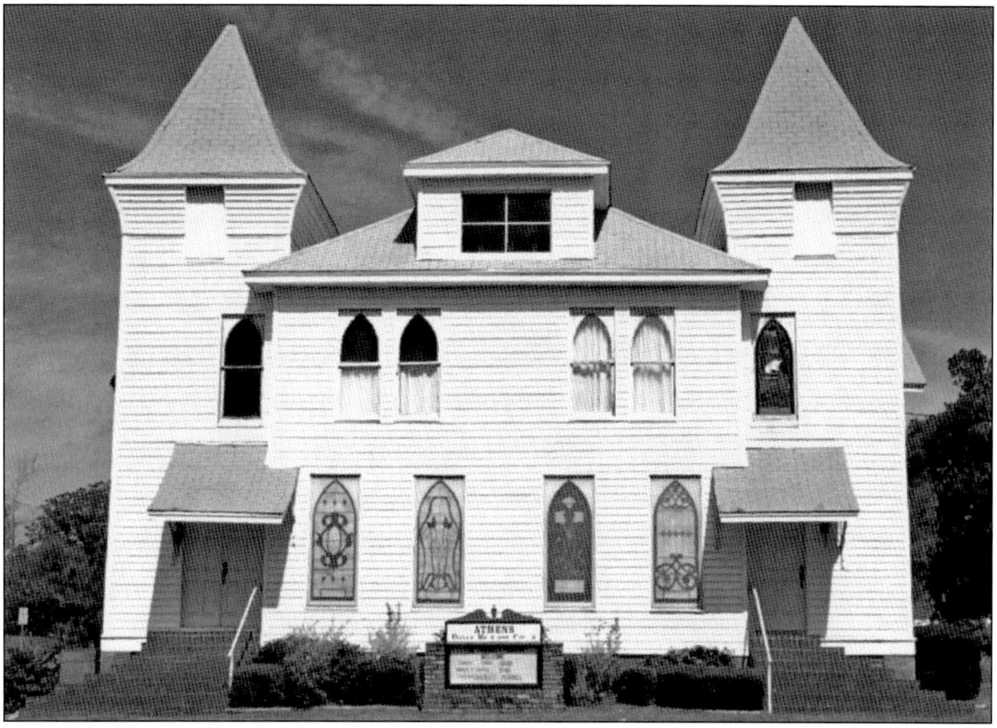

William Ashbrook organized the first Methodist society in Claiborne Parish in the late 1830s. The Methodists at old Athens gradually migrated to new Athens. William Henry Pace donated lumber from his sawmill and a prominent spot in the middle of Athens where the Methodists built their church in 1910. The building continues to serve the Methodist congregation of Athens as its place of worship. (Courtesy of the *Guardian-Journal*.)

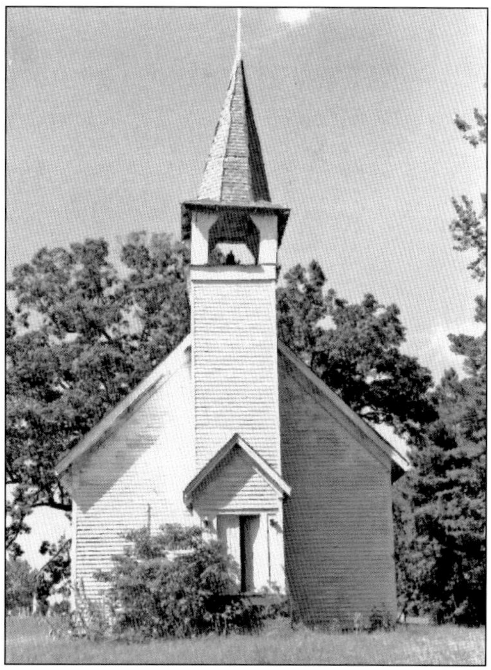

The Alabama Methodist Church stems from the Alabama Camp Grounds in the Weldon community, where annual revivals attracted large crowds of worshippers. Although services are no longer conducted at the Alabama Church, the building and its spire serve as a reminder that religion was a vital element in the lives of Claiborne Parish's early citizens. (Courtesy of Don Ceccarelli.)

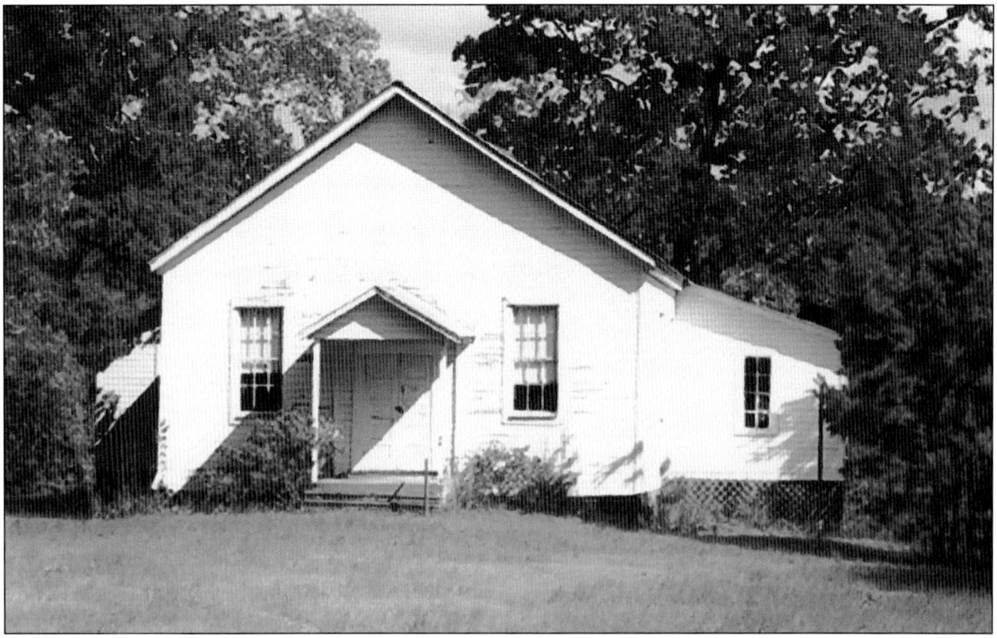

The first Bethlehem Methodist Church was constructed in 1868 on 3 acres of land donated by James Curry. The present building dates from 1877. For many years, the Baptist and Methodist congregations shared the building, using it on alternate Sundays. It was agreed that the first denomination to pay the $50 indebtedness would receive the deed to the church and land. The Methodists won out. The church was closed in 1999 as a result of declining membership. (Courtesy of the *Guardian-Journal*.)

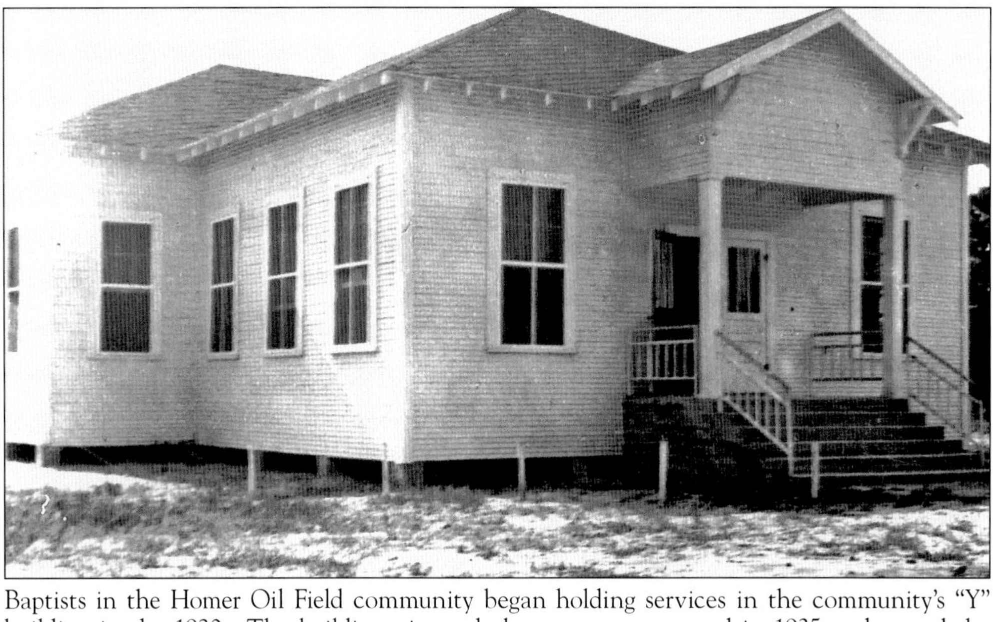

Baptists in the Homer Oil Field community began holding services in the community's "Y" building in the 1920s. The building pictured above was constructed in 1935 and served the Homer Oil Field Baptist Church as its meeting place until 1965, when the congregation built a new brick building on a site closer to town and renamed their church the Calvary Baptist Church. (Courtesy of A. T. Ferguson family.)

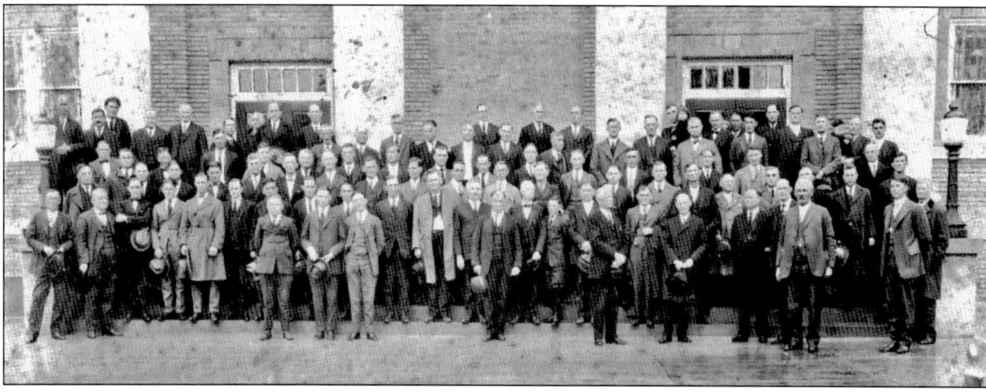

The Men's Bible Class of the Homer Methodist Church was first known as the Mutual Benefit Bible Class, with A. S. Ford as the teacher. While the present church building was under construction, the class met in the courthouse. In this 1924 photograph, members of the Men's Bible Class are shown standing on the steps of the newly completed Homer Methodist Church. (Courtesy of the Ford Museum.)

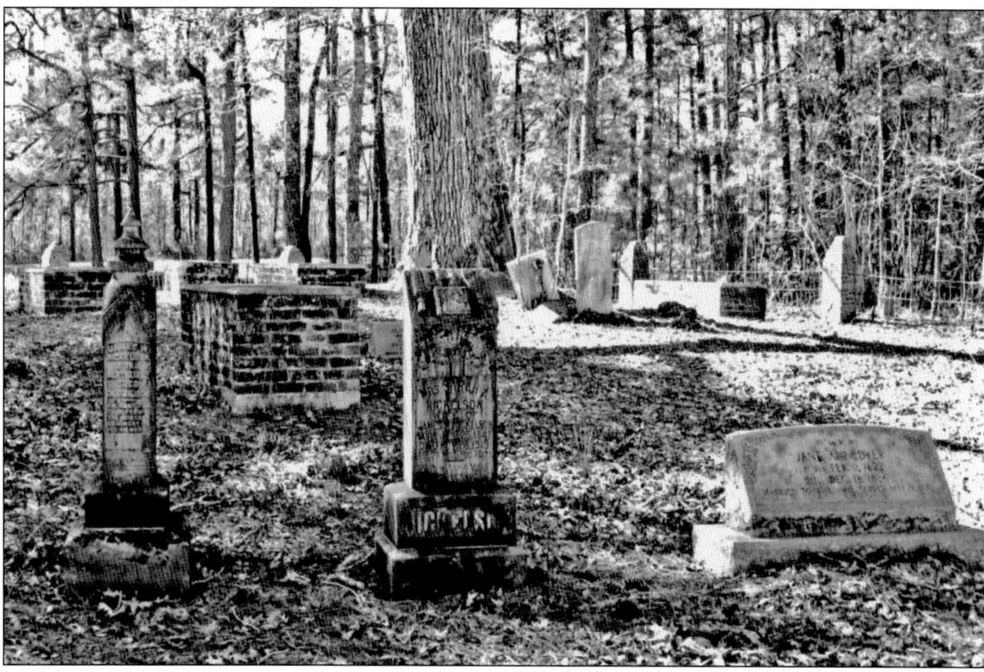

The Sack Pennington Gee family came to Claiborne Parish in 1836. Their reason for leaving Mississippi was to escape a gang of outlaws Gee helped capture. Gee was one of the wealthiest men in north central Louisiana. The Gee Cemetery was located a stone's throw from their mansion. Mary Ann Gee, the last surviving member of the family, died in 1873. Her two nieces and nephew sold the land, and vandals, looking for hidden silver and gold, tore the house down to the ground. (Courtesy of the Claiborne Parish Library.)

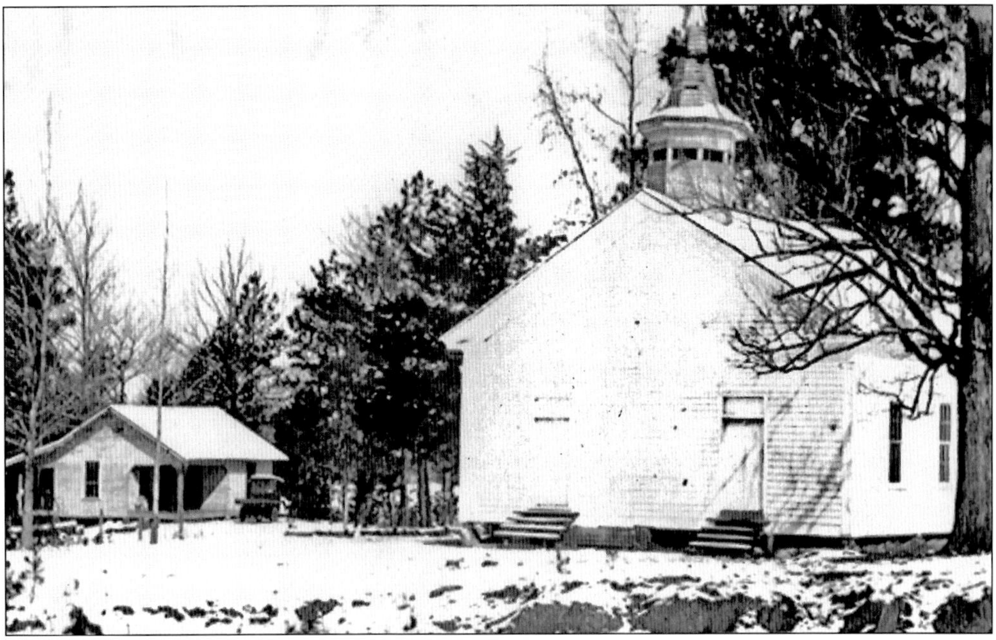

Summerfield Baptist Church was founded in 1881. Before the church building was constructed, the congregation met in the homes of church members. E. M. Corry deeded the land for the church on June 6, 1883. Services were held once a month on Saturday and Sunday. Records show that in 1909 a church member was sharply reprimanded by the church for selling soft drinks on Sunday. (Courtesy of Helen Campbell.)

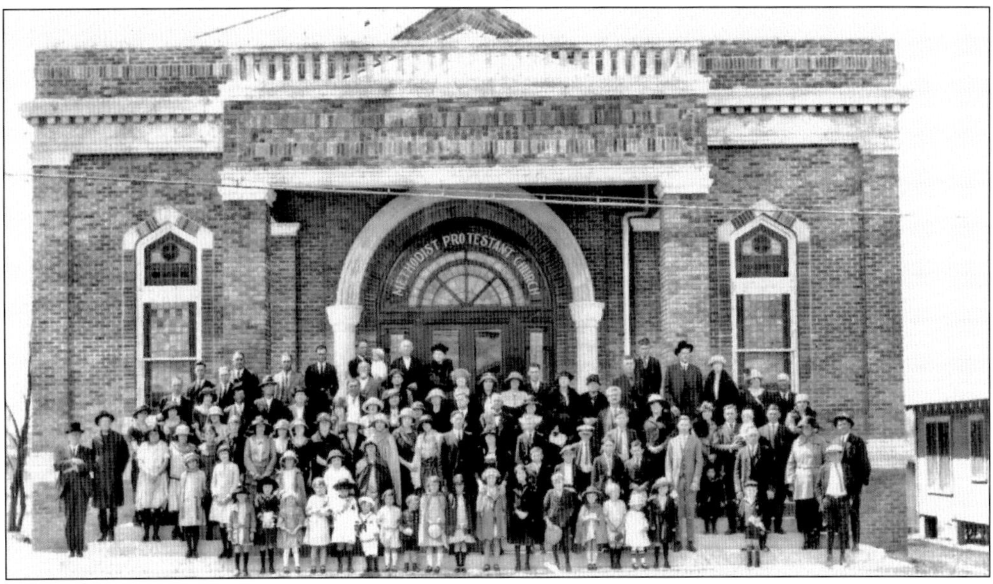

In 1939, the Methodist Episcopal Church, South (First Methodist Church) and the Methodist Protestant Church (Shady Grove Memorial Protestant Church) united as the Hayneville Methodist Church. From 1939 to 1957, the congregation used two church buildings and parsonages. Located only two blocks apart, one building was used for morning services and the other for evening services. In 1957, the former Methodist Protestant Church building and parsonage were sold to the United Pentecostal congregation. (Courtesy of Monte Banks.)

Six

Black Gold

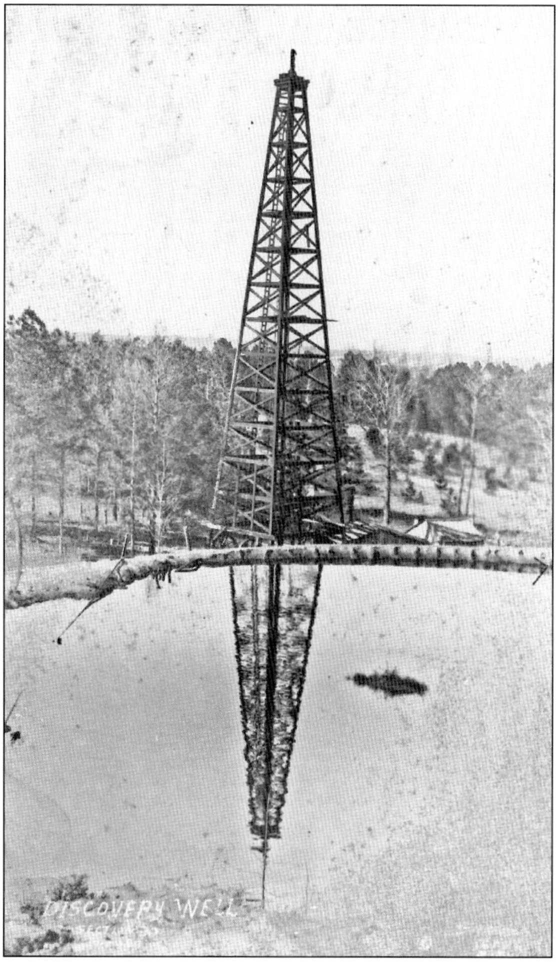

The oil boom of the 1920s brought major changes to Claiborne Parish. The discovery well of the Homer Field, drilled by Consolidated Progressive Oil Company on the Shaw lease, was brought in on January 12, 1919, pumping 2,500 barrels of oil and water from the Nacatoch sand at a depth of 1,409–1,416 feet. In May 1919, the Homer Field produced 10,034 barrels of oil per day and, by December of that year, was producing 879,960 barrels every 24 hours. (Courtesy of the Ford Museum.)

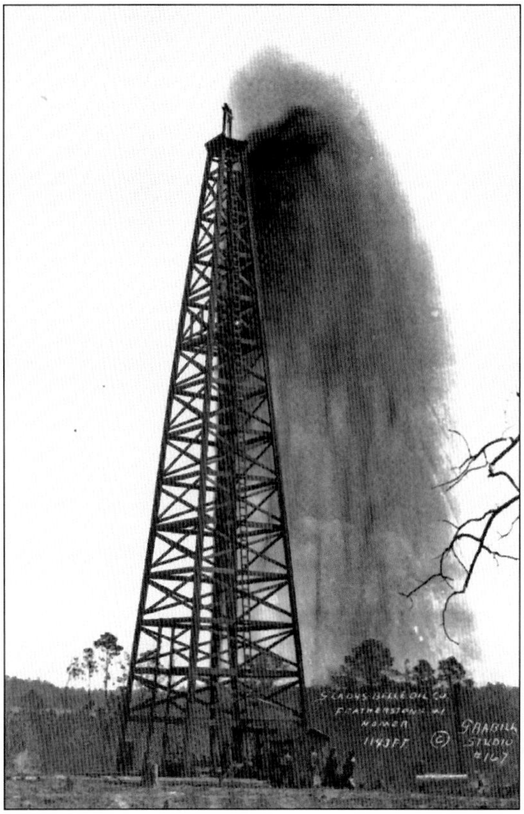

The Gladys-Belle Oil Company's Featherston No. 1 struck paying sand at 1,143 feet. In the early days, it was customary to let wells blow over the top, and a well that did not paint the derrick was considered practically a failure. In 1920, the Homer Field produced 21,508,000 barrels of the state's total annual production of 35,714,000 barrels, boosting Louisiana to third place among the nation's oil-producing states. (Courtesy of LSU Shreveport Archives—Noel Memorial Library.)

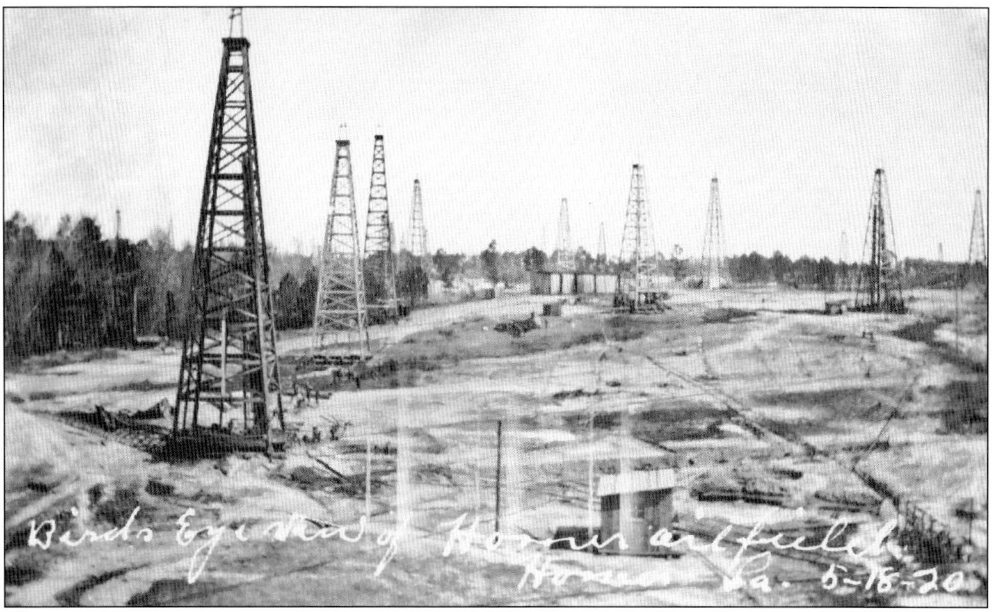

The Homer Field was eventually divided into the north field with 2,280 acres of production and the south field with 1,030 acres of production. By 1929, a total of 632 wells had been drilled. At one point, production from Claiborne Parish fields accounted for 97 percent of the oil produced in Louisiana. (Courtesy of Dr. Levelle Haynes.)

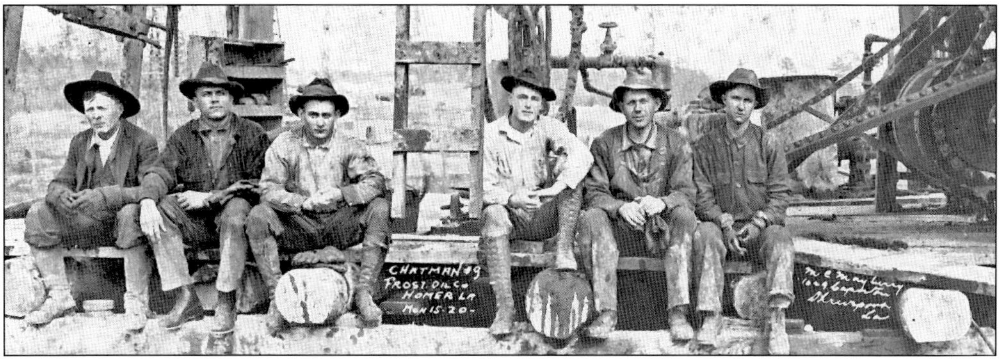

Six roughnecks stopped their work on the Chatman No. 9 to pose for this photograph on March 15, 1920. William Chatman, an African American, reaped great wealth from oil produced on his land in the Homer Field. Well No. 7, drilled on January 11, 1919, was the most prolific well on Chatman's property, producing 20,000 barrels of oil per day. (Courtesy of Bill W. Hightower.)

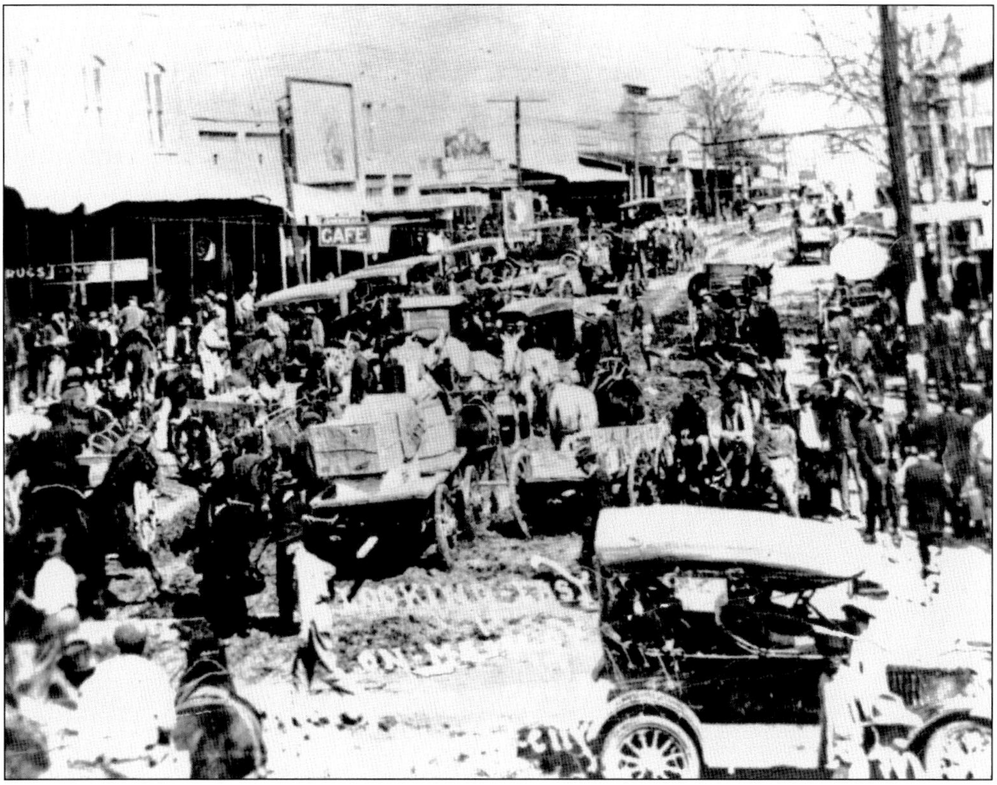

Oil speculators began drilling in the Haynesville area in early 1921. Shreveporters J. E. and C. B. Smitherman brought in the Taylor No. 2, the discovery well of the Haynesville Field, on March 30, 1921. Almost overnight, Haynesville mushroomed from a town of 1,000 inhabitants to a boomtown of 10,000. By November 1921, a week seldom passed without at least a dozen completed wells in the Haynesville Field. (Courtesy of J. R. "Snap" Oakes.)

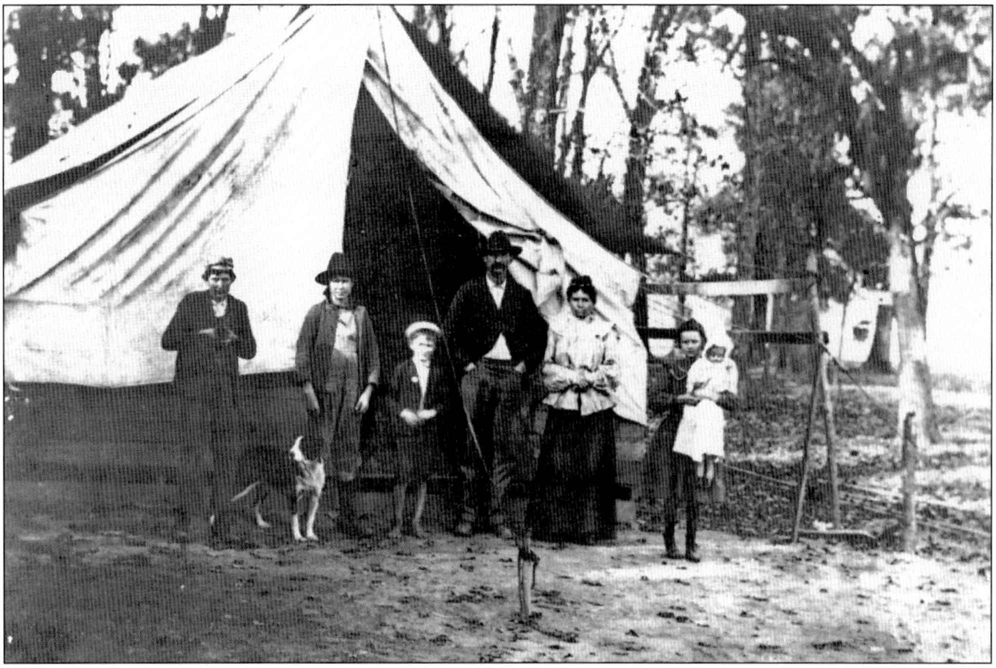

This tent is typical of the early housing arrangements used in the Homer and Haynesville Fields. Shacks, tents, and lean-tos were hastily erected on any vacant lot to provide lodging for the hundreds of people who came to Claiborne Parish to work in the oil fields. The population of Claiborne Parish reached 27,855 in the early 1920s. (Courtesy of the Ford Museum.)

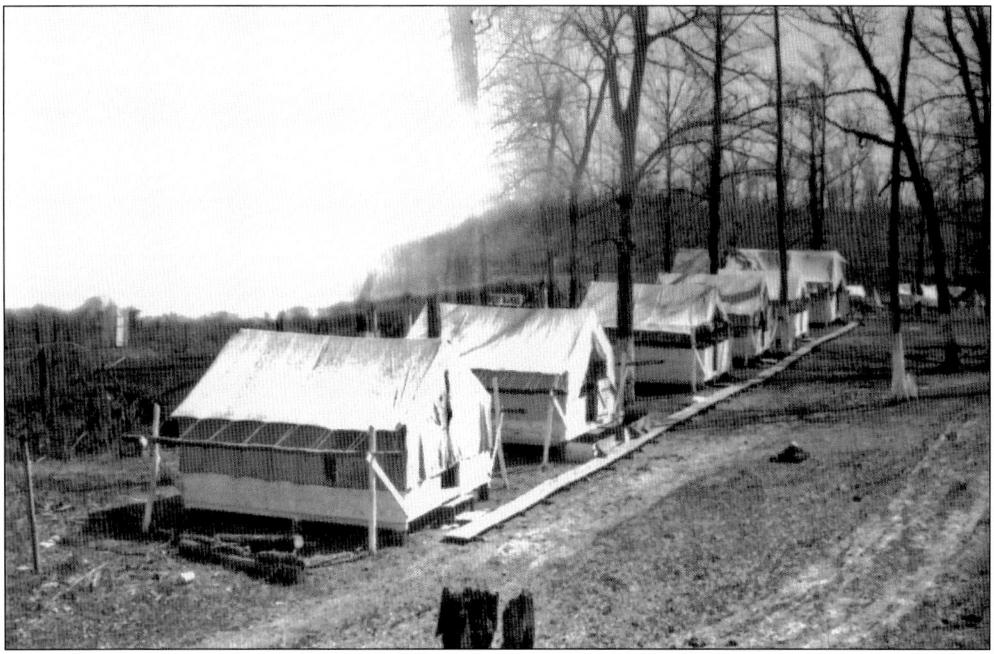

Ropes stretched between brace poles were used to support the roofs of these "elevated" tents. In this photograph, a plank sidewalk linked the tents together. Tent cities gradually disappeared as oil companies built permanent housing for their employees. (Courtesy of the Ford Museum.)

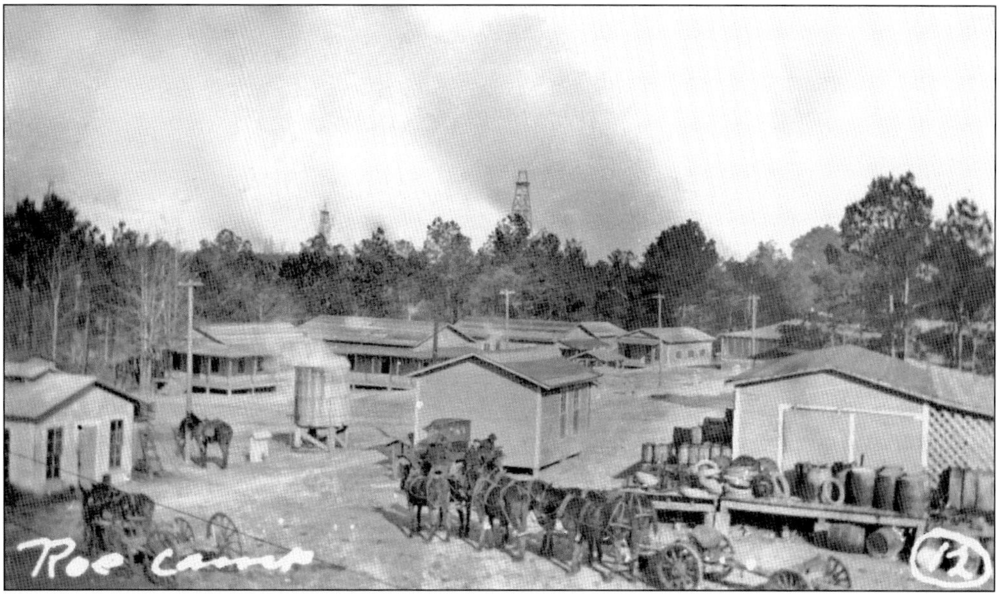

The Rowe camp near Homer was typical of the oil field camps that sprang up in Claiborne Parish. Many workers lived in the camps, since poor roads and inclement weather often hampered transportation to and from worksites. Men worked 12-hour days for $3.75 per day. (Courtesy of Dr. Levelle Haynes.)

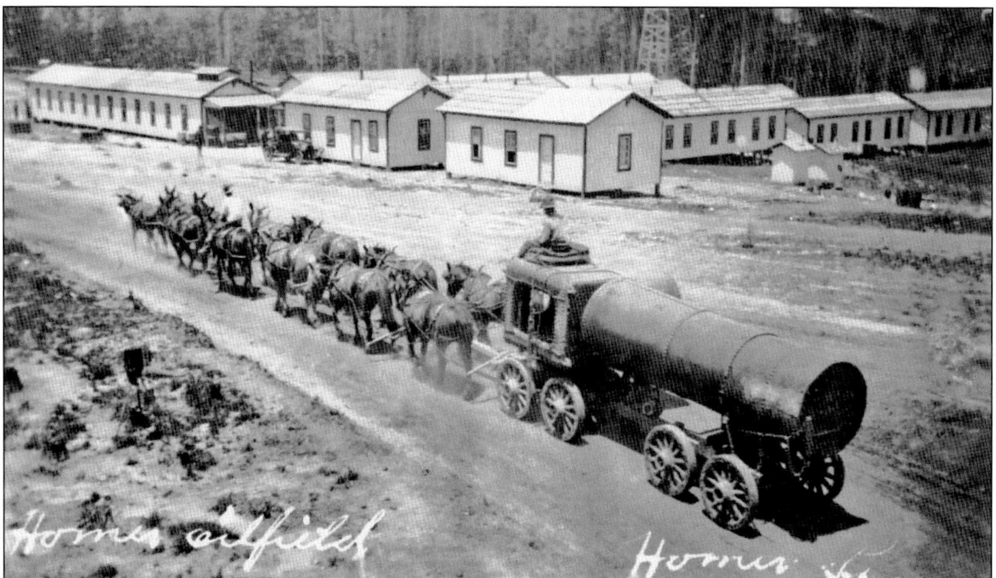

Mule-drawn wagons operated by teamsters were used to transport heavy equipment from the rail depots to the oil fields. Teams of as many as 20 mules might be hitched to a single wagon. This 12-mule team has hauled a load to a camp in the Homer Field. (Courtesy of Dr. Levelle Haynes.)

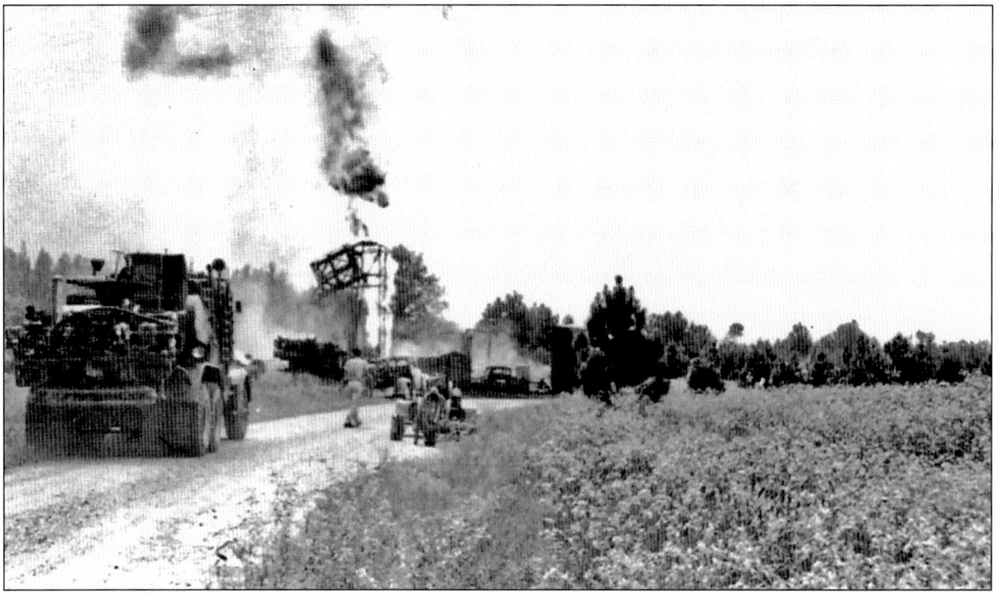

Fires on oil rigs were a frequent occurrence in the early days of the oil fields. Primitive technology and inexperience on the part of workers often combined to create accidents and explosions. When lightning strikes set storage tanks on fire, the tanks were usually left to burn themselves out. (Courtesy of Monte Banks.)

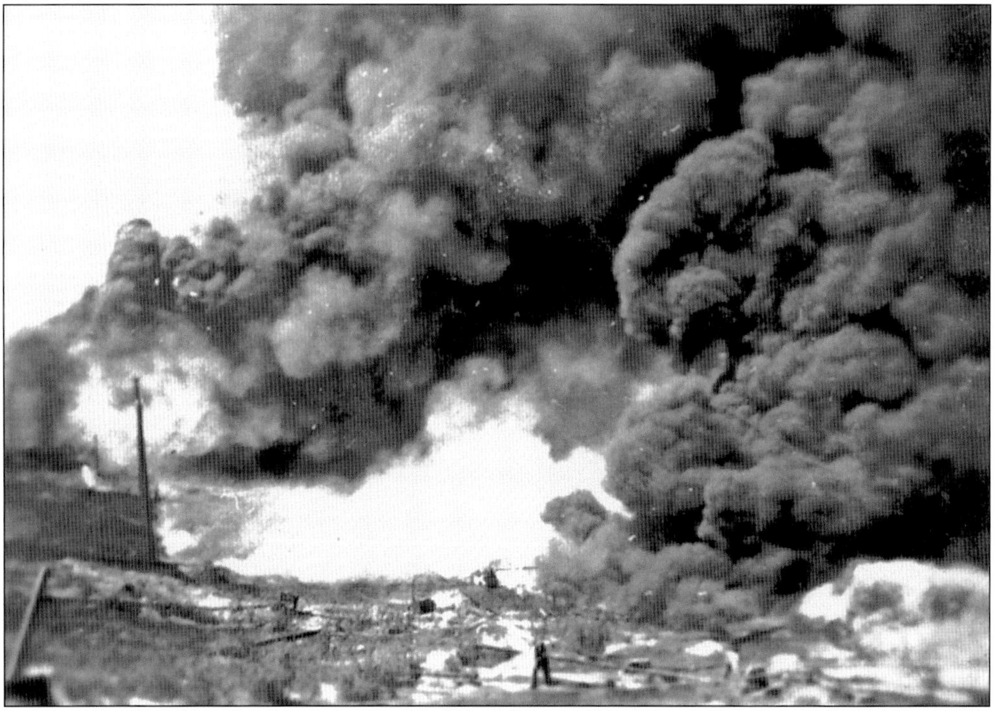

This blazing inferno created a black cloud of smoke that could be seen for miles. Special firefighting crews using high-pressure steam hoses might be called to extinguish the worst fires. An unsuccessful attempt to combat a blaze was once made in Caddo Parish by firing a cannon at a stuck well valve. (Courtesy of the Ford Museum.)

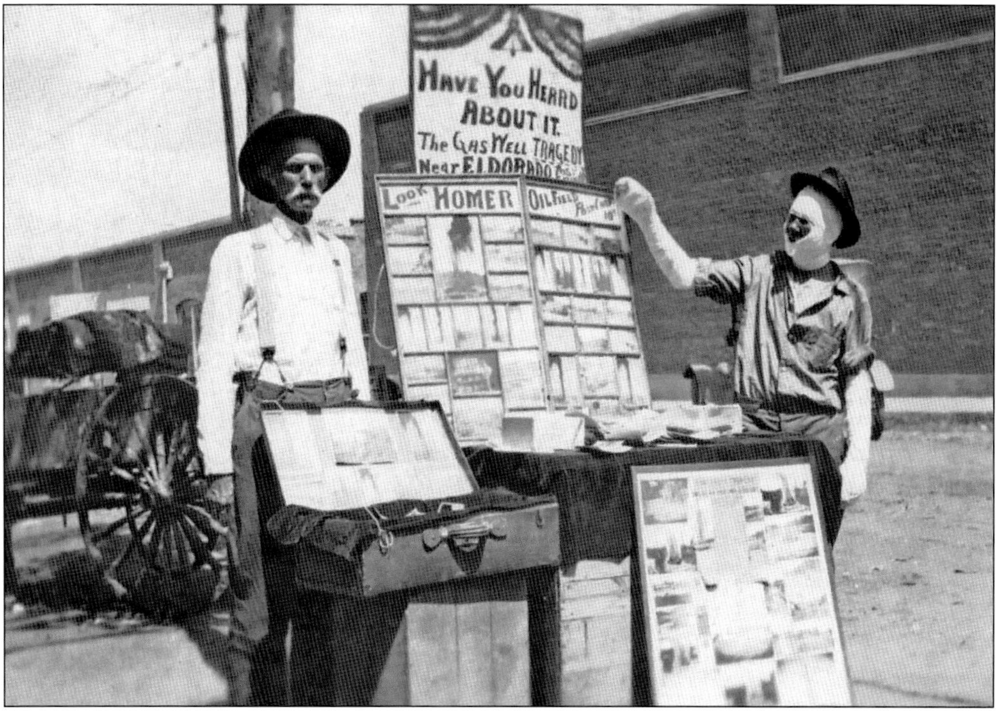

Oil field accidents occurred frequently, often producing tragic consequences. Oil companies sponsored safety and first aid training for their employees. This training was necessary, since it was often difficult to get a doctor in the event of an emergency. These men used an accident in the El Dorado Field to emphasize the need for safety. (Courtesy of Dr. Levelle Haynes.)

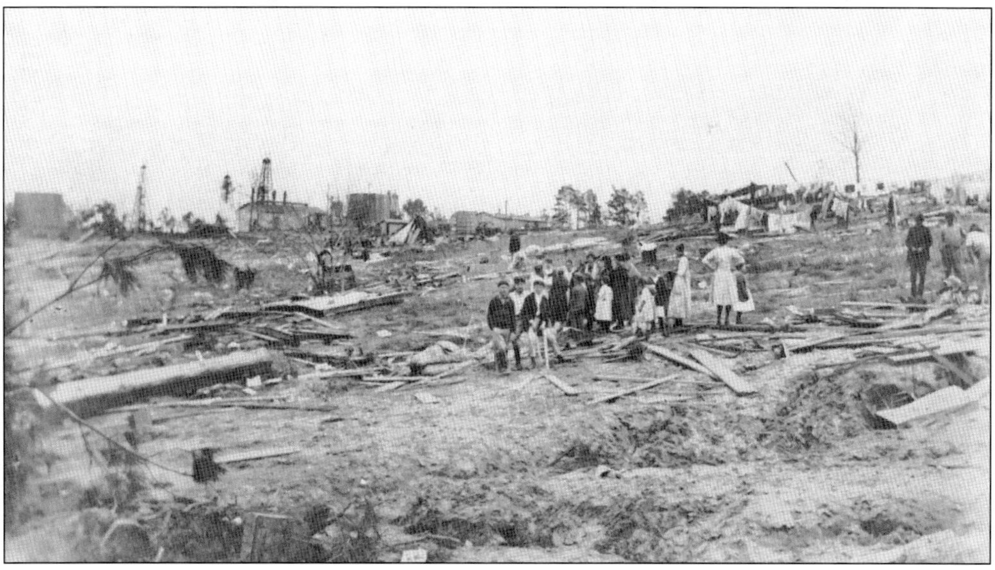

On the afternoon of November 25, 1926, Haynesville hosted Homer for the fourth annual Thanksgiving Day football game. That night, a cyclone struck the Ware's Chapel community and the Baucum Spur and Roxana oil camps. Seven people were killed, and 12 others were seriously injured. At Baucum Spur, a freight car loaded with 80,000 pounds of gas engines was overturned. Property damages neared $1 million. (Courtesy of the Ford Museum.)

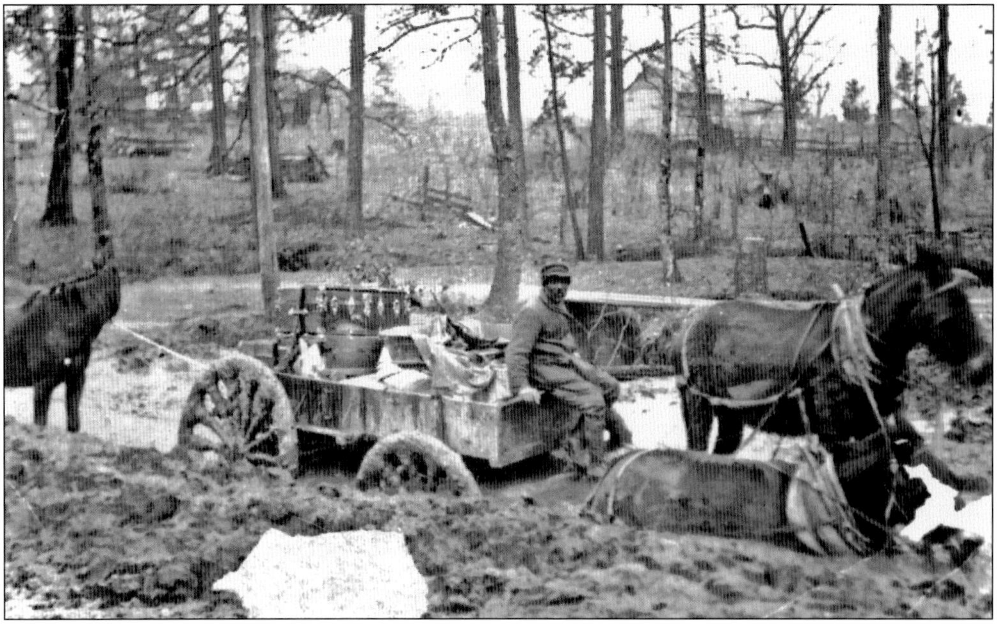

The year 1919 was known as the "Year of Rain, Mud and Mules." Some roughnecks vowed that it rained 40 days and 40 nights, rendering many parish roads impassable as a result of deep, thick mud. Here mules are attempting to pull a wagon through a muddy bog. The mule in the foreground is mired to his belly in mud. There were reports of mules buried under the streets of Homer and Haynesville because they could not be rescued. (Courtesy of J. R. "Snap" Oakes.)

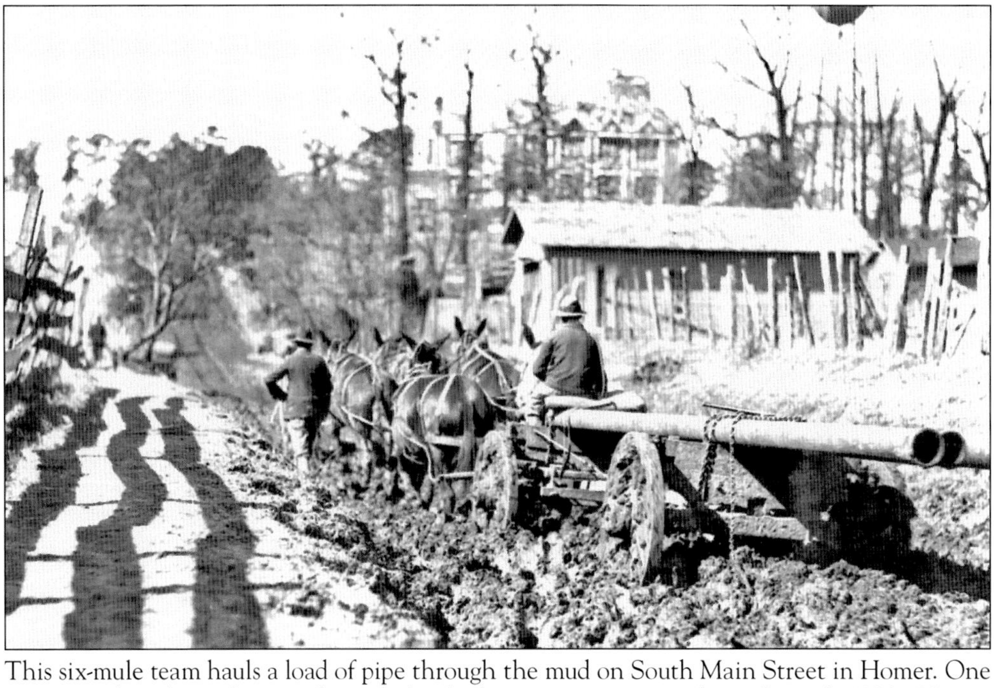

This six-mule team hauls a load of pipe through the mud on South Main Street in Homer. One man is guiding the mule team through the thick mire, a common sight in the early 1920s. Homer High School and Homer's first water tower appear in the top right of the photograph. (Courtesy of the J. J. Smith family.)

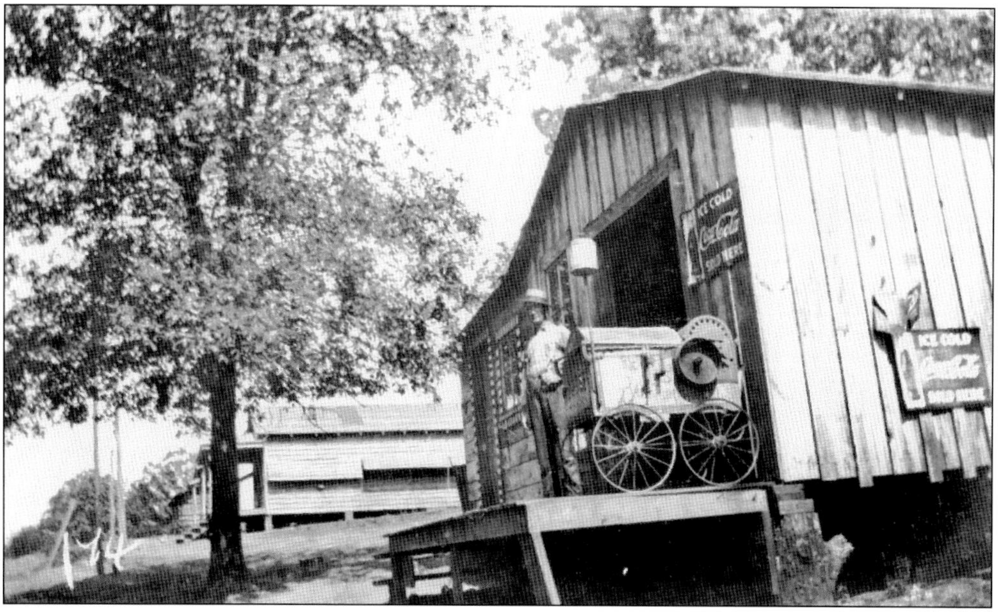

Many settlements in the oil fields became self-sufficient as oil company employees built their own stores, churches, and schools. Because transportation to the nearest town was often difficult, small stores such as the one above supplied the everyday needs of the men and women who lived and worked nearby. (Courtesy of Dr. Levelle Haynes.)

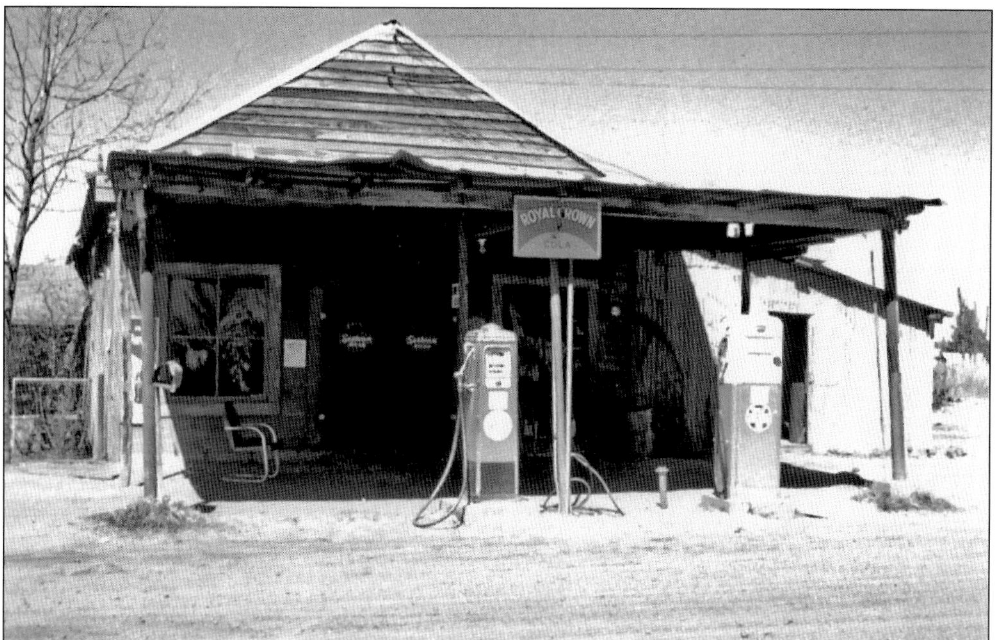

Built by W. J. Brown during the 1920s, this general store in the Homer Field was owned and operated successively by Jack Kimbell, Marvin Hanson, Charlie Pirtle, and J. T. Day. It offered gasoline and basic household supplies to neighborhood residents until it burned in 1964. (Courtesy of Ronald Day.)

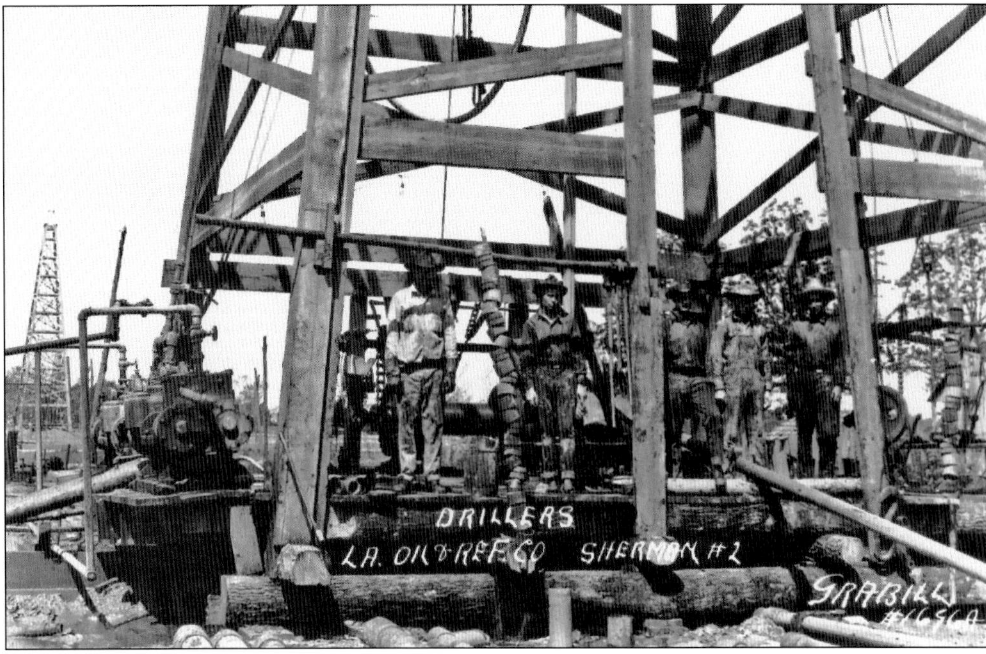

These drillers of the Louisiana Oil Refining Company posed for a photograph on the floor of the wooden derrick of the Sherman No. 2 in Haynesville. Rough-hewn logs support the drilling platform. Steel derricks were not commonly used until the 1930s. The LORECO Oil Company was eventually merged with Cities Service Oil Company. (Courtesy of Tom Crocker.)

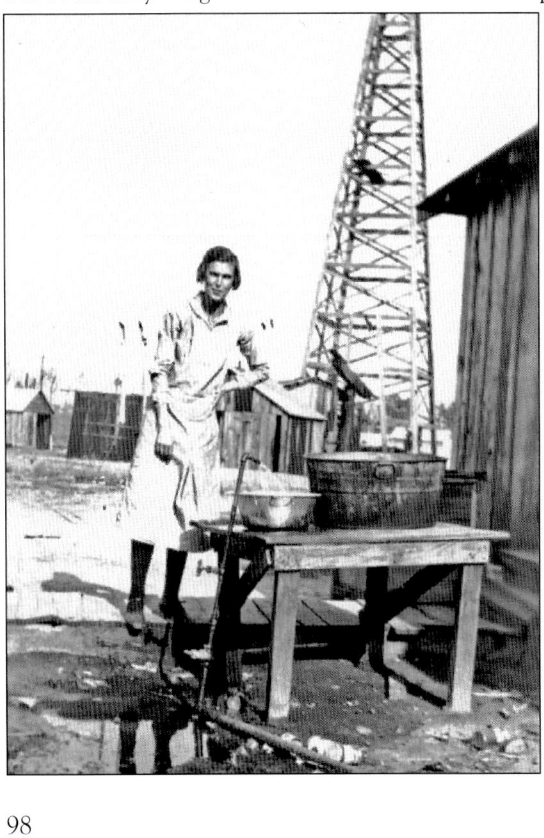

Company housing was offered free to employees of the oil companies. Living conditions were often difficult for the women of oil field families, whose days were spent keeping the family fed, the home clean, and the clothes washed and ironed. (Courtesy of the Barrow Estate.)

The oil boom introduced many new occupations to Claiborne Parish, ranging from unskilled roughnecks and roustabouts to skilled geologists and engineers. The men of the oil field developed their own vocabulary. Because most of the workers came from a farming background, a new hand in the field was called a "boll weevil." A "dog house" was a small shed where tools were kept and the men changed their dirty clothes. A "thribble" was a stand of three joints of pipe. (Courtesy of the Barrow Estate.)

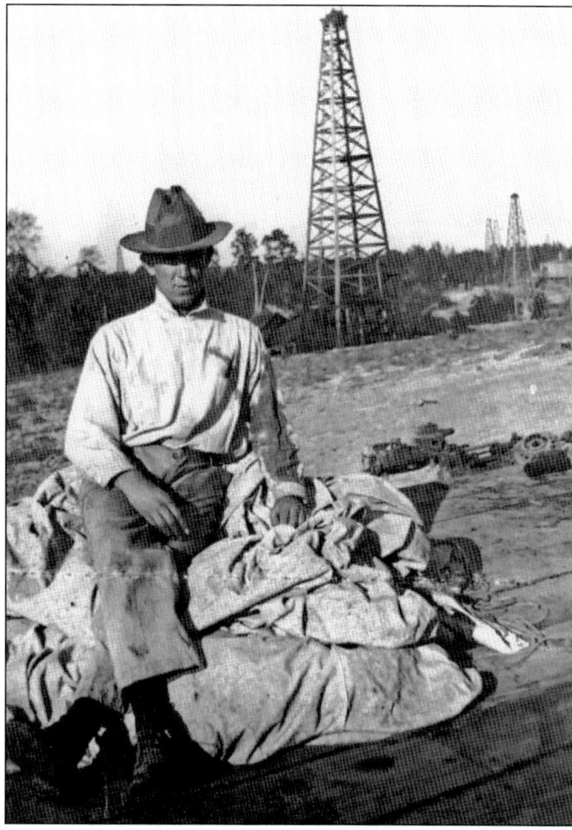

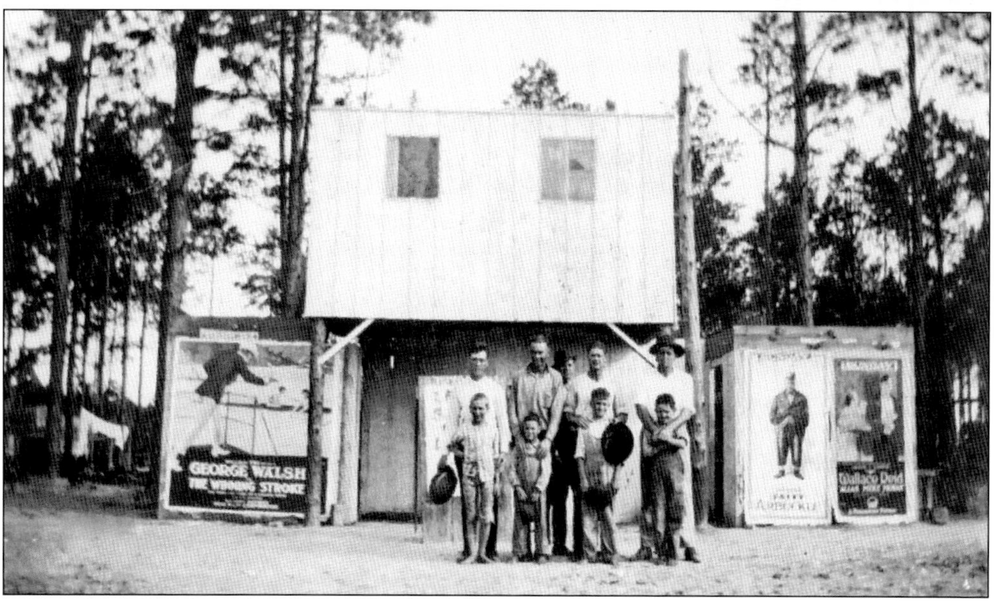

This group of men and young boys is waiting to see the latest motion picture at a cinema in the oil field. Posters advertising George Walsh starring in *The Winning Stroke*, Fatty Arbuckle, and Wallace Reid starring in *Alias Mike Moran* appear on the billboards. (Courtesy of Dr. Levelle Haynes.)

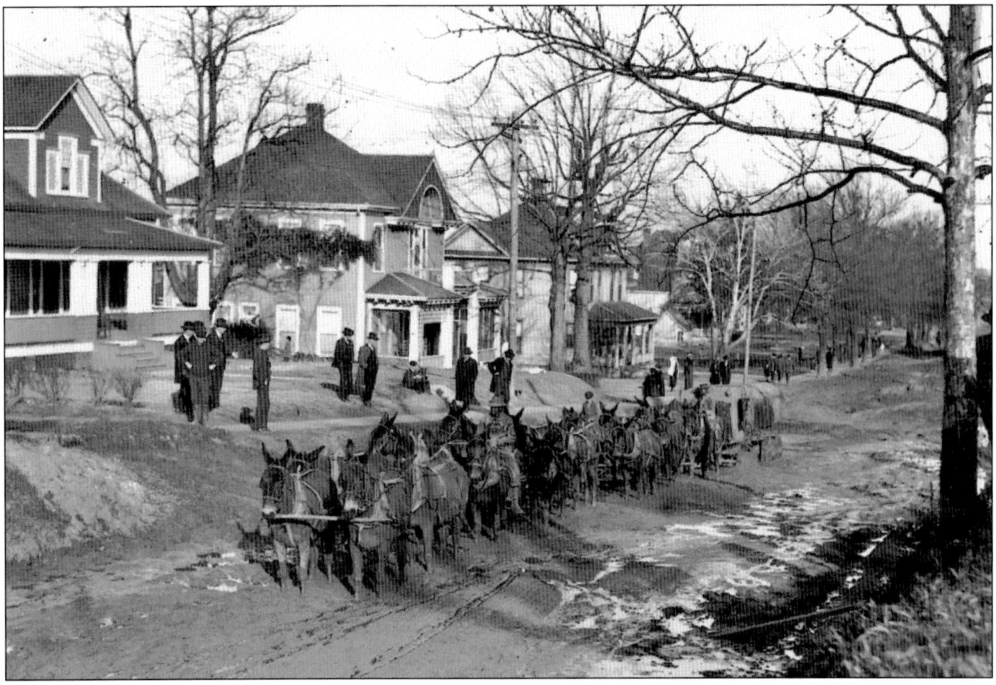

Long mule trains transporting equipment through the streets of Homer and Haynesville were a common sight during the days of the oil boom. This 12-mule team is pulling a large tank up North Main Street in Homer. (Courtesy of the J. J. Smith family.)

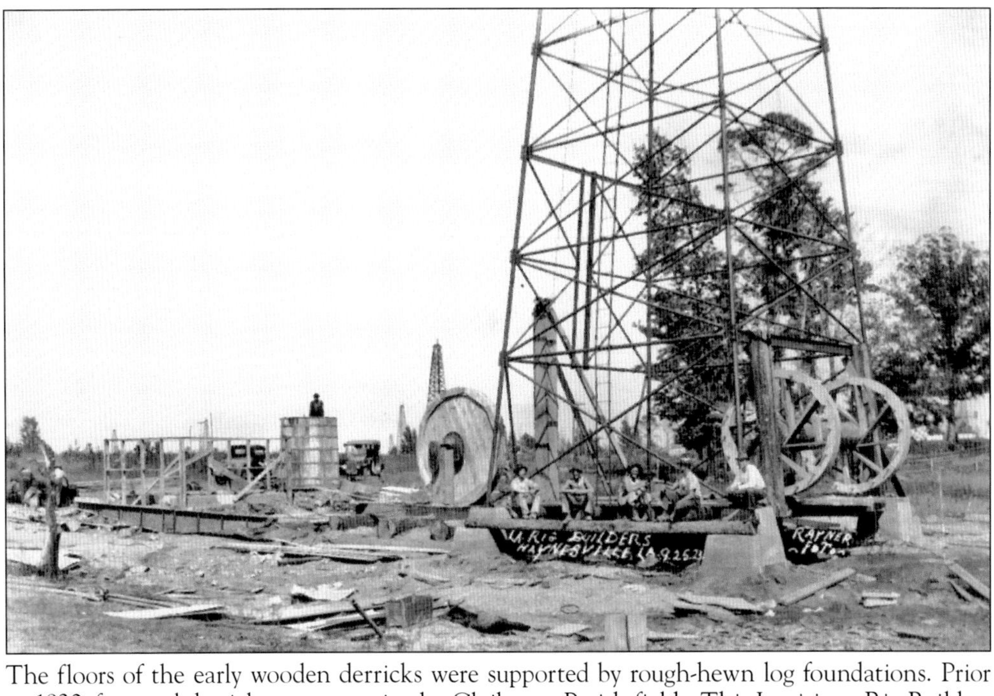

The floors of the early wooden derricks were supported by rough-hewn log foundations. Prior to 1930, few steel derricks were seen in the Claiborne Parish fields. This Louisiana Rig Builders crew is erecting one of the earliest steel derricks in the Haynesville Field. Large concrete piers were poured to support the derrick floor. (Courtesy of Bill W. Hightower.)

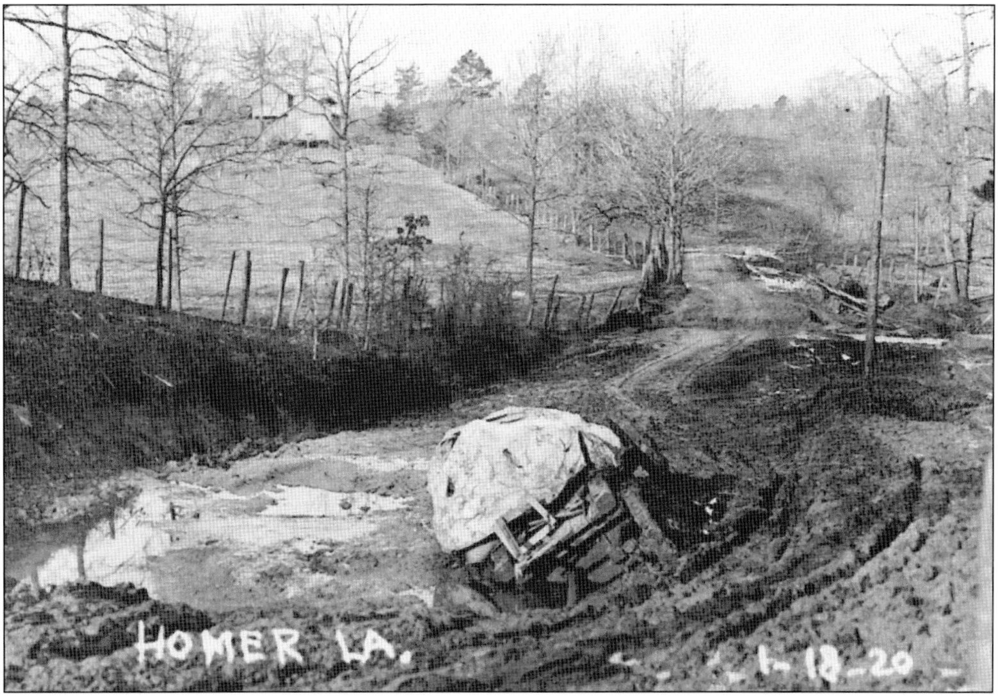

While the oil fields in Homer and Haynesville were booming, massive amounts of supplies and equipment were hauled to the fields, overburdening the area's unpaved roads. The driver of this wagon was forced to wait for additional mule power to free his supply wagon from the mud. (Courtesy of the W. M. Merritt family.)

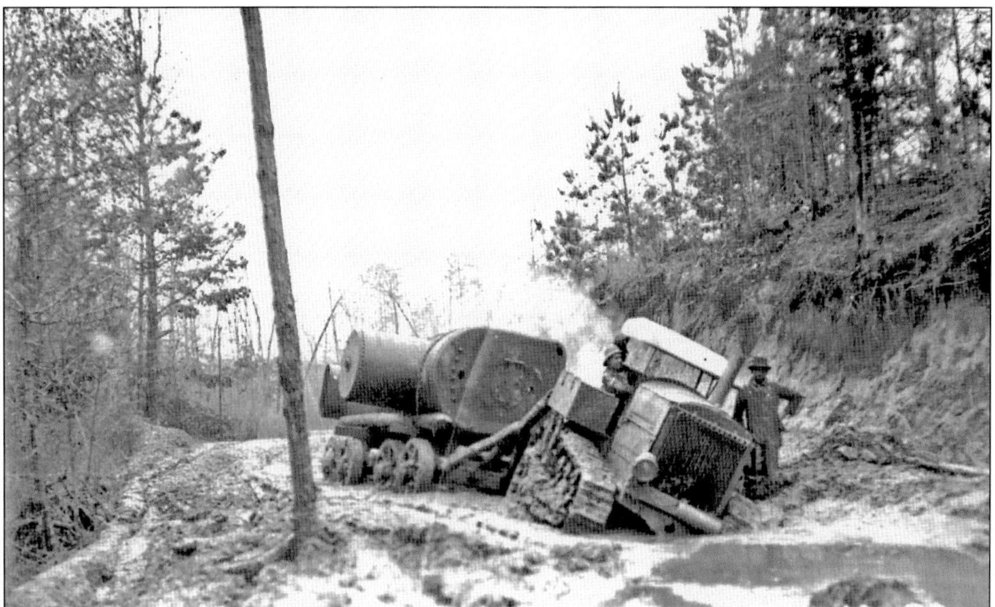

This engine-driven tractor did not fare any better on the muddy roads than the mule-drawn wagons. Heavy traffic damaged dirt roads throughout the parish, and rainy weather often turned the roads into quagmires. (Courtesy of Dr. Levelle Haynes.)

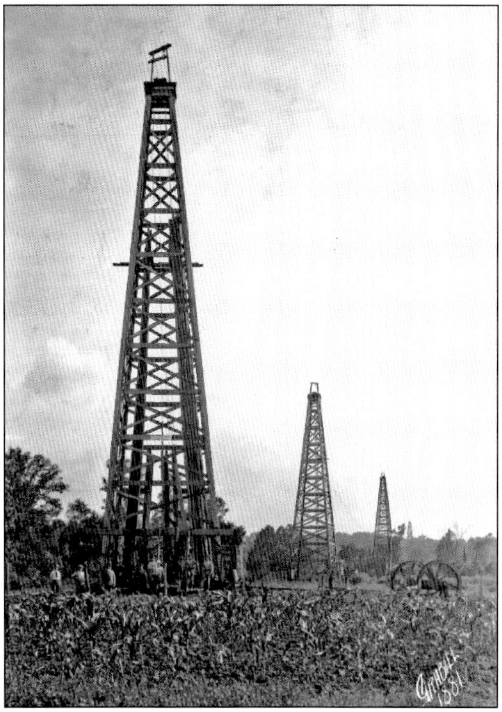

Much of the land leased by speculators and oil companies was farmland. It was not unusual to see derricks coexisting with cornfields and cotton fields. The price of a barrel of oil peaked at $3.19 in 1920 and gradually declined. During the years of the Depression, the price remained under $1 per barrel. (Courtesy of the Ford Museum.)

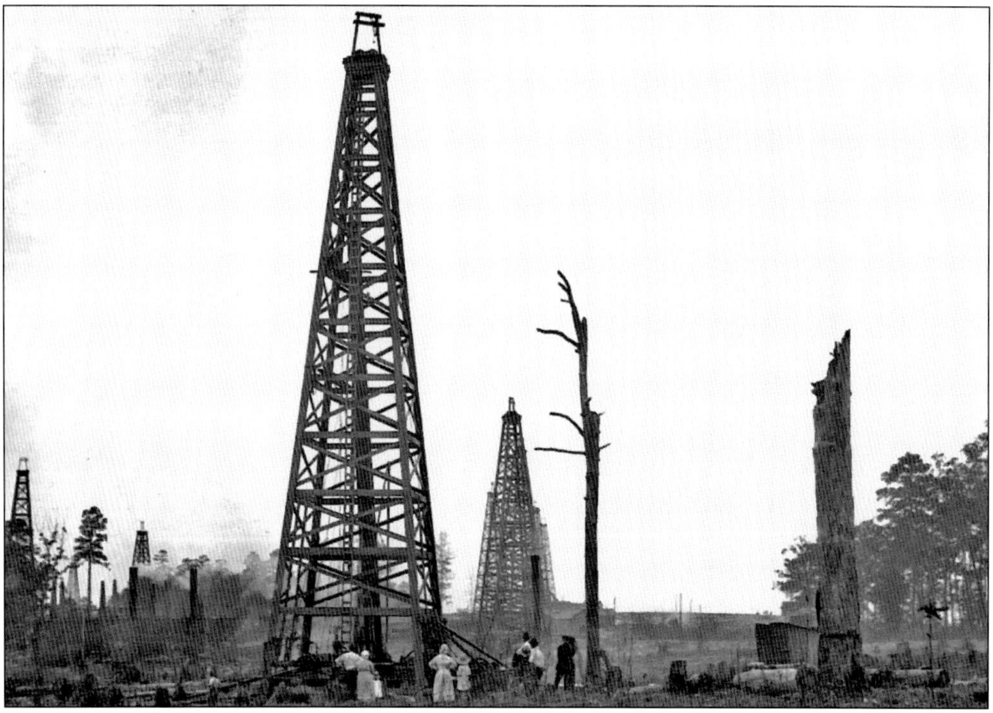

During the early days of the oil boom, little attention was given to environmental hazards. Oil and saltwater were allowed to flow freely, polluting ponds and streams and killing vegetation and wildlife. The Louisiana Legislature adopted its first conservation statutes in 1924. (Courtesy of the J. J. Smith family.)

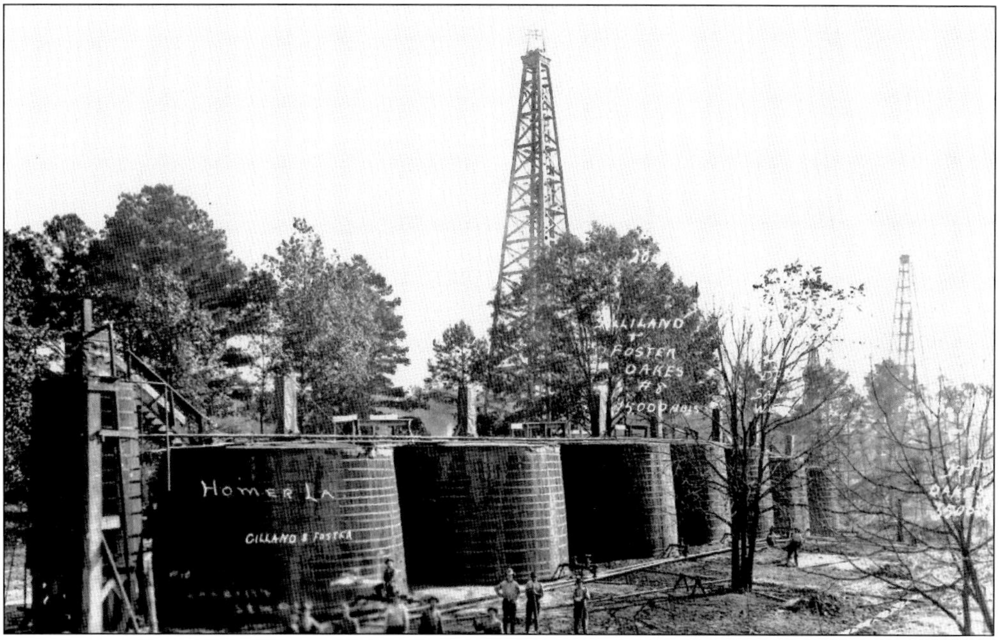

The Gilliland and Foster Oil Company owned these early storage tanks. Their No. 8 well produced 15,000 barrels of oil per day. Until adequate storage tanks and pipelines became available, oil was often stored in open-air pits made by damming natural ravines. (Courtesy of the Ford Museum.)

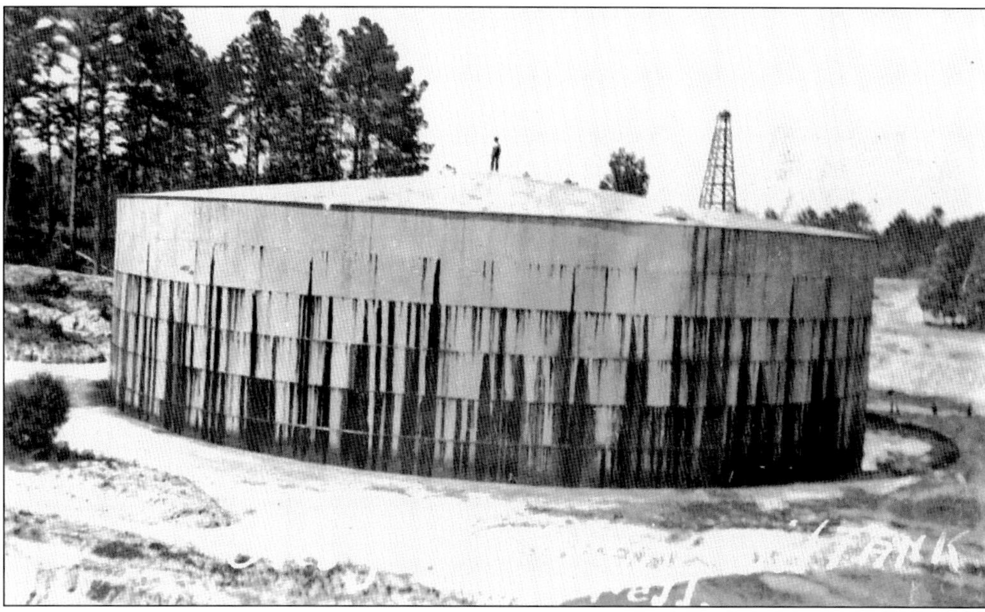

The man standing on top of this 55,000-barrel oil storage tank is dwarfed by the tank's size. At 42 gallons per barrel, this tank could hold 2,310,000 gallons of crude oil. Ten 55,000-barrel tanks were erected at the Weller Tank Farm in the Homer Field, and 52 storage tanks of this size were built in the Haynesville Field. It was reported in the mid-1920s that an employee measuring the oil level in a storage tank slipped, fell into it, and died before he could be rescued. (Courtesy of Dr. Levelle Haynes.)

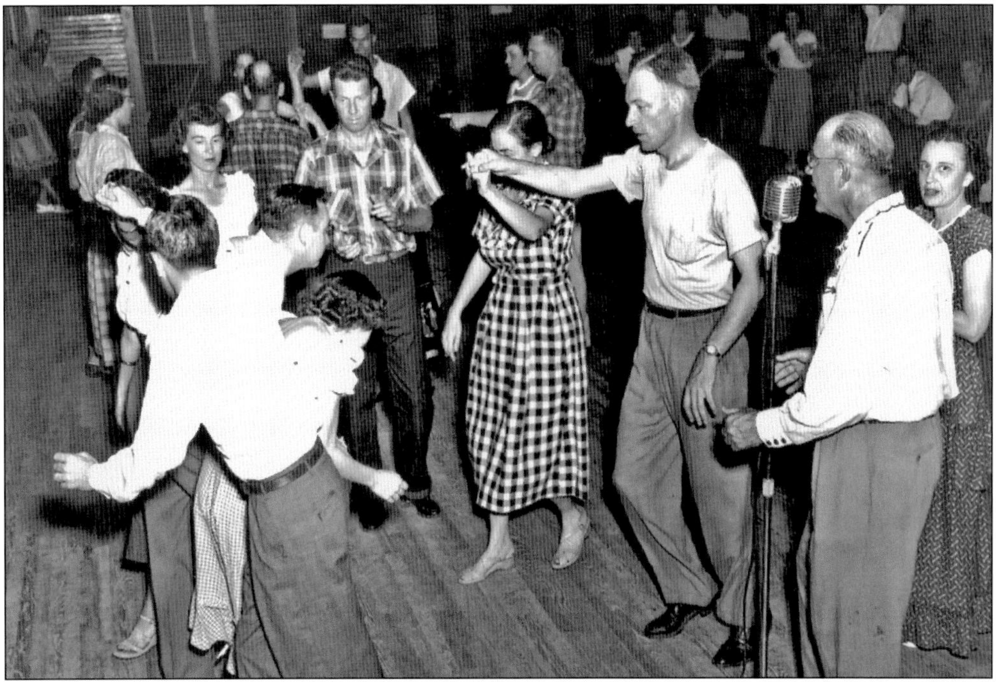

When the boom days ended, many workers and their families stayed in Claiborne Parish, raising their children and becoming invested in the community. The oilfield families were a close-knit group. Here couples enjoy a square dance. J. C. "Pop" Billingsley, who worked in the Homer Field, calls the dance at the microphone, with his wife, Sallie, beside him. (Courtesy of Maxie Garrett.)

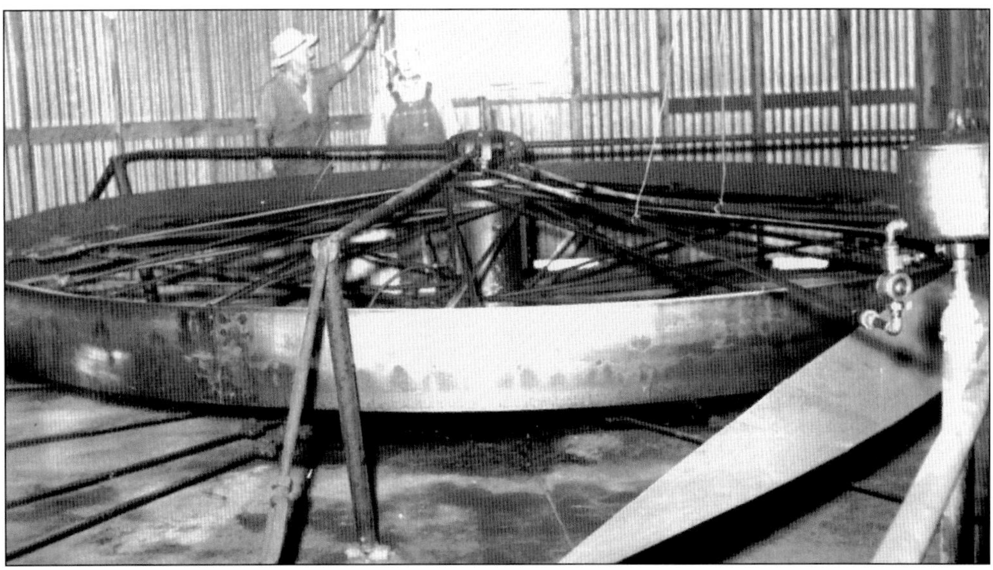

This giant wheel, known as a "widow-maker," operated rods that pumped oil out of wells. If a rod broke or became unattached, repairs had to be made to the wheel without shutting it down, hence its ominous nickname. The advent of electric motors eliminated the need for these large wheels. Pictured above are Ben Boyd and Harry Kimbell, employees of the Sinclair Oil Company. (Courtesy of Mac Brakefield.)

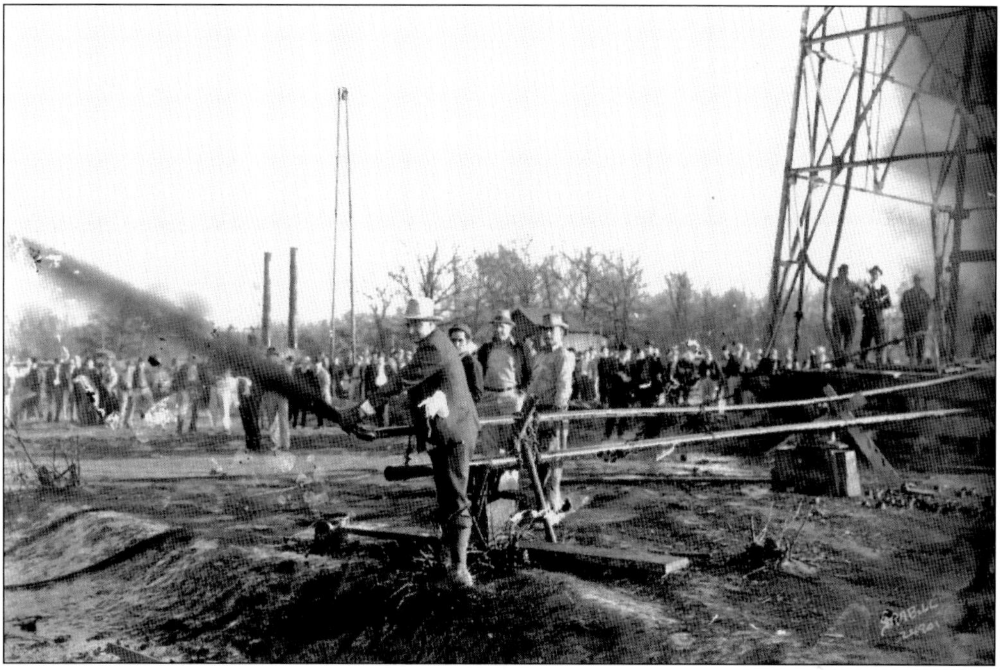

The discovery well of the Lisbon Field, the Maggie Patton No. 1, was brought in on December 18, 1936, by E. T. Oakes and John D. Caruthers Sr. In this photograph, Oakes directs oil into an earthen storage pit while an interested crowd of spectators looks on. (Courtesy of J. D. Caruthers Jr.)

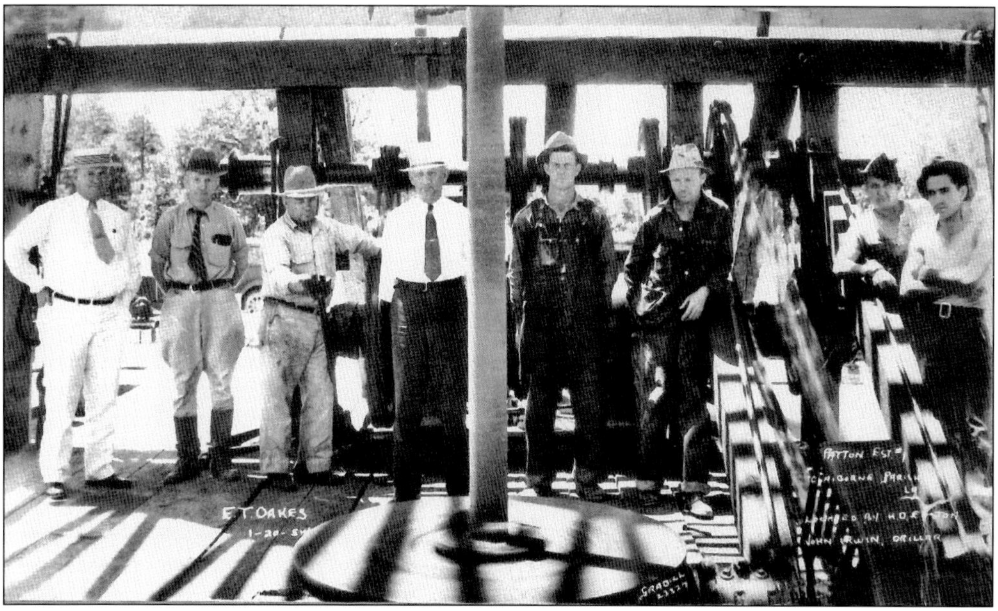

Posing on the derrick floor of the Maggie Patton No. 1 are, from left to right, operator E. T. Oakes, geologist H. D. Easton, driller John Irwin, Minor Patton, and four unidentified roughnecks. By 1948, much of the production from the Lisbon Field was being pipelined to the Claiborne Gasoline Plant to be processed into gasoline, naphtha, distillate, and butane products. (Courtesy of J. D. Caruthers Jr.)

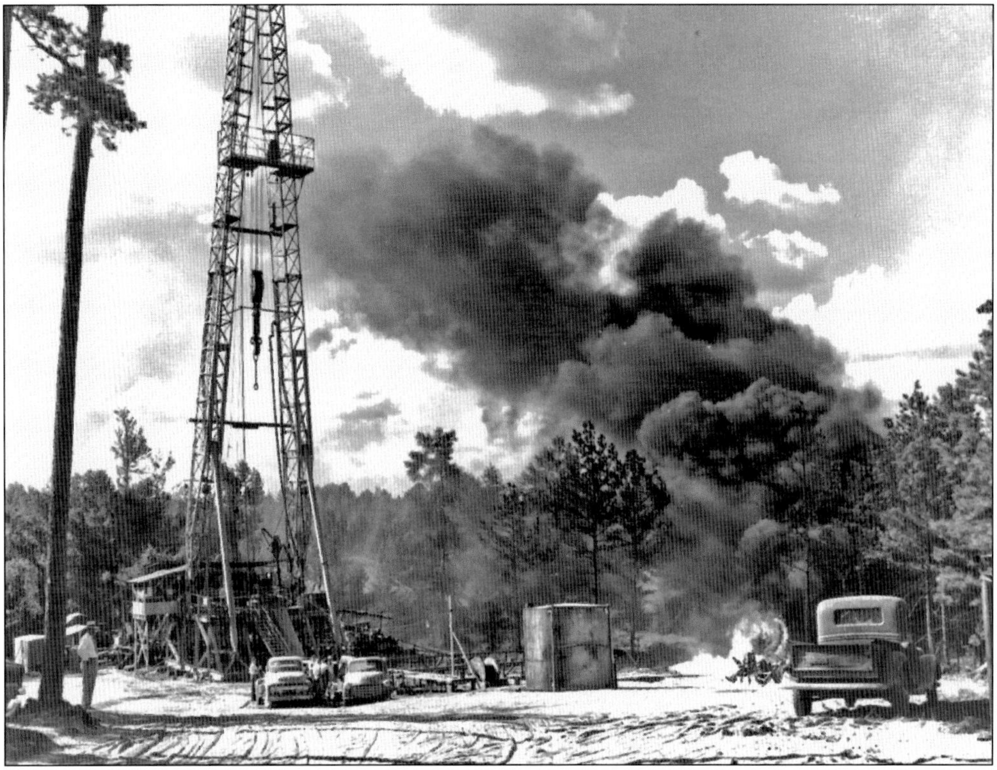

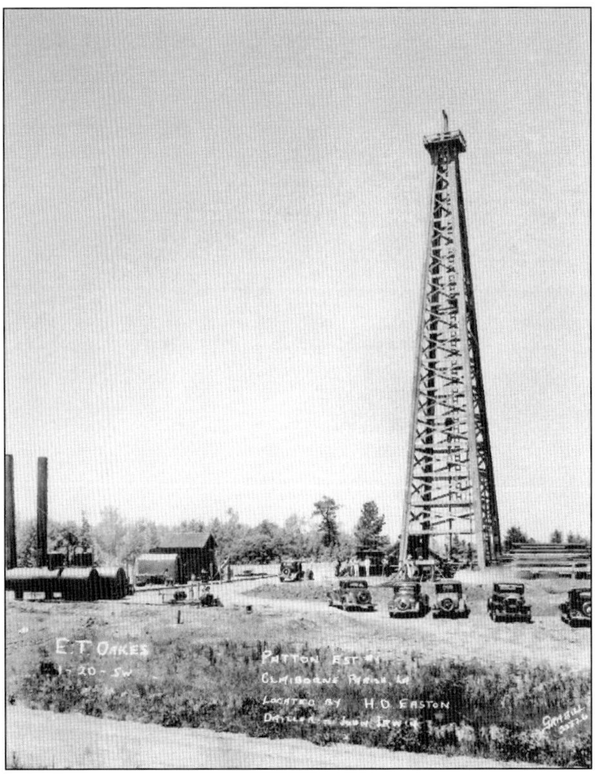

The discovery well in the West Lisbon Field, the Thomas Killgore No. 1, was brought in in 1955. In this photograph, J. D. Caruthers Jr. watches as the wind blows a flare from the Haynesville Sand back toward the work-over rig. Drilling activities can also produce coincidental discharges of oil, water, saltwater, natural gas, and sand. (Courtesy of J. D. Caruthers Jr.)

During Lisbon's brief history as the "Oil Metropolis of North Louisiana," temporary living quarters for newcomers were set up in the village's water office. Stores and cafés sprang up to furnish supplies and food to the hundreds of people who arrived to work in the fields. A temporary building was also constructed to serve as a satellite office for the sheriff's department and a jail for lawbreakers. (Courtesy of J. D. Caruthers Jr.)

Seven

REMEMBER WHEN

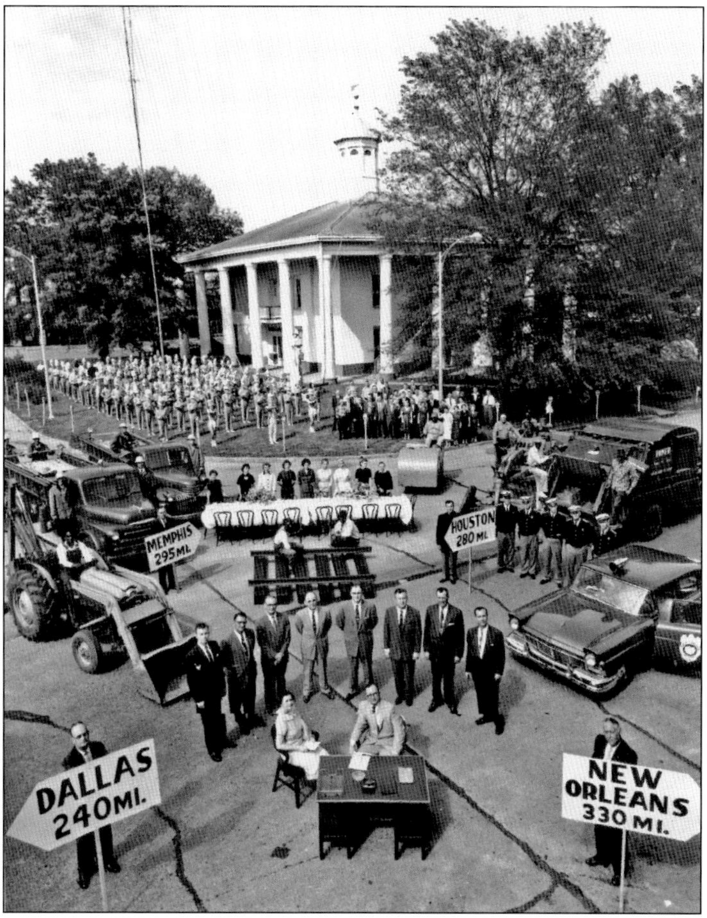

The Homer Development Corporation used various recruiting techniques to bring new businesses to Homer. This photograph, which appeared in the August 7, 1957, issue of *Life* magazine, features a broad range of local organizations gathered on the town square to promote Homer's image as a good location for families and businesses. (Courtesy of the Joe Robertson family.)

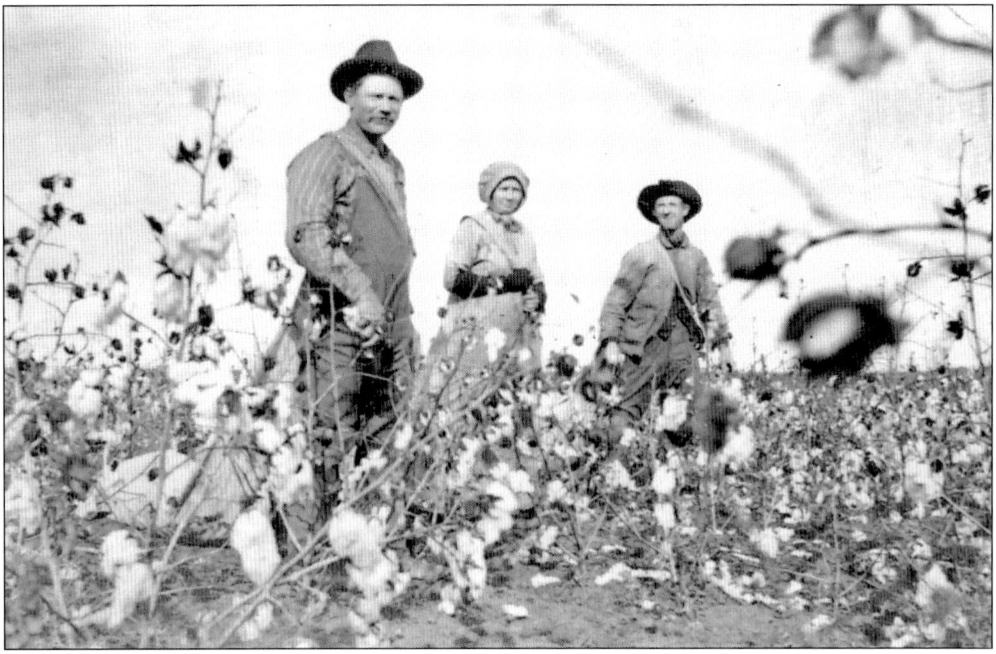

Claiborne Parish encompasses an area of 768 squares miles—755 square miles of land and 13 square miles of water. In 1929, there were more acres of cotton planted in Claiborne Parish than in any other cotton-producing county in the South. By the mid-1960s, cotton production in Claiborne Parish had virtually ceased. Cotton is no longer produced in Claiborne Parish. (Courtesy of the Ford Museum.)

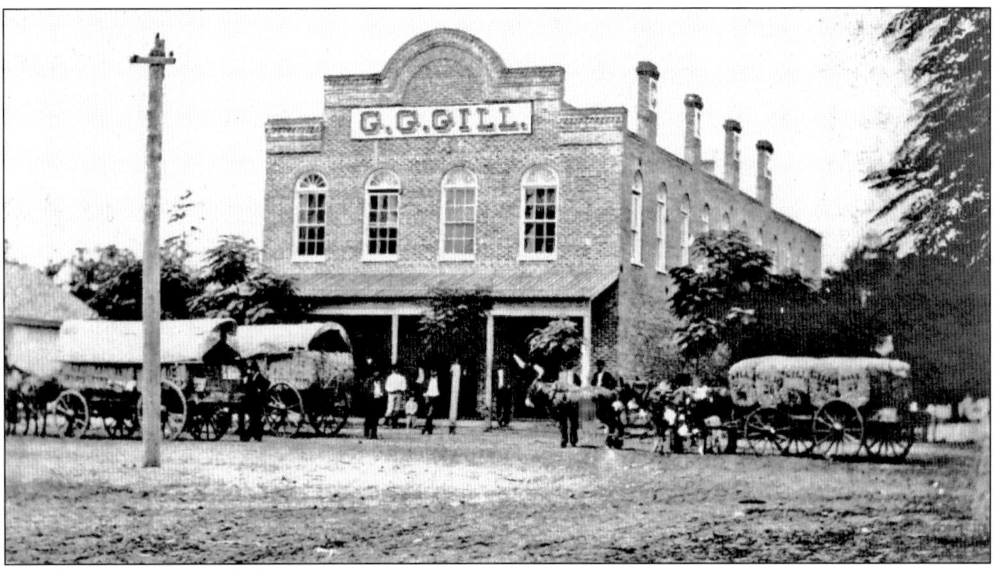

One of the oldest buildings on Homer's town square is the Gill-King building, completed by G. G. Gill in 1878. Gill's mercantile store offered a large stock of general merchandise for sale, including drugs, furniture, hardware, saddlery, and many other items. Gill also bought and sold cotton. In the foreground of this photograph, three wagons have stopped in front of the store with bales of cotton for sale. Note the Gill name painted on the four chimneys. (Courtesy of Joe Ellis Michael.)

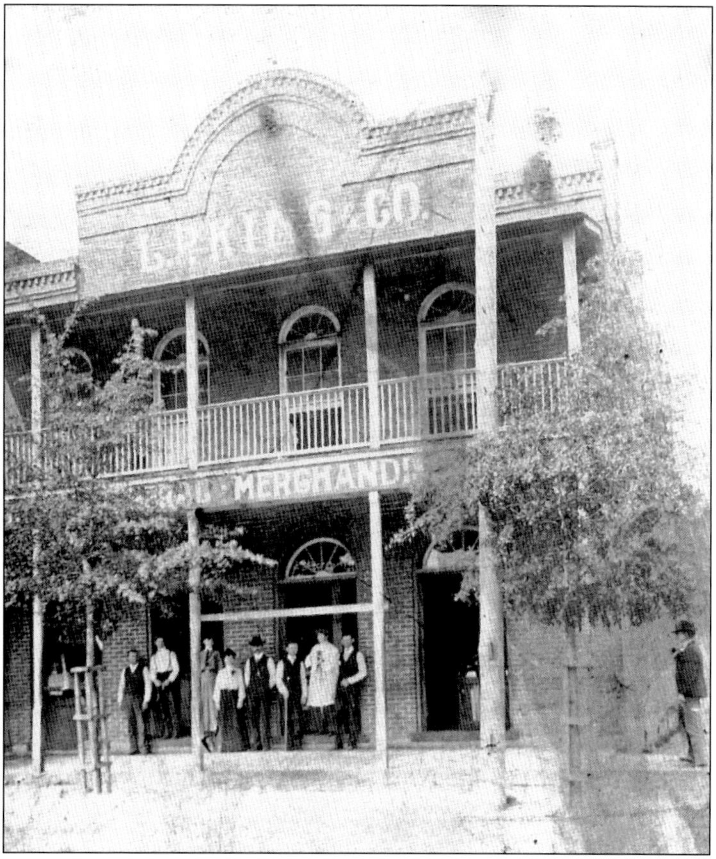

Over the years, business locations around the square changed owners, some more frequently than others. Leander P. "Bob" King purchased the Gill building in 1912 when he and his two brothers moved their mercantile business to Homer from Blackburn. (Courtesy of Ketha Woodard.)

Gas lamps suspended from the ceiling inside L. P. King and Company (below) help illuminate shelves and counters stocked with merchandise. From left to right are John Henry King, two unidentified, Bob King, and Franklin T. King. (Courtesy of Ketha Woodard.)

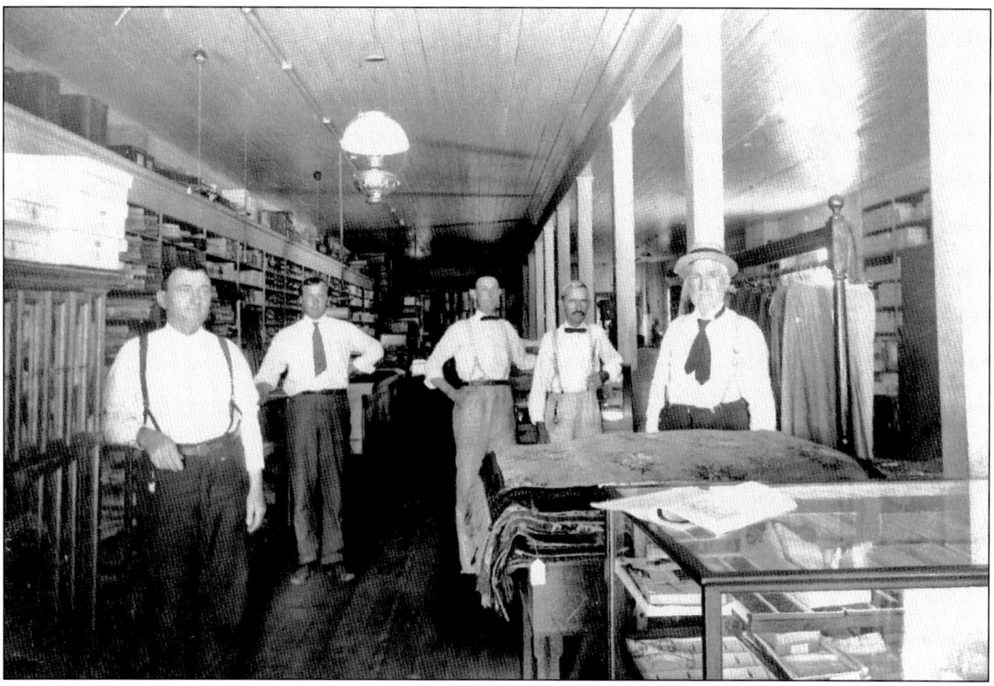

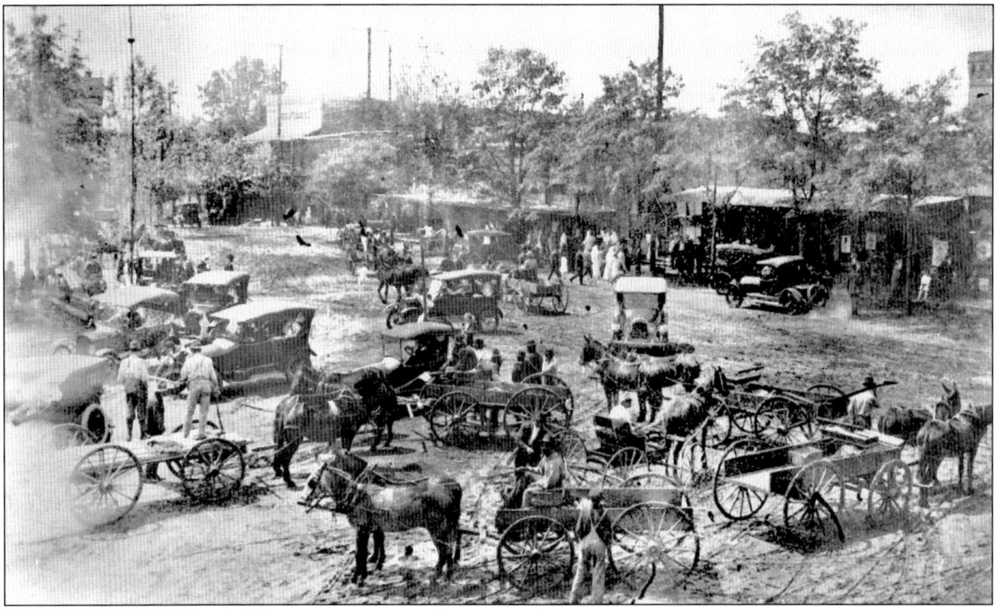

The American Red Cross experienced phenomenal growth during World War I. Membership grew from 17,000 to more than 20 million. More than $400 million in funds and materials were contributed by the American public to support Red Cross programs. Members of Homer's Red Cross chapter can be seen in the background of this photograph. (Courtesy of LSU Shreveport Archives–Noel Memorial Library.)

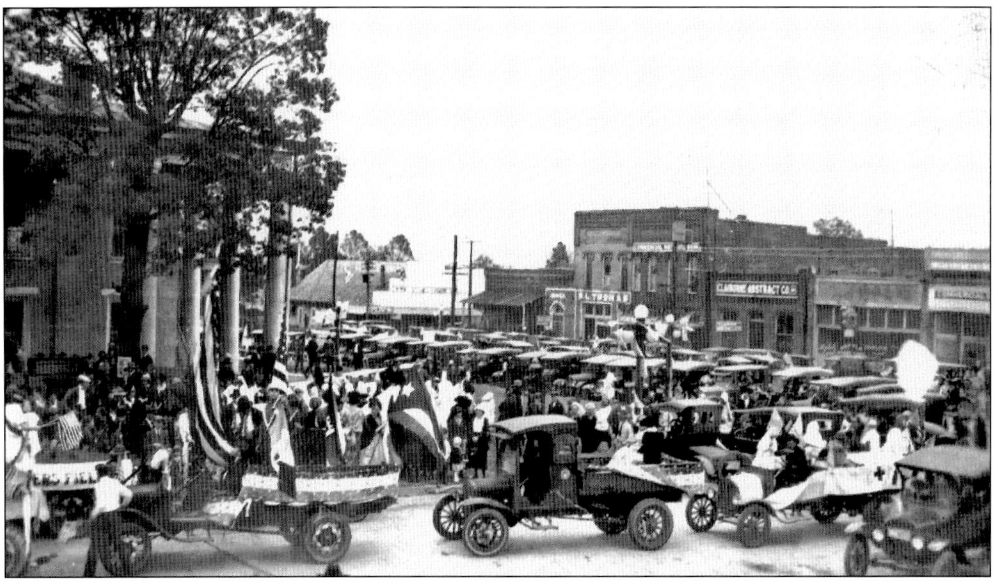

On November 11, 1918, Claiborne Parish residents gathered on the courthouse lawn to celebrate the armistice that marked the end of World War I. A patriotic parade was the highlight of the day. Six more months would pass before the terms of the Treaty of Versailles would be finalized. (Courtesy of Carolyn Thurmon.)

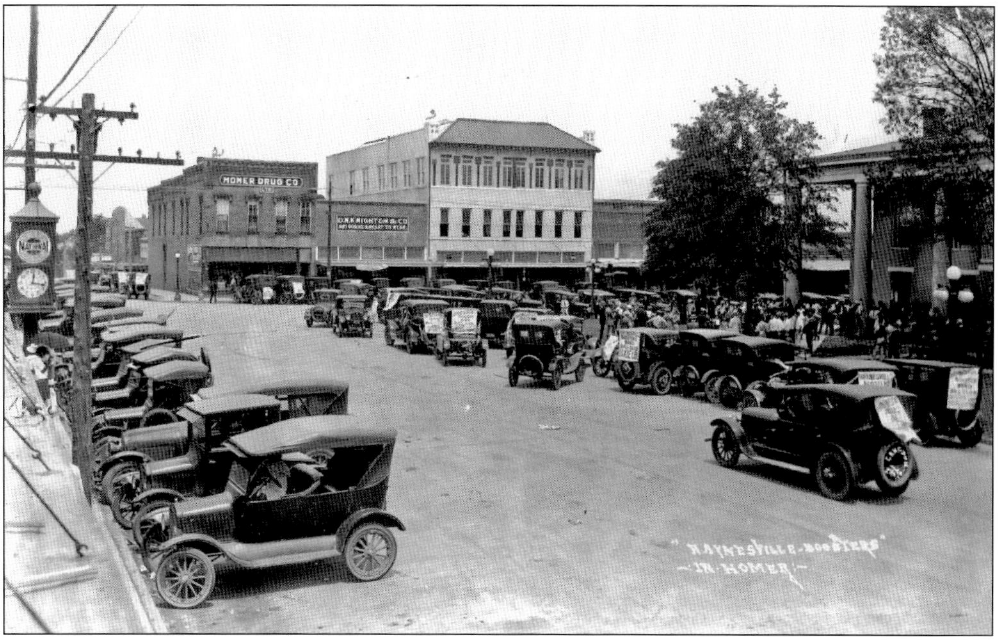

In this 1923 photograph, members of Haynesville's Football Booster Club have gathered on the courthouse lawn for a pep rally before the first annual Thanksgiving Day game between Homer and Haynesville. The marquee of the Woodbine movie theater can be seen behind the McCranie (Homer Drug) building. (Courtesy of the Claiborne Parish School Board.)

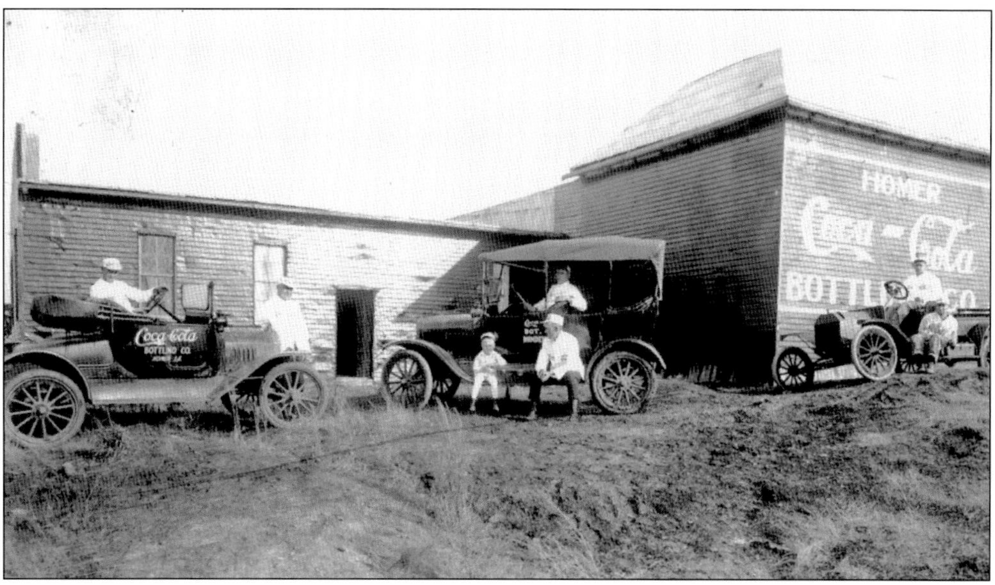

The Homer Coca-Cola Bottling Company's first building was located across the railroad tracks from its present site. The "Coke company" sold soft drink products to large retailers and small country stores throughout the parish. The young boy sitting on the running board of the center truck in this *c.* 1916 photograph is Joe Robertson, a future president of the company. (Courtesy of the Joe Robertson family.)

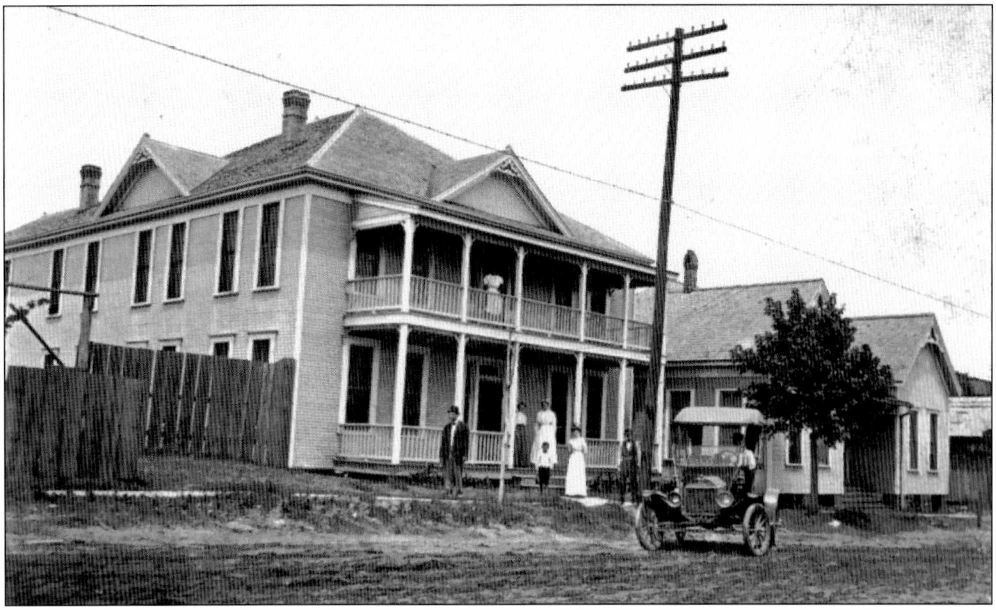

Dr. Philip Gibson opened his 20-room sanitarium on East Main Street in Homer in 1907. Gibson was graduated from Memphis Medical College in 1890, then returned to Millerton to begin his medical practice. He was the first medical doctor in North Louisiana to install an X-ray machine in his clinic. (Courtesy of Bill W. Hightower.)

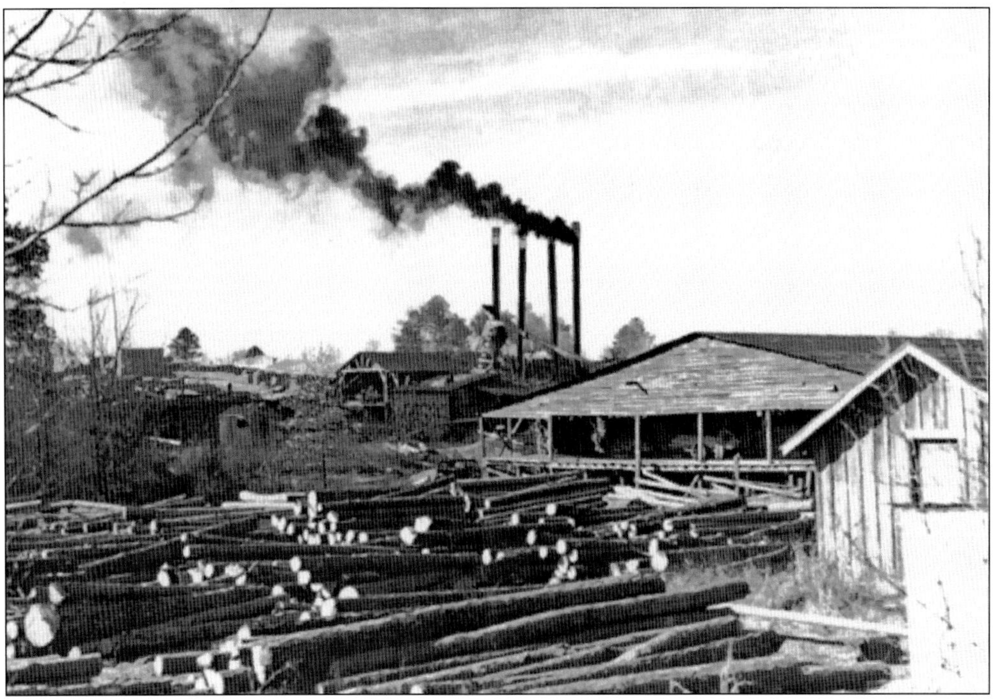

This sawmill was located on Highway 79 North on the lot presently occupied by the McLemore Shopping Center. It was a 7-inch gun mill with a capacity of 35,000 board feet per day. In 1948, it employed 95 people and had an annual payroll of $150,000. (Courtesy of the Claiborne Parish Library.)

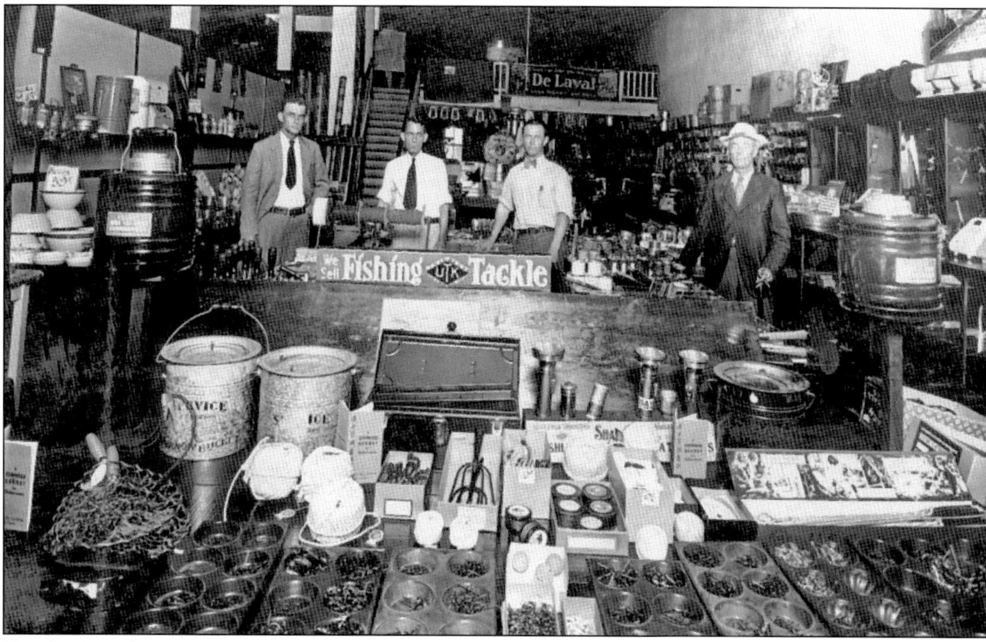

Fomby Hardware in Homer stocked a full line of merchandise for farm and home, including nails, lanterns, cream separators, pots, pans, fishing lures, and many other items. Before the days of funeral homes, Fomby Hardware also sold coffins, with Orie Kerlin providing undertaking services. Pictured in this May 1932 photograph are, from left to right, two unidentified, Oswald Fomby, and Walter L. Fomby. (Courtesy of the Ford Museum.)

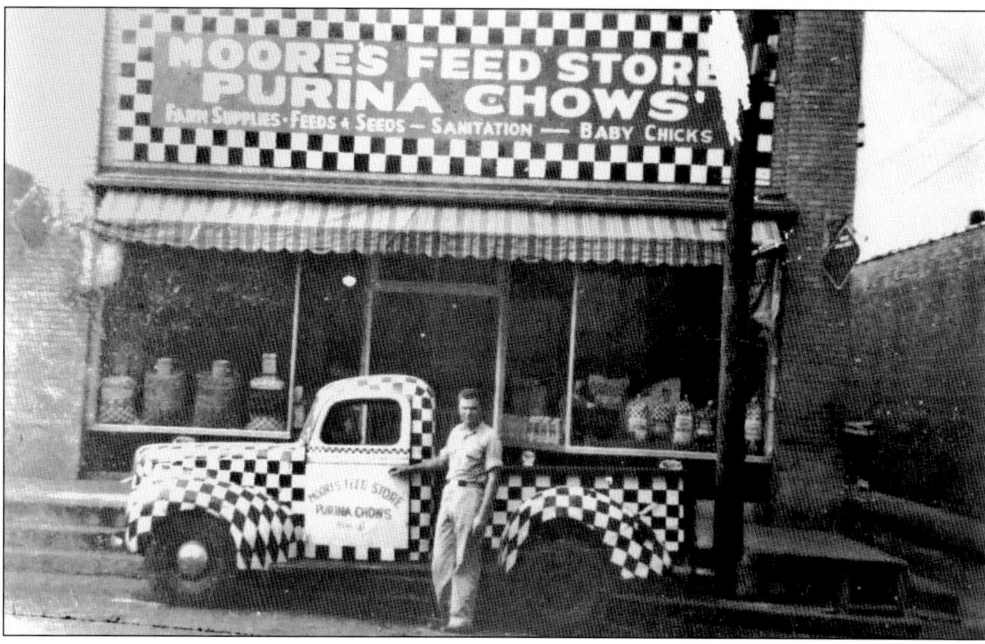

Moore's Feed Store, located just off the town square in Homer, carried farm supplies as well as feed for livestock. In this photograph, F. T. Hightower Jr. stands beside the store's delivery truck, colorfully painted with the familiar Purina checkerboard squares. (Courtesy of F. T. Hightower family.)

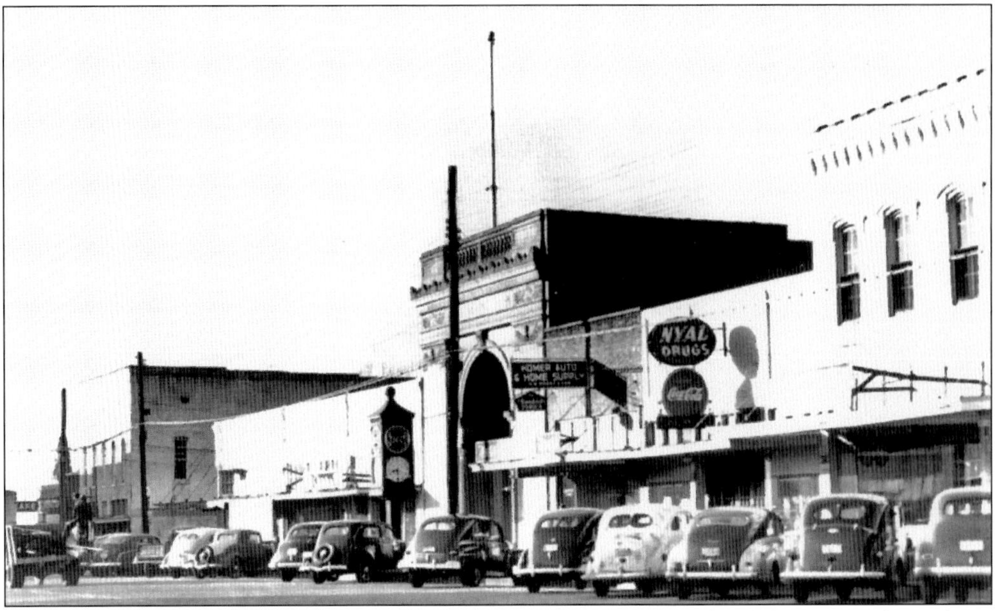

The Homer National Bank, founded in 1890, anchored the west side of the square throughout most of the 20th century. The building was completed in 1923 and the sidewalk clock installed the following year. Other businesses appearing in this photograph are the Homer Auto and Home Supply and Claiborne Drug Company. (Courtesy of Peggy Stovall.)

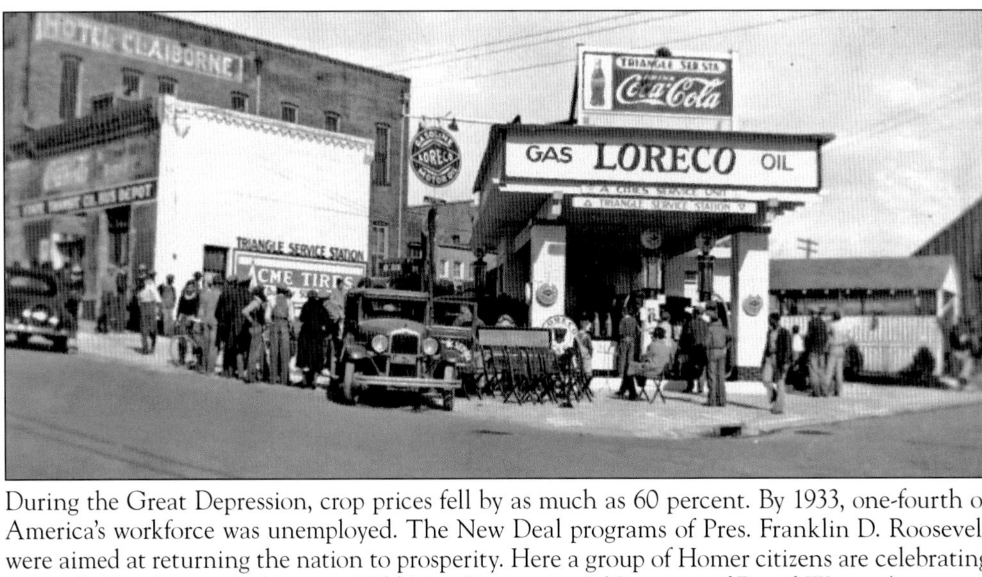

During the Great Depression, crop prices fell by as much as 60 percent. By 1933, one-fourth of America's workforce was unemployed. The New Deal programs of Pres. Franklin D. Roosevelt were aimed at returning the nation to prosperity. Here a group of Homer citizens are celebrating the end of hard times by hanging "Old Man Depression." (Courtesy of David Watson.)

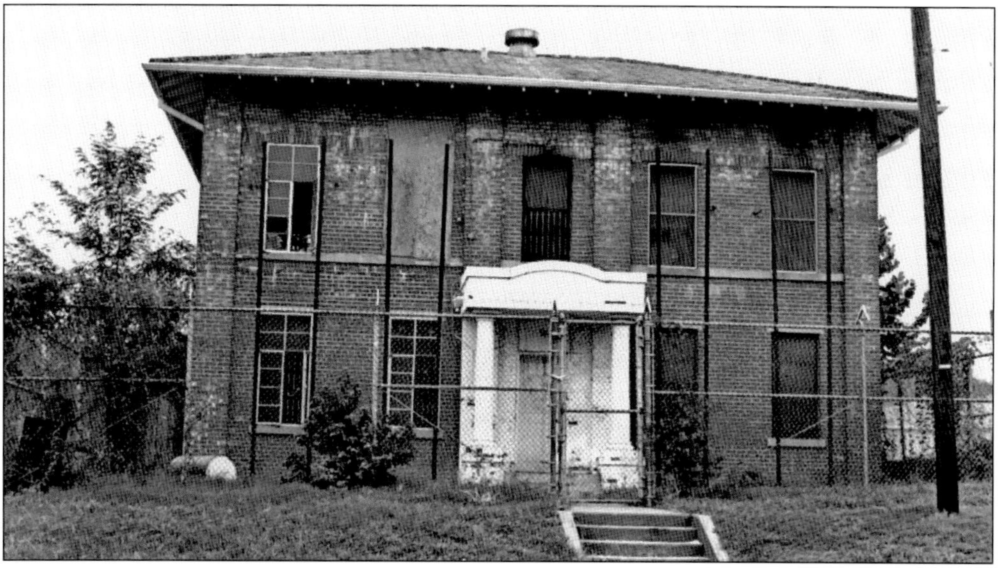

The first Claiborne Parish jail was a two-room wooden structure built in 1864 near the site of the present-day jail and sheriff's office. When a new jail was built on the east side of the square, the old wooden building was used as a "calaboose," or drunk tank, in which intoxicated persons were confined until they sobered up. The two-story brick building pictured here served as the Claiborne Parish jail from 1922 until 1971. (Courtesy of the Claiborne Parish Sheriff's Department.)

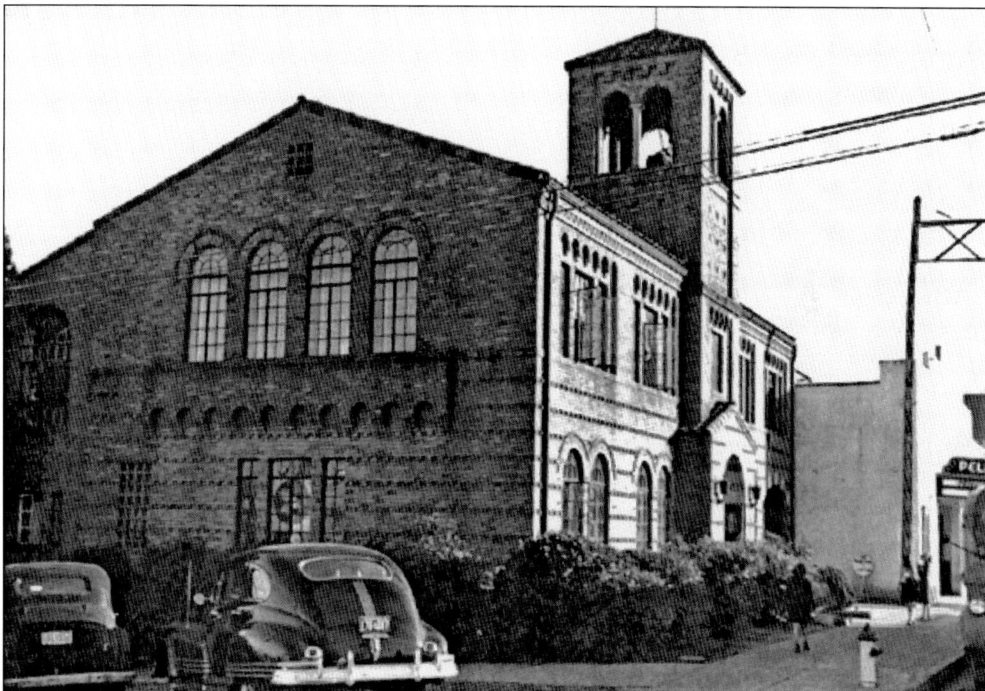

Homer's Mediterranean-style town hall was completed in 1929. In addition to spaces for town officials and employees, the building contained an auditorium and stage for public meetings and social events. The Pelican movie theater was located next door. (Courtesy of the Claiborne Parish Library.)

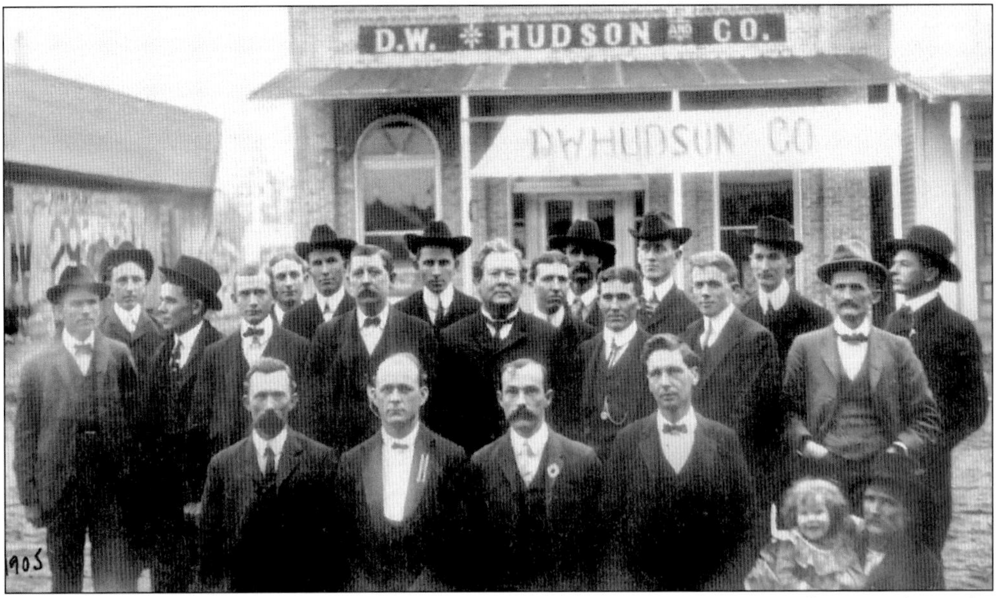

These men are engaging in what became a popular pastime in new Haynesville—watching the train come in. In this 1901 photograph are, from left to right, (first row) Dr. S. Waller, L. Yates, M. Foster, A. L. Brown, B. Phipps, and Phipps's daughter Bernice; (second row) Dr. L. Waller, L. P. Dawson, C. Taylor, S. B. Baucum, Judge Ben P. Edwards, J. Dawson, B. Reynolds, and H. Miller; (third row) M. Morgan, N. Baucum, P. Baucum, S. Baucum, S. E. Rankin, E. Evans, H. Sherman, and a cotton buyer named Hightower. At the back on the left is L. Beene. (Courtesy of Monte Banks.)

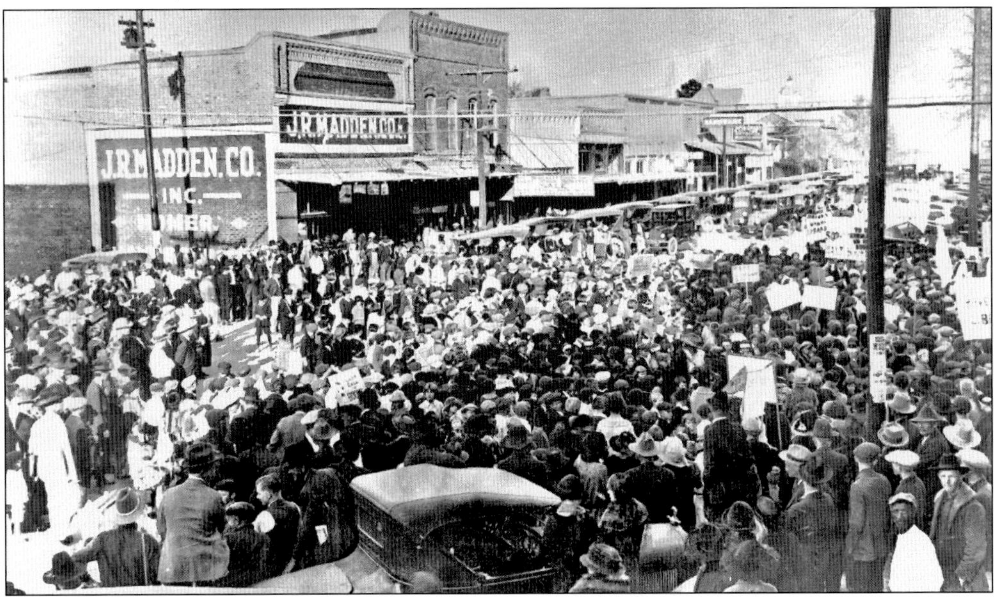

In this *c.* 1924 photograph, a large crowd carrying signs has gathered to show support for constructing a library in Haynesville. On the corner is the J. R. Madden building, the present location of Killgore Pharmacy. Visible in the distance is the dome of the First Baptist Church. The dome was removed in 1925 when the building was enlarged. (Courtesy of the Claiborne Parish School Board.)

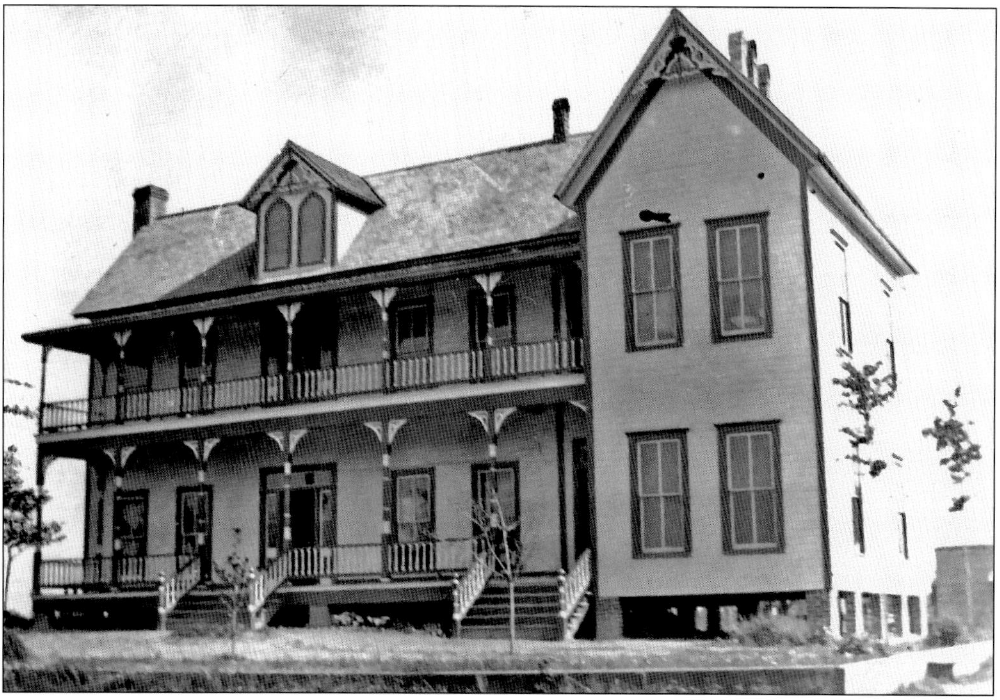

This Haynesville hotel was built in 1904 by J. C. Powell, the man who installed the first bathtub and private waterworks in town. It stood on the south side of Main Street, catercorner to the First Baptist Church. When Charles Bridgeman bought the hotel in 1908, he renamed it the Bridgeman Hotel. Later it was bought by John L. Garrett and renamed the Elgin Hotel. The building burned in 1934. (Courtesy of Monte Banks.)

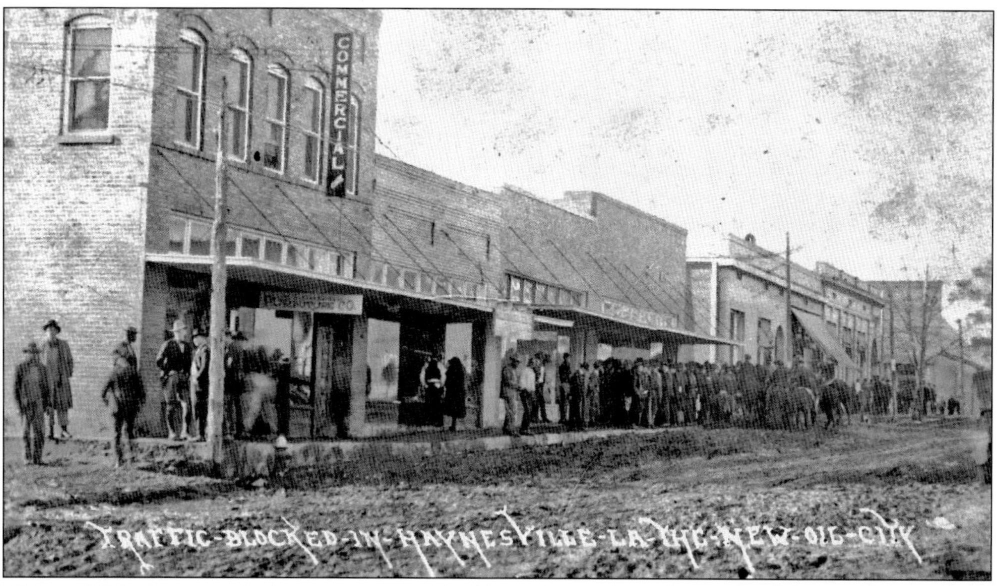

This *c.* 1921 photograph shows a group of buildings located on the west side of Highway 79 one block north of Haynesville's present-day post office. The discovery of oil in the Haynesville Field created a surge in all business activities. At the far end of the block is the Planters Bank building. (Courtesy of Don Terry.)

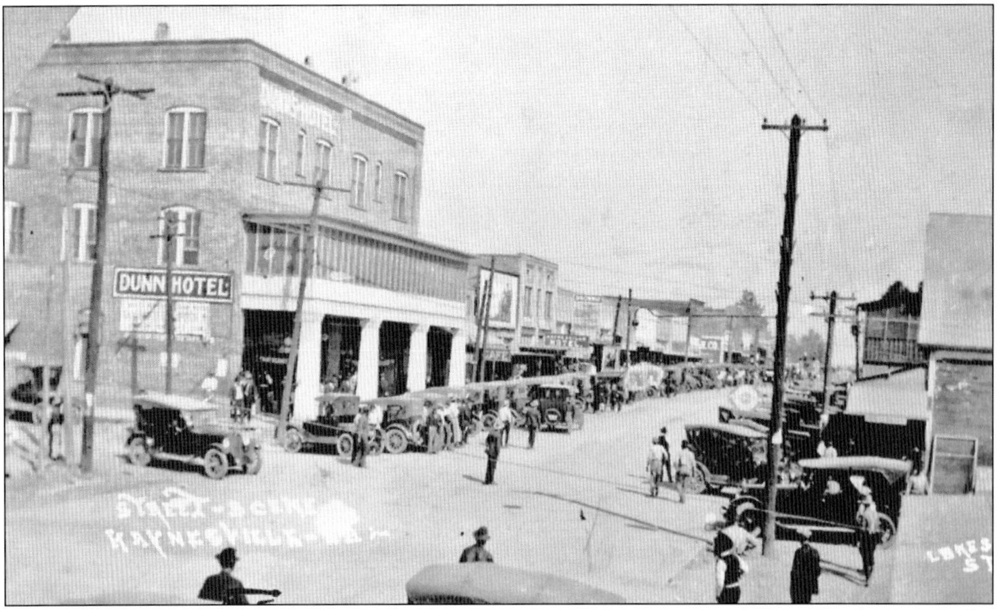

Haynesville's business district on Main Street thrived following the discovery of oil near the town in 1921. The Dunn Hotel was completed in 1913 by L. C. Bolen. In 1917, M. J. Dunn bought the hotel and equipped it with gas heat and hot and cold running water in every room. Down the street, the Haynesville Hotel can be seen next to the Brownie movie theater. (Courtesy of Monte Banks.)

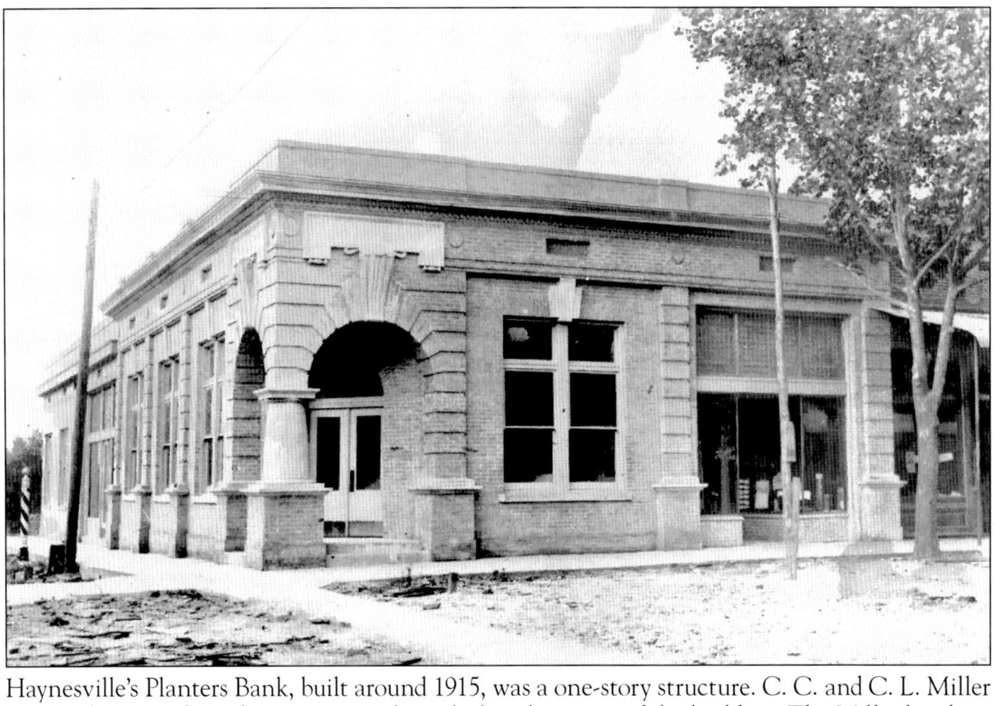

Haynesville's Planters Bank, built around 1915, was a one-story structure. C. C. and C. L. Miller operated a men's furnishings store in the right-hand portion of the building. The Miller brothers also owned a barbershop where the striped barber pole can be seen at the far left. (Courtesy of Tom Crocker.)

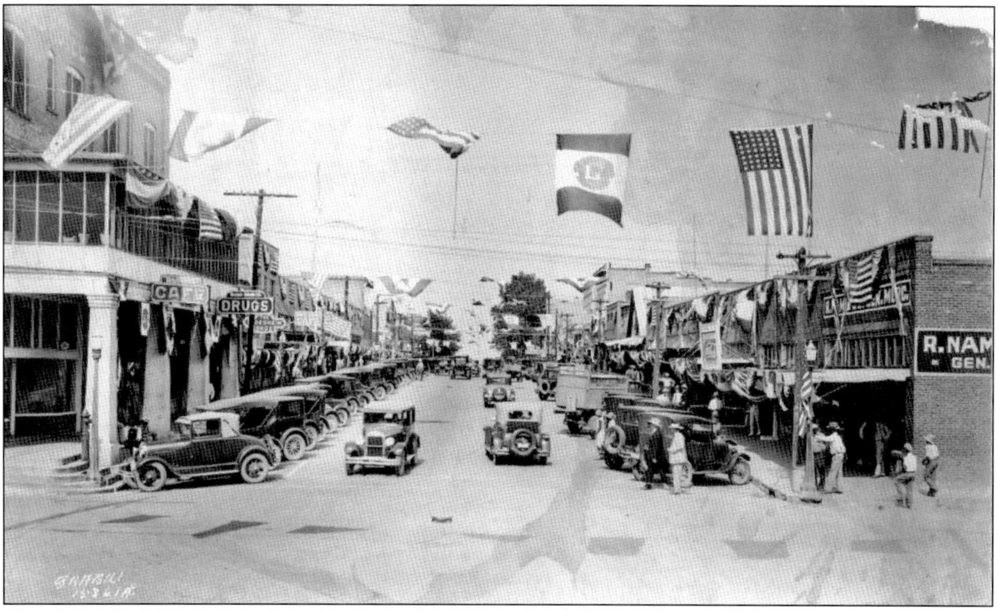

Flags and banners line Haynesville's Main Street for a Lions Club convention in May 1928. Businesses visible on the north side of the street include the Dunn Hotel and Café, Bond Drug, a Florsheim Shoe store, the White House Café, and City Drug. On the south side of the street, businesses that can be identified are R. Namie's General Merchandise store and Miller Drug. A Dixie Mist Ice Cream truck appears in the line of cars on the right. (Courtesy of Tom Crocker.)

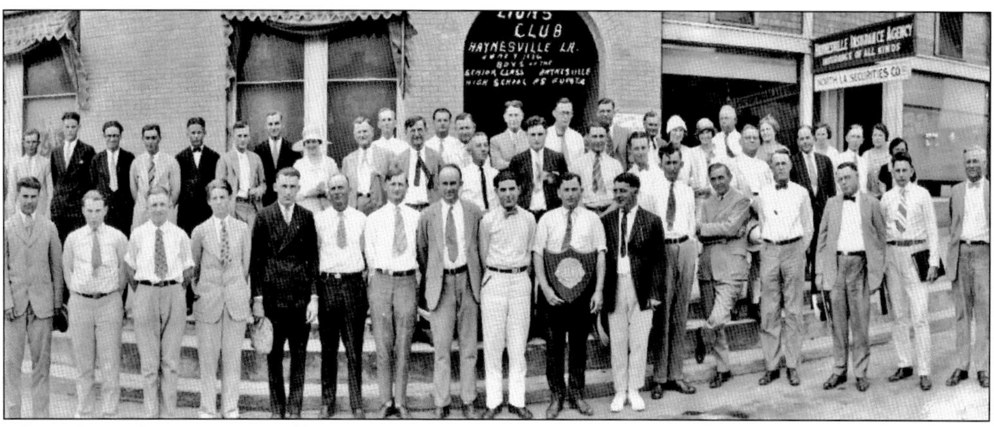

These boys from Haynesville High's senior class were the guests of the Haynesville Lions Club on June 9, 1926. They are pictured here on the east side of the Planters Bank building. A breeze is blowing the men's ties and stirring the new awnings over the windows. (Courtesy of Monte Banks.)

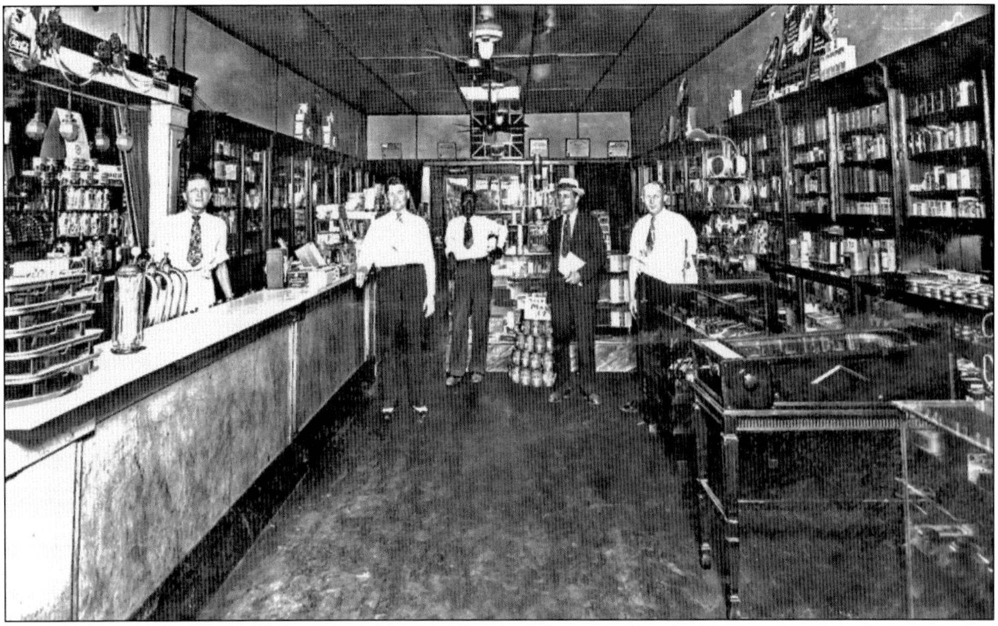

A favorite gathering place in the 1930s was the marble-topped soda fountain inside Haynesville's Miller Drug Company, where a soda jerk stood ready to fill requests. Mounted on the walls are glass-front cabinets holding a variety of health and beauty aids. At the rear of the store, framed licenses and diplomas are displayed above the pharmacy window. (Courtesy of Monte Banks.)

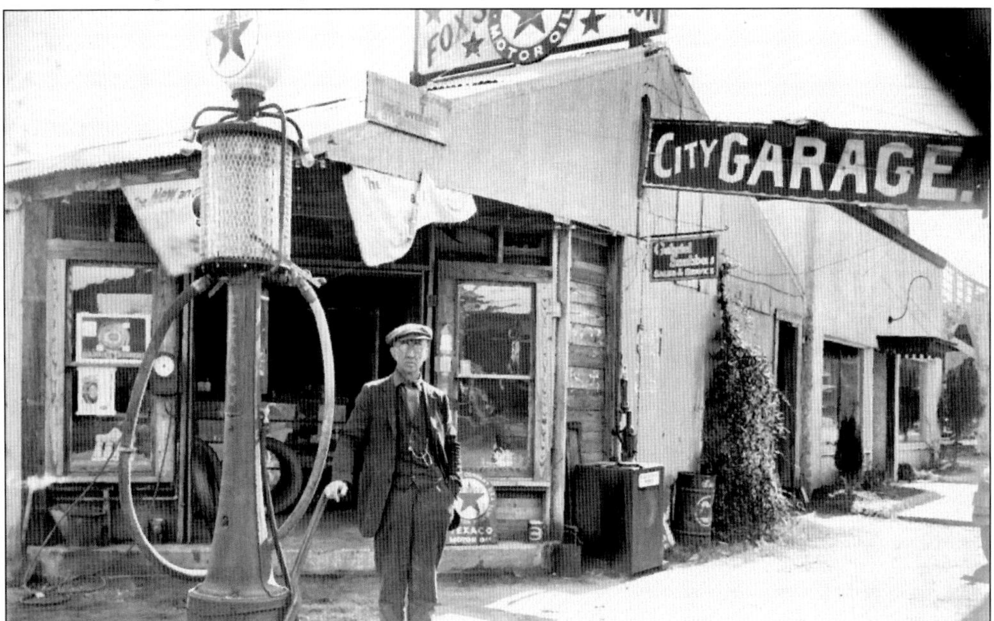

In 1927, Fox's Station in Haynesville offered full service to its customers. Texaco gasoline was available from the tall gravity-fed pump, and an air hose was mounted on the wall behind the gas pump. The station also sold Kelly tires and other Texaco products. A mechanic was on duty for automobile repairs. Inside the station, customers could buy a variety of soft drinks and snack products. (Courtesy of the Ford Museum.)

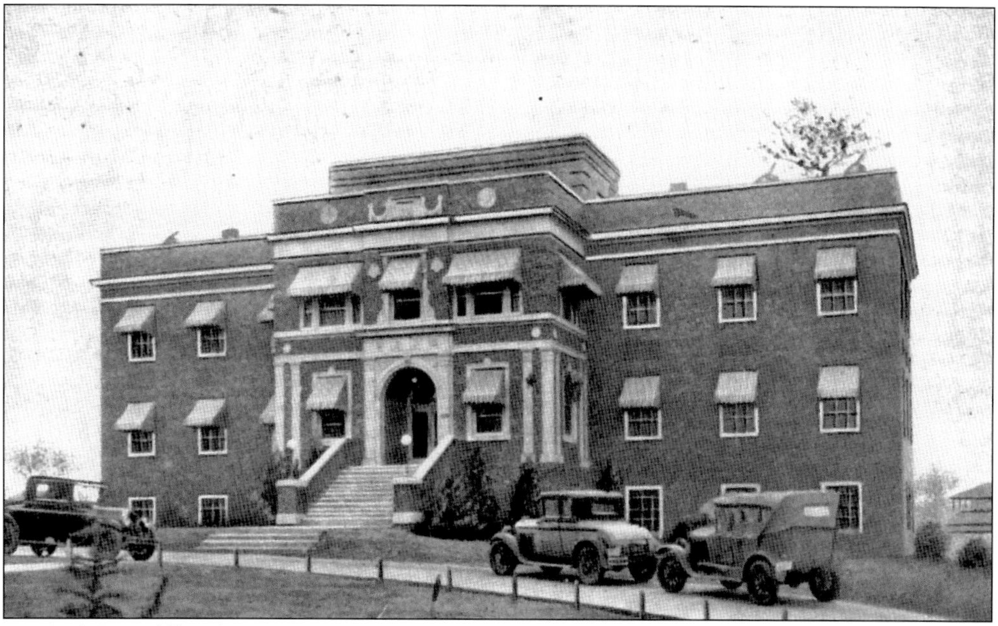

Dr. Carl O. Wolff and Dr. M. J. Rivenbark played key roles in building the three-story Haynesville Sanitarium in 1926. Until Homer Memorial Hospital was opened in 1949, Haynesville Sanitarium served as Claiborne Parish's only hospital. The 40-bed sanitarium also had eight bassinets for newborns. (Courtesy of the Ford Museum.)

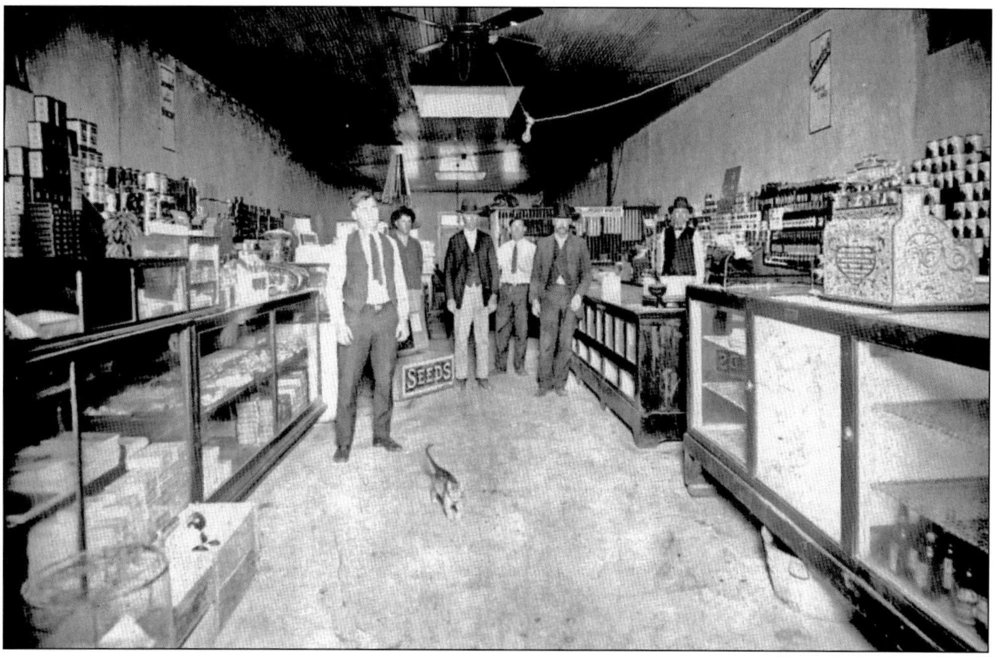

At one time or another, T. U. Norton pursued a variety of occupations, including running a farm, blacksmith shop, sawmill, general store, and Haynesville's first cotton gin. Pictured inside Norton's general store are, from left to right, John H. Garrett, Shack Hartsell, Hugh Talley, Jim Garrett, Hugh Hunt, and T. U. Norton. The cat in the foreground helped keep the rodent population in check. (Courtesy of Ardece Sanders.)

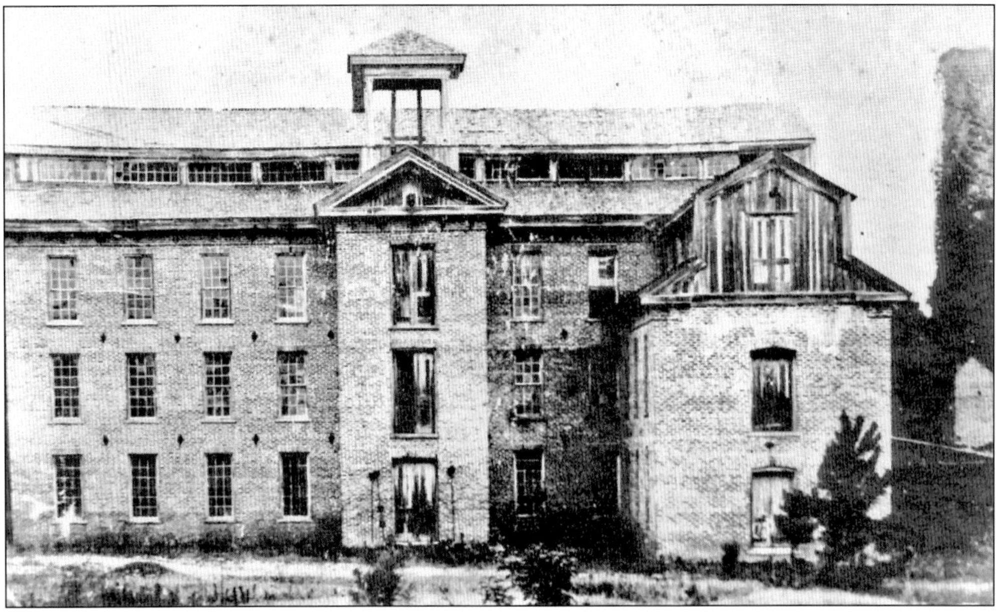

The Claiborne Cotton Manufacturing Company, known locally as the "Arizona Cotton Factory," was built around 1867 in the Arizona community. In the three-story factory building, workers made thread and 1,000 yards of Osnaburg cloth per day. Inadequate transportation and lack of skilled workers were the main factors contributing to the company's decline. (Courtesy of Bill W. Hightower.)

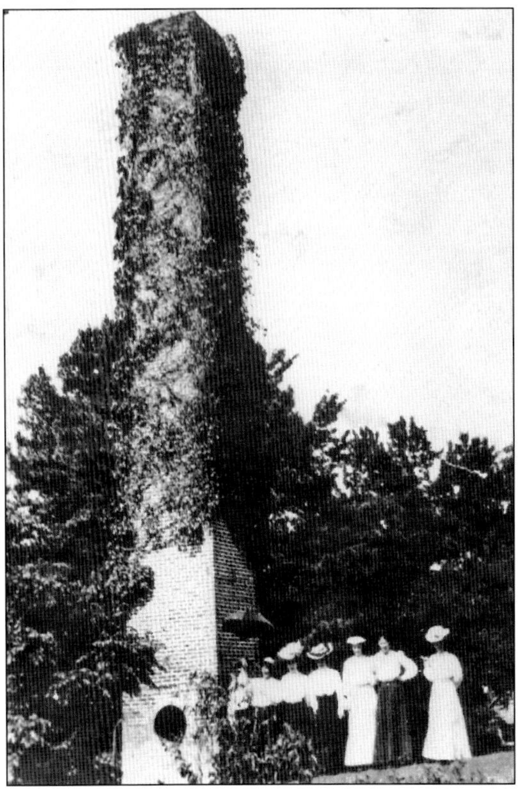

The Arizona Cotton Factory was closed in the early 1870s and sold at auction to John Chaffe of New Orleans. The building was torn down in 1900, leaving only the tall brick chimney as a reminder of the entrepreneurial spirit of the factory's founders. (Courtesy of the Ford Museum.)

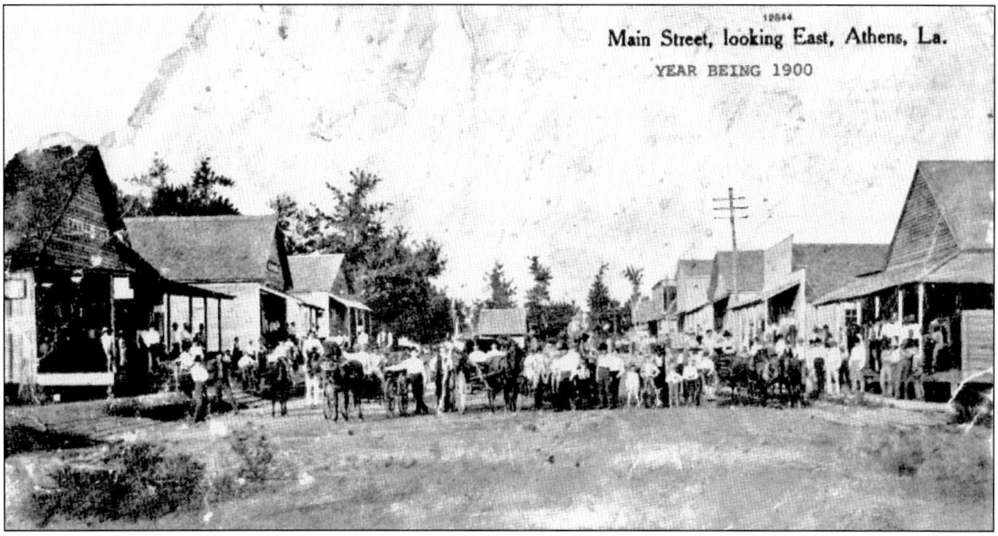

These citizens have gathered on the main street of downtown Athens for this 1900 photograph. Businesses on the left are the Baker Brothers store, Dillon and Martin's store, and John Beauchamp's jewelry store. On the right are Will Pace's store, the post office, Simpson Brothers drugstore, and the commissary of the Johnson Lumber Company. The town well is in the center of the street. (Courtesy of the Ford Museum.)

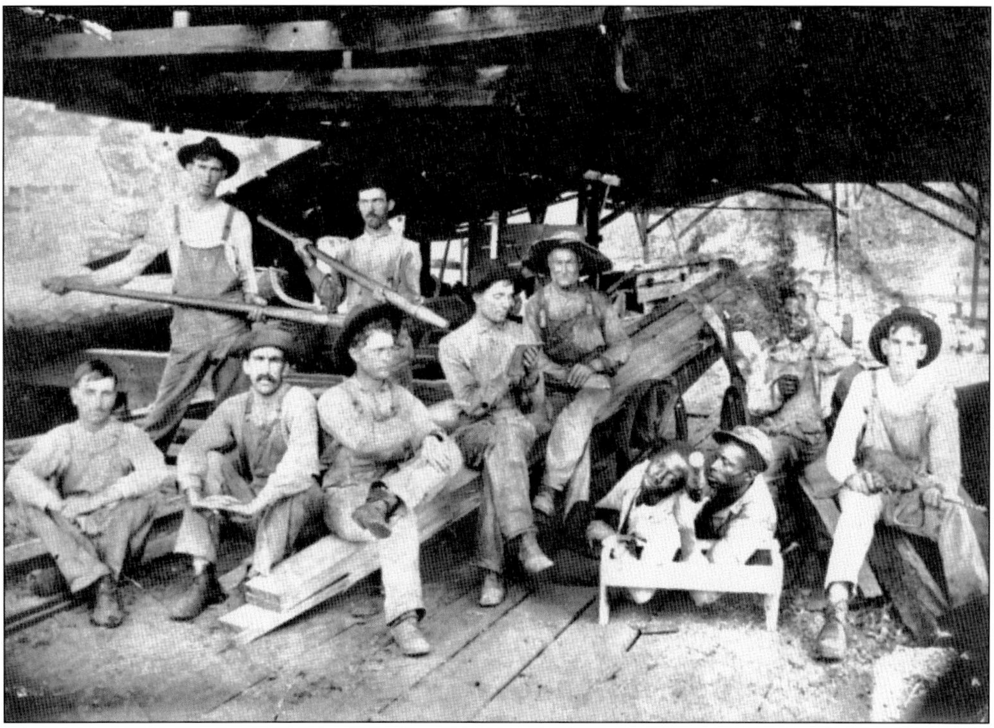

The Pace Lumber Mill began operations in 1904. The two men who are standing are holding cant hooks—leverage tools used to shift and move logs. The three men in the center are seated on newly cut planks piled on a two-wheeled cart. The man at the far right holds an early brace and bit. (Courtesy of the Ford Museum.)

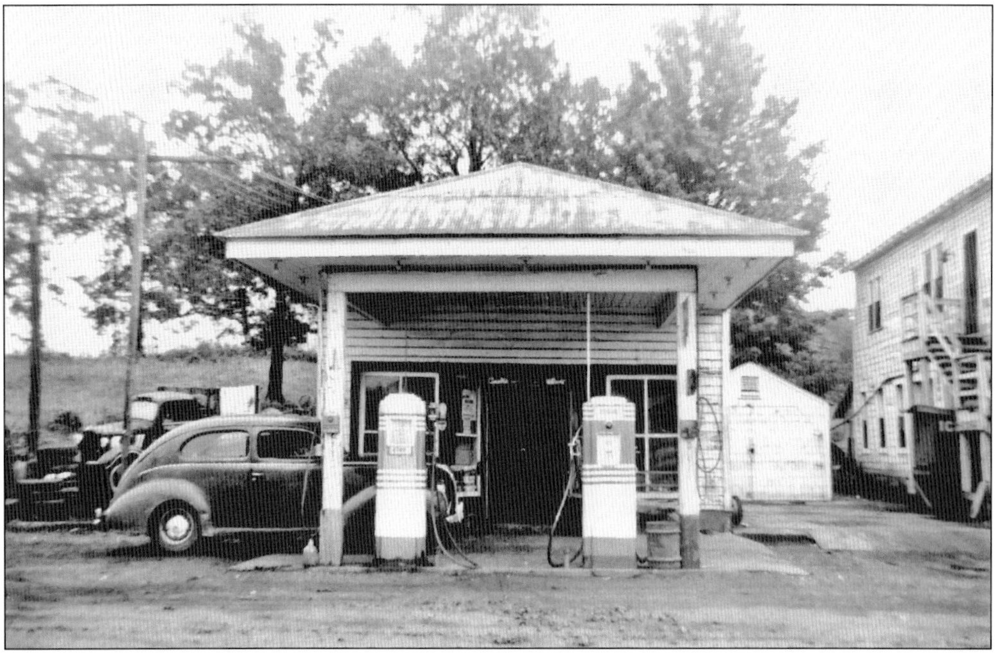

This Cities Service gas station provided automobile fuel and service for residents in Athens. Cities Service bought out Louisiana Oil Refining Corporation in the 1930s. (Courtesy of the Horace Watson family.)

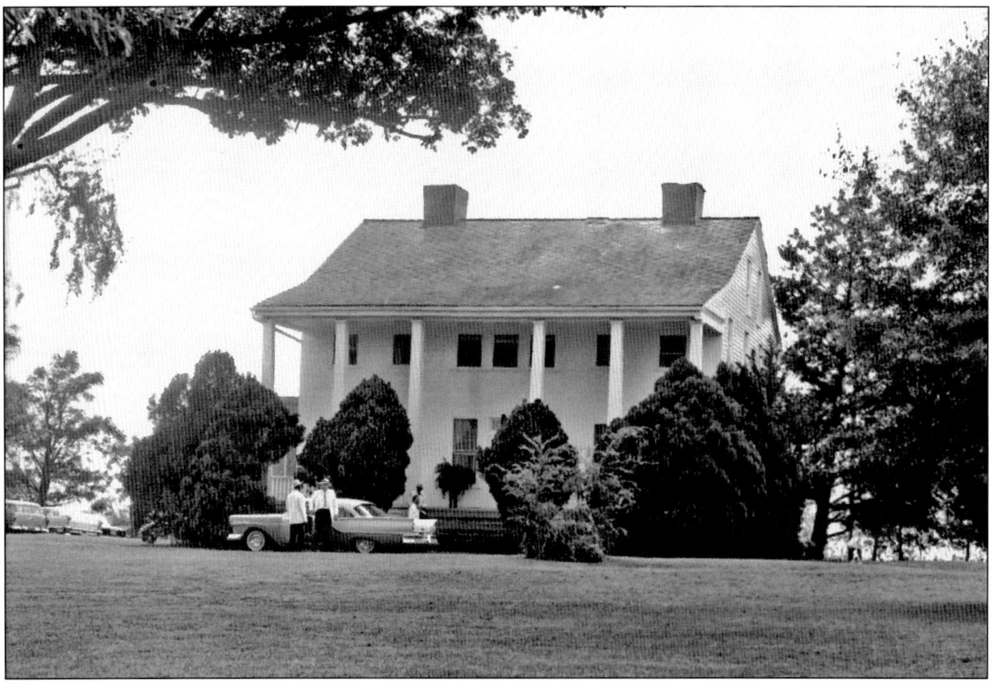

The Killgore house, a two-story Greek Revival structure located in Lisbon, was built in 1859 by Charles A. Killgore. Featuring square columns across the front gallery, the house was built with virgin timber from the Killgore homestead. It has remained in the Killgore family since its construction. (Courtesy of Edith K. Kirkpatrick.)

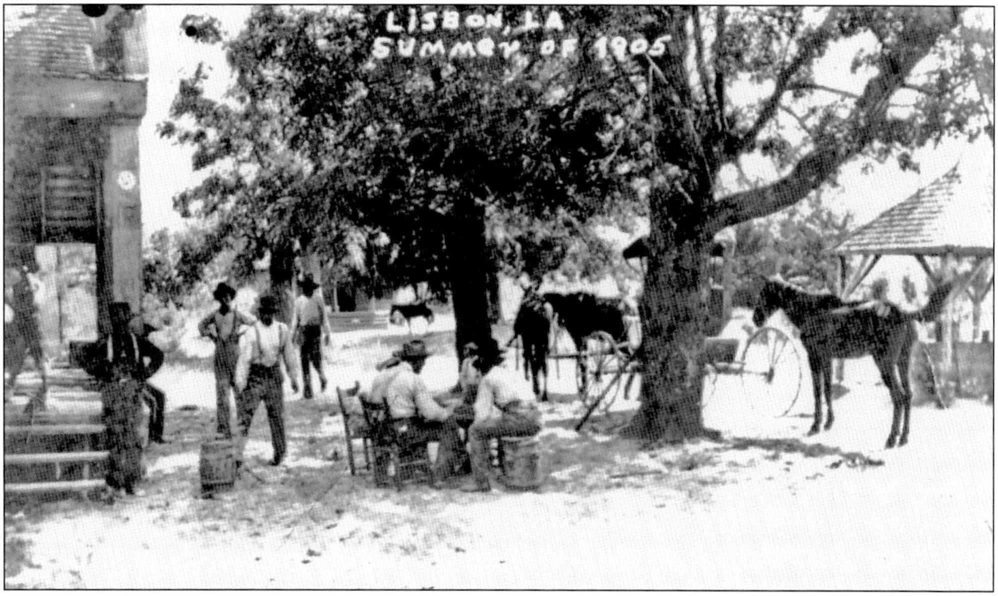

In this photograph, a Saturday evening game of checkers is being played in downtown Lisbon during the summer of 1905. The town well with its shed can be seen at the far right. During this period, horses, mules, wagons, and buggies provided the primary means of transportation. (Courtesy of Shelley Malsam.)

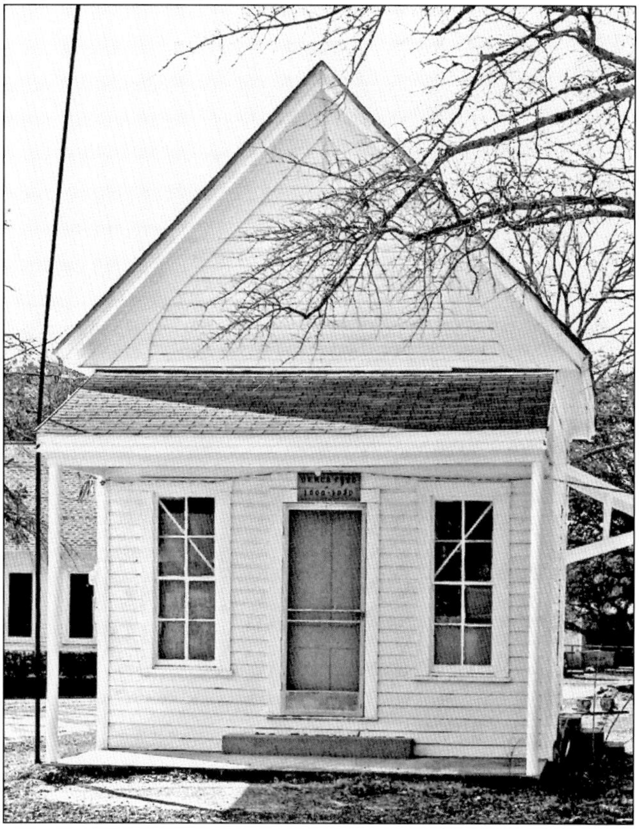

The office of Dr. Willis C. R. Ford, with its distinctive steep roof, has become a landmark in Lisbon as one of the few older buildings remaining of what was once a thriving town in Claiborne Parish. Dr. Ford was well known in the Lisbon community. Records from Ford's office indicate that his fee for delivering babies was $3. He died at the age of 46 in 1920 from a ruptured appendix. (Courtesy of Frank and Jane Speer.)

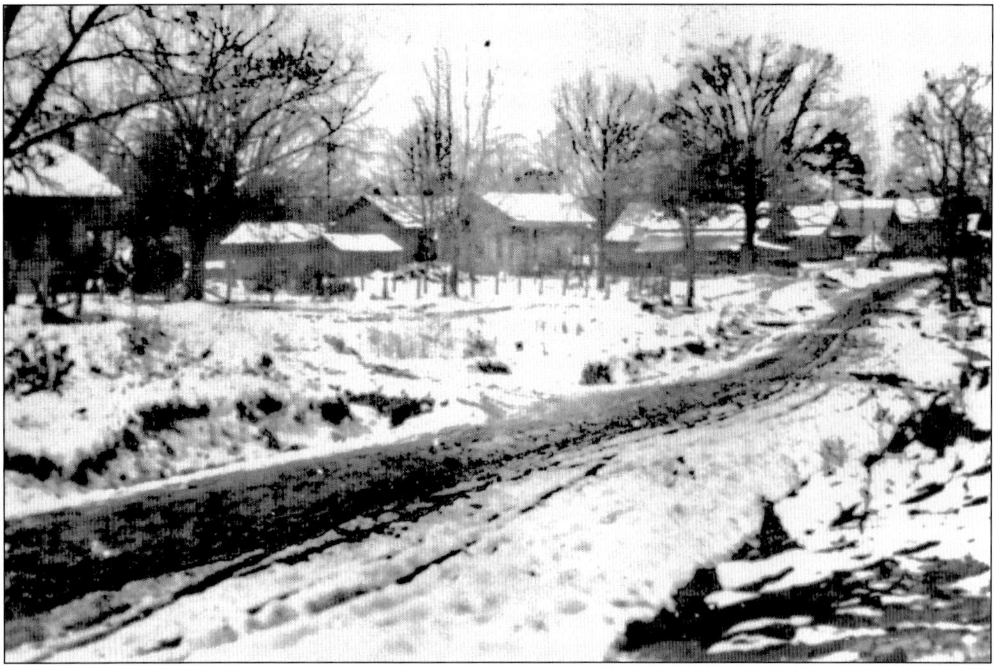

On a snowy day in 1918, traffic has turned the dirt road through Summerfield into a muddy trail. In this photograph, the first house on the left was owned by Dr. J. C. Allgood. The third building from the left was owned by Will Gray and used as a boardinghouse for teachers. A well for watering horses is situated in the fork in the road. (Courtesy of Butch Bays.)

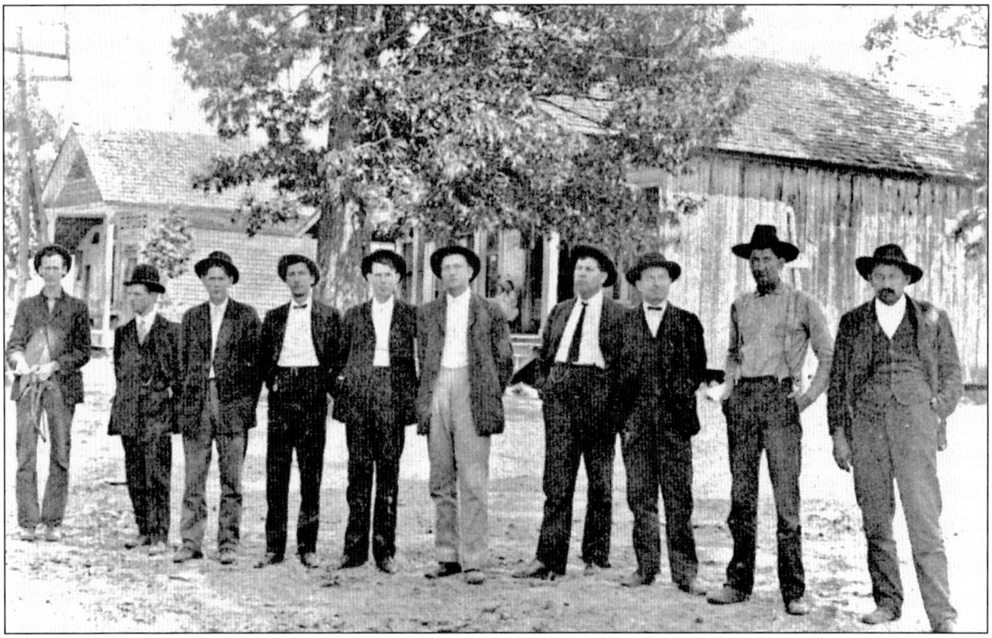

Pictured in downtown Summerfield in 1908 are, from left to right, J. Pat Smith (holding reins), Dr. J. F. Tanner, Will Gully, Will R. Davidson, Ed C. Hightower, Lucius M. Davidson, Dr. J. C. Allgood, Eugene Raley, John Y. Davidson, and Jasper Allgood. A doctor's office and a general store can be seen behind the men. (Courtesy of Kate Sherman.)

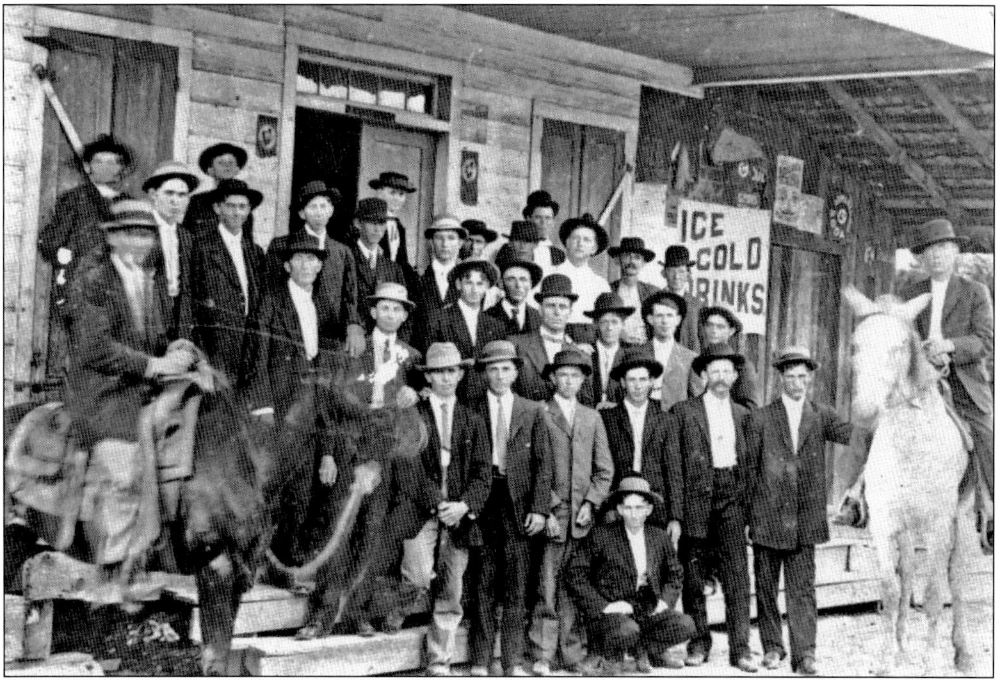

Men are gathered in front of a Summerfield store in this *c.* 1910 photograph. A number of advertising signs can be seen on the wall of the store, including five Arm and Hammer Baking Soda advertisements. Another sign touts Golden Salve, a patent medicine developed in the 1860s. (Courtesy of Bill W. Hightower.)

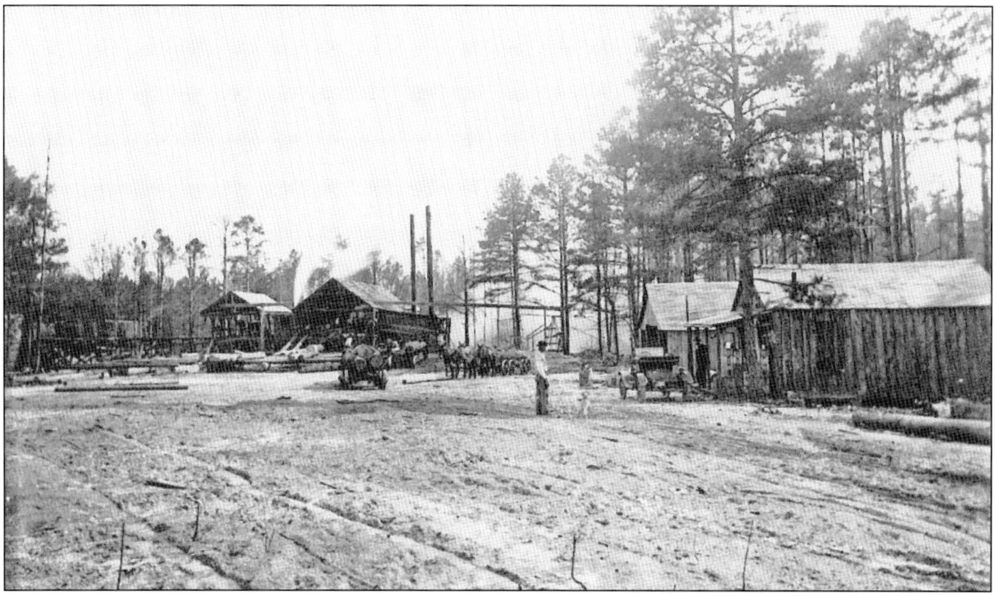

Sawmills, such as this one located near the home of John W. Monday in the Antioch community, were once a common sight throughout Claiborne Parish. Trees were cut using crosscut saws, double-bit axes, mauls, and wedges. Once a tree was felled, the limbs were removed and the tree was cut into logs of manageable lengths. The logs were then hauled to a sawmill to be sawed into planks. (Courtesy of Helen Campbell.)